inv.dk. 11/2006

1/ Nov '07
3 Jan '08
3 Nov '09

D0072139

THE FILMS OF
KENNETH BRANAGH

Samuel Crowl

PRAEGER

Westport, Connecticut
London

Library of Congress Cataloging-in-Publication Data

Crowl, Samuel.
   The films of Kenneth Branagh / Samuel Crowl.
      p. cm.
   Includes bibliographical references and index.
   ISBN 0-275-98089-8 (alk. paper)
1. Branagh, Kenneth. I. Title.
   PN2598.B684C76   2006
   791.4302'33092—dc22   2006001445

British Library Cataloguing in Publication Data is available.

Library of Congress Catalog Card Number: 2006001445
ISBN: 0-275-98089-8

First published in 2006

Praeger Publishers, 88 Post Road West, Westport, CT 06881
An imprint of Greenwood Publishing Group, Inc.
www.praeger.com

Printed in the United States of America

The paper used in this book complies with the
Permanent Paper Standard issued by the National
Information Standards Organization (Z39.48-1984).

10 9 8 7 6 5 4 3 2 1

For Charlie, Aidan, Theo, Audrey, and Miles

"If we shadows have offended,
Think but this, and all is mended:
That you have but slumbered here,
While these visions did appear."

CONTENTS

Preface   ix

1   The Actor as Filmmaker   1

2   *Henry V*   19

3   *Dead Again*   37

4   *Peter's Friends*   55

5   *Much Ado About Nothing*   73

6   *Mary Shelley's Frankenstein*   95

7   *A Midwinter's Tale*   113

8   *Hamlet*   129

9   *Love's Labour's Lost*   149

Appendix 1   Interview with Kenneth Branagh   **167**

Appendix 2   Kenneth Branagh Filmography   **179**

Appendix 3   A Chronology of Kenneth Branagh's Work as an Actor, Writer, and Director on Film, Stage, and Television   **183**

Notes   **187**

Index   **199**

PREFACE

This study owes its inception to Eric Levy, the former film editor at Praeger Publishing. He believed Kenneth Branagh's films deserved a full-length critical treatment and approached me about the project. When I resisted, he pressed his case. In an attempt to end the exchange, I finally said, "Eric, can you imagine writing thirty pages on *Peter's Friends*?" He emailed right back with this rejoinder: *"Peter's Friends* has one of the great opening shots in recent films, wouldn't writing about it be a pleasure?" I admired his persistence, his admiration for Branagh's films, and his memory for detail (that opening shot is remarkable) so I relented and said yes. I have not regretted my decision. Dan Harmon, who inherited this project from Eric, has provided support and suggestions for improvement as the manuscript neared completion.

This work is the first comprehensive account of Kenneth Branagh's feature films to appear in English. Branagh is the first British actor of his generation to join the growing list of Hollywood stars, including Clint Eastwood, Robert Redford, Mel Gibson, Warren Beatty, and Kevin Costner, who have transformed themselves into major, award-winning film directors. Branagh expands and enlarges Orson Welles's legacy of taking his Mercury Theater Company from New York to Hollywood and into the world of film. Welles's attempt was short-lived and ended after his first three pictures, yet Branagh has sustained the company ideal through eight feature films with the promise of many more to come. Branagh has distinguished himself as a filmmaker by successfully mixing and mingling classical (*Henry V* and *Hamlet*) and commercial (*Dead Again* and *Mary Shelley's Frankenstein*) projects and has sought to erase the line between films made for the art house and the multiplex. Branagh has created an audacious and energetic film style noted for its fluid, sweeping camera style, a reliance on robust and romantic filmscores, and the use of a core group of British and American actors.

I want to thank the editors of the Ohio University Press for their permission to lean, lightly I hope, on material on Branagh's Shakespeare films I have previously published in *Shakespeare at the Cineplex*. That volume placed Branagh's Shakespeare films in the context of the dramatic revival of the genre in the 1990s. Here my interest is in how those films fit into the context of Branagh's career as a film director. My chapters on Branagh's Shakespeare films are an attempt to rethink and reevaluate earlier judgments and to expand upon ideas only casually suggested in *Cineplex*. I also want to thank the members of the Shakespeare Association of America's annual film seminar, especially H. R. Coursen, John Ford, Kathy Howlett, Douglas Lanier, James Lake, Laurie Osborne, Courtney Lehmann, Kenneth Rothwell, and Lisa Starks, for challenging and expanding my ideas about Branagh's qualities as a filmmaker.

This book was written in London and Athens and profited from conversations with friends and colleagues on both sides of the Atlantic, including Ed and Carolyn Quattrocchi, Don and Anne Stevens, Charlie and Claire Ping, Will and Ann Lee Konneker, Russell Jackson, Mark Thornton Burnett, Ramona Wray, Dean and Alvi McWilliams, Andrew Escobedo and Beth Quitslund, Tom Carpenter and Lynne Lancaster, and Stuart and Anne Scott. The former English Department Chair at Ohio University, Kenneth Daley, was interested in this project from its inception and found creative ways large and small to aid in its completion. My students in recent graduate seminars on Shakespeare and film (focused on Branagh and his contemporaries) were quick to share their own enthusiasms for (and reservations about) Branagh's work. The College of Arts and Sciences at Ohio University generously provided me a research grant that allowed for the hiring of three resourceful research assistants, Sara Pennington, Alicia Sutliff, and Athena Castro-Lewandowski, to help track down Branagh material buried in newspaper and magazine interviews. Patty Colwell prepared the manuscript and remains a wizard at reading my hurried scribble. I owe a special debt of gratitude to Mark Thornton Burnett who kindly allowed me to examine material in the Branagh Archives at Queen's University–Belfast, much in advance of the formal opening of that collection. Mark White's biography of Branagh appeared when this work was in press. I am sorry not to have included some of his insights into Branagh's talents as a film director in this study, but I am pleased that our judgments about Branagh's achievements often coincide.

I have known Kenneth Branagh for almost fifteen years. Our relationship is formal and professional rather than personal, as befits a critic and his subject. I want to acknowledge here his remarkable generosity, as a man and an artist, in responding to my queries in correspondence and in conversation. He has a genuine ability to articulate his passion for Shakespeare and for filmmaking in a manner that is both challenging and engaging—qualities that are obviously apparent in his work as well. His personal assistant, Tamar Thomas, has also been extremely helpful in answering questions about Branagh's career and in scheduling our meetings. I owe her more thanks than this mention can convey.

Branagh's stage performances and his films have communicated powerfully to the young. My students responded passionately to his *Henry V* and delighted in his *Much Ado About Nothing*; Branagh spoke to them much as Olivier and Welles spoke to my generation. Younger scholars such as Sarah Hatchuel, Courtney Lehmann, and Douglas Lanier have staked out the terms of the debate about Branagh's films and his talent as a film director. In keeping with this spirit I am delighted to dedicate this book to our grandchildren in the hopes that Branagh, or one of his successors, will relight the Shakespeare on film torch and keep it burning for their generation.

As always, Susan Crowl was a coconspirator on this project and made a significant contribution to my understanding of the important role of Patrick Doyle's film scores in Branagh's work.

Chapter 1

THE ACTOR AS FILMMAKER

Kenneth Branagh was born on December 10, 1960, in Belfast, Northern Ireland. His mother (Frances Harper) and father (William Branagh, Jr.) came from large families who lived in York Street, a rough and tumble Protestant and Catholic neighborhood that bordered Belfast's famous dockyards. Branagh's maternal (Speedy Harper) and paternal (Pop Branagh) grandfathers were well known local eccentrics who worked in and around the Belfast Docks and migrated daily between their York Street homes, the dockyards, and the local pubs.

Branagh begins his youthful stab at autobiography, *Beginning*, with a tough-minded but nostalgic evocation of the Branagh and Harper clans and their hard but lively York Street life. The downside of their existence was stereotypically Irish: alcoholism and large families. Speedy Harper left most of his daily wage at the pub on the way home from the docks. His wife died from complications following the birth of her eleventh child, Branagh's mother. The upside of York Street life was the sense of extended community it provided and the power of storytelling it provoked from its denizens. The Branaghs and Harpers were Protestants, but in Branagh's account their Irish thirst for a jar and a tale was much more prominent than their religion.

Branagh's father escaped the often brutal life of the dock worker by being apprenticed to a joiner (a carpenter). He eventually became a skilled construction worker who found steady employment first in Belfast, then in "the South," or Republic of Ireland, and eventually in England. When Branagh was ten and the Troubles were erupting in Northern Ireland,

William Branagh moved the family to Reading, England, where they have remained.

The move from Belfast to Reading was the key event in Branagh's young life. The natural York Street bonds with extended family and community were severed, and the Branaghs were thrust into a new world less threatening than Belfast's sectarian violence but far from brave. Branagh quickly intuited the rub of national differences in his new environment and learned to suppress his Belfast identity by managing "to become English at school [while remaining] Irish at home."[1] Sports, especially rugby and football (soccer), provided Branagh's initial entry into his new environment. Later, becoming involved in school theatricals and writing local newspaper reviews of novels for teenagers further consolidated his standing in his adopted landscape and culture.

This brief biographical sketch is helpful in understanding the development and direction of Branagh's career as an actor, director, and filmmaker. Branagh's genius as a film director is bound up with his powers of synthesis. He draws energy and inspiration, rather than paralysis, by finding himself straddling rival legacies, traditions, and cultures: Protestant and Catholic in Belfast; English and Irish in Reading; and Stratford and Hollywood in his film career. He inherits from his grandfathers the gift of storytelling, the delight in entertaining others. He came to understand that stories, particularly film stories, have the power to reach far beyond national boundaries to unite their varied audiences in common dreams and aspirations.

In Reading, Branagh developed the ability, common to many young actors, to hide in public. What was uncommon about his experience was that he found a way to express his new English identity in sport as well as theater. Branagh's answer to his outsider status was to give himself rather fully to a public role at school while preserving more introspective activities for home: writing stories and reviews, watching endless Hollywood movies on television, and writing letters to his performance heroes (the first went to the British comedy team of Morcambe and Wise and the last to Laurence Olivier). From the beginning of his school career Branagh nourished his identity as a risk-taker. That quality would come to dominate his life as a student at RADA (the Royal Academy of Dramatic Arts), his career as a young actor, and his eventual move into filmmaking. It is important to recognize that institutional high culture was never present in Branagh's immediate environment. His Irish past gave him access to folk life and storytelling and the family television opened up the world of popular British entertainers and American movies; the interest in the classical theater and Shakespeare he fashioned for himself. Acting became, for

Branagh frames a shot on location for *Peter's Friends*. [Photographer: Clive Coote, Courtesy of Photofest]

Branagh, the ultimate means of synthesizing his native Irish bravado with his adopted English tradition.

Branagh's leap from acting to filmmaking followed a similar pattern. Even though he was the Brancroft Gold Medal prize winner at RADA, and he moved immediately from graduation into the cast of a lauded West End play (Julian Mitchell's *Another Country*), and then found himself playing *Henry V* at Stratford as a member of the Royal Shakespeare Company (RSC), all by the age of twenty-three, it became obvious that acting did not absorb all of his energy and ambition. The artist might have been satisfied with his early stage career, but the former rugby and football captain was not. By Branagh's own account, he was a poor company member in his one season with the RSC. He felt that the Company lacked a cohesive sense of community; that the actors were more hired hands than partners in the enterprise; and that the leadership (Trevor Nunn and Terry Hands) was distant and too often otherwise engaged. As a result, his dissatisfaction expressed itself in challenge and revolt, ranging from complaints about pay to writing and producing a mocking satire about the organization. Eventually the only answer was to strike out on his own.

Bolting from the RSC was a radical move. Over the years the RSC had nourished a series of young stars, such as Ian Richardson, Judi Dench,

Alan Howard, Ben Kingsley, and David Suchet, allowing them to grow and enlarge their talent in a series of leading roles stretched out over three or four (or more) seasons. That pattern would repeat itself in the career of Anthony Sher, the other young star (playing Richard III) in the company with Branagh in the 1984–1985 season. But Branagh was restless and chafed under what he regarded as the impersonality of the RSC; his massive energies were not challenged by the actor's limited role in the large repertory enterprise that since the 1960s had been run largely by university-educated directors: Peter Brook, Peter Hall, Trevor Nunn, and Adrian Noble, rather than actor–managers.

English stage actors have thrived in the repertory system, and though they complain, like all artists harnessed to institutions they don't fully control, they also tend to get on with the work rather than revolting. Branagh's Irish moxie, loosely disguised by his English assimilation, allowed him to break free of the RSC to establish his own actor-led Renaissance Theatre Company in 1985. Over three seasons the company produced Branagh's own play, *Public Enemy*, and seven of Shakespeare's: *Romeo and Juliet*, *Twelfth Night*, *Much Ado About Nothing*, *As You Like It*, *Hamlet*, *A Midsummer Night's Dream*, and *King Lear*. All the productions were directed by actors, a rarity in current English theatrical practice. Branagh himself directed several, and he recruited Judi Dench, Geraldine McEwan, and Derek Jacobi to direct others. During this same period Branagh acted in several small-budget films and the highly successful television mini-series, *Fortunes of War*, which helped to establish his name and reputation to an audience beyond Shakespeare and the classical theater.

One overlooked element in Branagh's combination of talents is his ability to write. From the stories he wrote as a kid to his reviews of books for teenagers to his first play to his early autobiography, Branagh found himself comfortable with written as well as spoken language. While he was mocked by some in the English press for the hubris of publishing an autobiography at twenty-eight, *Beginning* is skillfully told. Branagh creates an interesting and compelling persona, something of a hard task when recounting a success story. Most writing by the young depends upon having a sensational personal narrative to confess: drugs, incest, bulimia, poverty, abuse. Branagh's trajectory more closely resembles Horatio Alger's than Huck Finn's, and yet he manages to convince us of the uncertain, at-times overwhelmed lad wrapped in the tiger's hide. There are modest Shakespearean parallels dancing in the air here and they only add to the book's charm. When Branagh, then, made the biggest leap of his young career, the leap into film, he did so not only as an actor and director, but as a writer as well.

Branagh's auteur status as a filmmaker derives as much from his role as a screenwriter as from the unique elements of his directorial style and the interesting thematic continuities between his films. He has written the screenplays for five of his eight feature films (*Henry V*, *Much Ado About Nothing*, *A Midwinter's Tale*, *Hamlet*, and *Love's Labour's Lost*) and for one of his shorts (*Listening*).[2] He was nominated for an Academy Award for Best Adapted Screenplay for *Hamlet*. As that film is famous for using a full text of the play, this nomination was greeted derisively in some quarters.[3] However, reading the screenplay reveals Branagh's intimate understanding of Shakespeare's material and his uncanny sense of how to translate it into the language and rhetoric of film.

Branagh's daring decision to take his Renaissance Company into film mirrored the Shakespearean tale he sought to capture, *Henry V*. Though now, over fifteen years later, the decision has become a crucial part of the history of Shakespeare-on-film, it bears repeating. The Shakespearean film genre had been dead for almost two decades after the critical and commercial failure of Roman Polanski's *Macbeth* in 1971.[4] Shakespeare was regarded as box office poison in Hollywood. Not only was filmed Shakespeare deadly, the particular Shakespeare Branagh intended to make had already been definitively inscribed on the screen in 1944 by the century's greatest Shakespearean actor, Laurence Olivier. Branagh had the drive and chutzpah to take on two English legends and, with a little help from some important friends (the producer Stephen Evans and the noted actors Paul Scofield, Ian Holm, and Judi Dench), miraculously created a dynamic film that brought a fresh conception of a more natural Shakespeare (tough, lean, gritty, and emotionally charged) to a new audience. The film, made for six million dollars, was universally praised and was nominated for three Academy Awards, including Best Actor and Best Director nominations for the brash, Irish unknown who was suddenly a hot item in Hollywood and the world of film.

The unexpected success of *Henry V* (1989) created a renaissance for the Shakespeare film, and the decade of the 1990s proved to be the richest for the release of Shakespeare films in the one-hundred-year history of the genre. The decade also proved to be the period in which Kenneth Branagh made his mark as a film director. He made eight major films between 1989 and 2000 ranging from self-financed independent films such as *Peter's Friends* (1992) and *A Midwinter's Tale* (1995); to more Shakespeare's such as *Much Ado About Nothing* (1993), *Hamlet (1996)*, and *Love's Labour's Lost* (2000); to Hollywood fare such as *Dead Again* (1991) and *Mary Shelley's Frankenstein* (1994). Branagh also appeared as an actor in eight other films in this period, again working across a range of films from low budget independents such as *How to Kill Your Neighbor's Dog* (2000), to Hollywood extravaganzas such as *Wild Wild West* (1999). Often, Branagh chose to work in films made by directors with unique film styles, such as Barry Sonnenfeld (*Wild Wild West*), Robert Altman (*The Gingerbread Man* [1998]), and Woody Allen (*Celebrity* [1998]). Branagh was clearly interested in seeing first-hand how very different directors worked—from Altman's improvised dazzle to Allen's minimal camera set-ups and controlled focus on the screenplay. The most interesting dynamic developed between Branagh and Altman, though the finished product only had flashes of brilliance rather than sustained momentum.

Branagh's work in the 1990s, as he moved through his thirties, was prodigious. He knew he was a hot property and he wanted to maximize his ability to leverage as much funding for his film projects—especially Shakespeare—as possible. As a result, as the decade progressed, he moved away from the stage and more thoroughly and deeply into film. His last stage role in the 1990s was the Hamlet he did for the Royal Shakespeare Company in the 1992–93 season, where he was again linked with Adrian Noble who had previously directed him in *Henry V.* He did not return to the stage until his highly lauded performance of Richard III at Sheffield's Crucible Theatre in 2002. As an example of Branagh's relentless activity during the 1990s, here is his schedule for 1992:[5]

January 6–12	Recorded audio version of *Hamlet* at BBC Maida Vale
February 1–9	Shooting for *Swing Kids* in Prague
February 24 to March 28	Shot *Peter's Friend's* at Wrotham Park, North London
March 30	First rehearsal for *Coriolanus* in London
May 4	First preview for *Coriolanus* in Chichester
May 13	First night of *Coriolanus*; performed in repertory until June 27, 1992
June 6–8	Shot short film *Swan Song* at Criterion Theatre
June 27	First rehearsal for *Much Ado About Nothing* at Villa Vignamaggio, Greve, Tuscany
August 3 to September 19	Shot *Much Ado About Nothing*
October 5	First rehearsal for *Hamlet* at the RSC, Clapham, London

December 12	First preview at the Barbican
December 18	First night of *Hamlet*; played in repertory until March 11, 1993 at the Barbican before moving to Stratford where it played until May
December 21	Screened *Much Ado* for Sam Goldwyn at the Pavilion Theatre, LA
December 24	*Peter's Friends* opened in New York

The 1992–93 period is not only illustrative but, perhaps, marks the moment when Branagh's star, artistically and personally, was in its ascendancy. His marriage to Emma Thompson had made them the most famous theatrical couple in England since Laurence Olivier and Vivien Leigh. Branagh's performance of Hamlet played to packed houses in London and Stratford from December of 1992 until May of 1993. The production was particularly popular among the young, with many queuing all night to snap-up day tickets and standing room places when the box office opened each morning. In March of 1993 Emma Thompson won the Academy Award for her portrayal of Margaret Schlegel in the Merchant-Ivory film of *Howard's End*. In May, Branagh's film of *Much Ado About Nothing*, starring Thompson as Beatrice, opened to ecstatic reviews and became the first Shakespeare film since Zeffirelli's 1968 *Romeo and Juliet* to capture a large teenage audience and become a commercial success. In less than three years, from the golden summer of 1992 until the spring of 1995, though Branagh's work-pace had not slowed, the glow had evaporated from his career. The English press had turned on the glamorous couple they had helped to create; *Mary Shelley's Frankenstein* had been released to dismissive and often savage reviews; and the Branagh-Thompson marriage had dissolved.

As an answer to this private turmoil, Branagh turned again to those resources that fired his creative engine—the synthesis of his Belfast boyhood with the sustaining powers of a theatrical company. He wrote his one completely original screenplay, *A Midwinter's Tale*, which celebrated the crazy, mad, exasperating, and glorious life of a group of itinerant actors coming together for a benefit performance of *Hamlet* in a rural English village. As Branagh retorted when a recent interviewer chided him for insisting on his Irish heritage, "But I feel Irish. I don't think you can take Belfast out of the boy. I came from the kind of street where everyone knew everyone else. Surrounded by dozens of cousins and friends, it was like living in a large extended family. Maybe that's why I was drawn to the theatre, as another way of belonging to a large family."[6] A *Midwinter's Tale* celebrates that family by telling a series of loving backstage stories about actors and their insecurities and eccentricities. Branagh financed the film himself, with all the cast and crew being paid the same salary and all having equal shares in the profits the film ultimately generated when it was sold to Castle Rock Entertainment for distribution. Two young scholars interested in the intersection of Shakespeare and popular culture, Douglas Lanier and Courtney Lehmann, have both written compellingly about the importance of community in Branagh's film aesthetic. Lanier thinks Branagh is largely successful in putting Shakespeare to work in the service of a communal ideal, while Lehmann has strong reservations about Branagh's achievement, but both are right to sense that creating community is at the heart of Branagh's artistic ambition.[7]

Branagh closed this active decade with two daring decisions. The first was to shoot a three hour and forty-five minute full-text *Hamlet*, and the second was to take the Shakespeare film genre in a stunning new direction by making a musical comedy version of *Love's Labour's Lost*, set in the long summer of 1939 as Hitler rolled into Eastern Europe. Branagh used many of the great and lasting popular songs of the 1930s by George Gershwin, Irving Berlin, and Cole Porter as a modern expression of ideas about wooing and love at work and play in Shakespeare's text. In both films Branagh was leading his audience in new directions in the Shakespeare film genre, but they did not follow. Neither film was able to build on the audience Branagh had found for *Henry V* and greatly expanded for *Much Ado About Nothing*, though *Love's Labour's Lost* managed to recoup its production costs. Though Branagh signed a three-picture deal with Miramax in 1998, the only film of that projected trio to be made is *Love's Labour's Lost*. After the intense film-directing activity of the 1990s, Branagh returned to his roles as an actor (on stage and in film) and theater director in the first years of the new century. As this study goes to press, Branagh's filmmaking career is once again in motion with his film version of *As You Like It* (see my interview with Branagh at the back of the volume), financed by HBO Films currently in post-production, and a treatment of Mozart's *The Magic Flute*, set against the backdrop of World War I, scheduled to begin shooting in January of 2006.

Branagh has been compared most often with Laurence Olivier and Orson Welles, his great predecessors in creating and defining the Shakespeare film genre. Welles and Olivier were unique in their generation as actors turned filmmakers. Their work with Shakespeare on stage provided the inspiration for trying successfully to translate him into film, especially

Branagh seated on the crane preparing for the elaborate extended steadicam and crane shot that ends *Much Ado About Nothing*. [Photographer: Theo Westenberger, Courtesy of Photofest]

faced with the largely unsatisfactory efforts to do so in the 1930s in both America and England. Olivier, of course, never found in film the same satisfaction, as actor or director, that he did working in the theater. He only directed one non-Shakespearean film, *The Prince and the Showgirl* (1956), and the experience of working with his troubled co-star Marilyn Monroe permanently soured his interest in directing popular films. Olivier is universally recognized as one of the great stage and film actors of his age, but his films are more prized by Shakespeareans than cineastes.

Welles's legacy, of course, runs counter to Olivier's. Welles will always be remembered as one of the giants of twentieth-century film, while his work in the theater in the 1930s has become a historical footnote rather than career-defining. Once he moved into film with *Citizen Kane* (1941), he only returned to the theater three times—to play Othello in 1951, Ahab in *Moby Dick* in 1955, and King Lear in 1956.[8] Welles was a great innovator as a film director and Olivier paid him the high compliment of borrowing the deep focus technique that Welles had pioneered in *Citizen Kane* as a central ingredient in the cinematography of his 1948 film of *Hamlet*.

Branagh's dual career as a classical actor and filmmaker does have its source in the work of Olivier and Welles. To that legacy he adds a third strong influence from the history of Shakespeare on film, Franco Zeffirelli's operatic neo-romanticism. Branagh creates his own unique style, what Pauline Kael called his "flamboyant realism," from his synthesis of the elements at work in the films of his powerful predecessors.[9] Olivier and Welles were unique in their era as actors who became film directors. This crossover was undoubtedly dictated by their experiences of directing, as well as acting, in the theater and their commitment to Shakespeare as the central figure in the development of their art. None of their actor-contemporaries on either side of the Atlantic, on stage, or on screen, attempted to combine both worlds. Great Hollywood actors such as Clark Gable, Jimmy Stewart, Humphrey Bogart, Cary Grant, Katharine Hepburn, Spencer Tracy, or Jimmy Cagney never attempted to direct a film of their own. Only John Wayne was tempted, and the result, *The Alamo*, was a failure. Similarly, none of Olivier's contemporaries, John Gielgud, Ralph Richardson, Alec Guinness, or Michael Redgrave, ever directed a movie.

Branagh came of artistic age in a different era. The collapse of the old Hollywood studio system in the 1950s and 60s not only opened the door for younger, more independent directors such as Francis Ford Coppola, George Lucas, and Stephen Spielberg, but made it much more possible for actors to find funding for films they wished to direct. Beginning in the early 1970s with Clint Eastwood and his *Play Misty for Me* (1971), major Hollywood actors began careers as directors. Eastwood remains, thirty-five years later, at the head of the class, having directed twenty-seven films including winning the Academy Award for Best Picture and Best Director for *The Unforgiven* (1992) and *Million Dollar Baby* (2004). Other actor-directors whose films have claimed Hollywood's top prize for Best Picture and/or Best Director include Woody Allen, Robert Redford, Kevin Costner, Mel Gibson, and Warren Beatty. Nothing similar has happened in the British film world. Albert Finney did make one venture into directing, *Charlie Bubble* (1967), and then returned exclusively to acting. But Branagh's chief film influences, with one or two exceptions, always flowed from Hollywood commercial films rather than from the work of directors such as Tony Richardson, Lindsay Anderson, Karel Reisz, and Richard Lester who created a revolution in British films in the 1960s. Branagh linked the tradition established by Olivier and Welles, as actors who directed Shakespeare films, with the newer American practice of established actors seeking to expand their careers by directing.

As Sarah Hatchuel and others have pointed out, Branagh, as a movie director, is deeply attracted to Hollywood film codes, conventions, and genres.[10] He draws energy and inspiration from the popular Hollywood films he remembers watching, primarily on television, as a boy growing up in Belfast and Reading. When asked about the obvious influence of Hollywood films on his particular style of filming Shakespeare, he responded, "I'm absolutely unembarrassed about that. . . . I was inspired by the fact that Shakespeare himself can legitimately be called a populist. The theater he worked for was subject to the rule of box office, something that is interestingly and comically treated in *Shakespeare in Love*. . . . he seemed to be a man who had a commercial instinct."[11] Branagh has been fearless in trying to rescue Shakespeare from the small art house audience and reclaim him for the modern cineplex that draws a crowd similar in its range to the one that flowed over London Bridge to the Rose and the Globe on an Elizabethan summer afternoon.

Branagh's four Shakespeare films all have Hollywood models: the war film for *Henry V* ; the screwball comedy for *Much Ado About Nothing*; the intelligent epic, such as David Lean's *Doctor Zhivago* (1965) or *Lawrence of Arabia* (1962), for *Hamlet*; and the American film musical comedy, a mixture of Fred Astaire and Gene Kelly, for *Love's Labour's Lost*. His four other feature films also draw upon established models: the noir detective thriller for *Dead Again*; the country weekend house party for *Peter's Friends*; the gothic-romantic horror film for *Mary Shelley's Frankenstein*; and—in a quieter, more local, and less obvious vein—the Ealing Studio comedy for *A Midwinter's Tale*. Branagh is an auteur in the popular, rather than art house or avant-garde, tradition. His films bear no resemblance, nor do they gather energy from such obvious auteurs as Fellini, Bergman, or Truffaut. He is, however, a keen student of the Shakespeare film, and thus one can detect in his film style the occasional influence of the work of the great Japanese and Russian directors, Akira Kurosawa and Grigori Kozintsev. But he is much more of a cross between Clint Eastwood and Woody Allen. Like Eastwood he is drawn to established Hollywood commercial genres; like Allen he frequently works with the same group of actors and has developed a clearly recognizable film style, though one quite different from Woody's clean, formalist lines and static camera.

Branagh's Shakespeare and non-Shakespearean films all draw upon the same core group of actors—Richard Briers, Derek Jacobi, Michael Maloney, Emma Thompson, Ian Holm, Geraldine McEwen, Nicholas Farrell, Robin Williams, Richard Easton, Judi Dench, and Branagh himself. This is Branagh's attempt to create a film company based on his experience in England's stage repertory system. The only, and short-lived, classical model for what Branagh has accomplished in company continuity over a series of films was Orson Welles's attempt to transport his Mercury

Theater Company from New York to Hollywood. They became his principal players in his first three films, *Citizen Kane* (1941), *The Magnificent Ambersons* (1942), and *Macbeth* (1948), but that was the extent of their collaboration as Welles left Hollywood for Europe in the 1950s. In the commercial film world, as mentioned previously, Branagh participates in the pattern of using a core group of actors across several films, as established in Hollywood by John Ford and revived in our time by Clint Eastwood and Woody Allen.

Branagh's eight films can be broken into two distinct groups based on landscape and focus. *Henry V* (1989), *Peter's Friends* (1992), *A Midwinter's Tale* (1995), and *Love's Labour's Lost* (2000) all share a company ethos in substance and style. Branagh's camera work is as vivid in these films as in those with a wider sweep, but it is less romantically intoxicated. The focus, with a few notable exceptions, is more generally on the group experience than on the individual. Henry V is defined through camera work and editing as much by his relationship to others (the Boar's Head Tavern crew, the traitors, his band of brothers, Emma Thompson's Katherine) as by his solitary screen moments. The other three films concentrate on group experience and, particularly in *A Midwinter's Tale*, Branagh repeatedly positions his cast to capture as many of them in the composition of the frame as possible. These four movies are Branagh's most personal films. They all reveal his ethos of community as he strives to create harmony out of disparate and disruptive energies. *Henry V* was his bold, against the odds, first venture into filmmaking where reliance upon crew and cast was essential for the novice director; *Peter's Friends* and *A Midwinter's Tale* are ensemble films in content and structure and were shot on shoe-string budgets largely financed by Branagh's work in other films; *Love's Labour's Lost* necessitated the creation of a mini-dramatic academy for the cast who devoted themselves to an intensive period of singing, dancing, and voice lessons before the formal shooting began. With the exception of Berowne's long speech on love, ladies, and learning, the camera's attention is always on the group rather than the individual. Shakespeare's comedies celebrate communal rituals rather than private agonies and *Love's Labour's Lost* emphasizes this social reality by featuring four sets of lovers. Branagh's film intensifies this experience by transforming the lovers into various versions of Fred and Ginger, or Gene and Leslie; dancing becomes the image of the heaven-on-earth harmony romantic comedy aspires to achieve.

Branagh's other four films, *Dead Again* (1991), *Much Ado About Nothing* (1993), *Mary Shelley's Frankenstein* (1994), and *Hamlet* (1996), expand into wider landscapes and, while still tied to the communal experience, they open up avenues for more idiosyncratic personal exploration. Not surprisingly, these films also had much larger budgets to work with, ranging from *Much Ado About Nothing*'s fifteen million dollars to *Mary Shelley's Frankenstein*'s forty-million-dollar budget. In these films Branagh's camera expands into vaster physical and psychological territory. *Dead Again* is Branagh's only film actually shot in Hollywood (on the same Paramount sound stage where Welles had shot *Citizen Kane*), and it moves back and forth between the 1940s and the 1990s and between black and white and Technicolor photography, investigating a tangled tale of music, mystery, and murder. The film allows for some bravura displays of acting by Branagh and Emma Thompson as they double the roles of Roman Strauss and Mike Church (Branagh) and Margaret Strauss and Amanda Sharp (Thompson). While Branagh managed to get Derek Jacobi into the cast, once Donald Sutherland had left the film, as the villain Franklyn Madson, *Dead Again* took a big step away from Branagh's Renaissance Company. The film's focus was clearly on Branagh and Thompson's characters and their intriguing double lives, even though it also featured cameo roles for Andy Garcia, Robin Williams, and Hannah Schygulla, the star of many Werner Fassbinder films.

Much Ado About Nothing returned many of the Renaissance crew to film along with the American screen stars Denzel Washington, Keanu Reeves, Michael Keaton, and Robert Sean Leonard. Branagh's film vocabulary was enlarged by shooting the entire picture on location at the Villa Vignamaggio in Tuscany in the summer of 1992. The film is robust and vivid from its opening sequence of the women enjoying the summer sun on a Tuscan hillside as their potential mates come pounding home from war in the valley below. As Branagh's slow-motion camera catches the men lifting provocatively in and out of their saddles, they pump their fists triumphantly in the air—the Magnificent Seven galloping into Shakespeareland—as Patrick Doyle's score soars on the soundtrack. This giddy, romantic, populist energy is maintained throughout the film and is capped by the final dazzling steadicam shot of the reunited lovers and their fellow wedding celebrants swirling out into the villa's gardens as confetti dances in the air. *Much Ado* was the first Shakespeare film since Zeffirelli's *Romeo and Juliet* in 1968 to become a commercial success, particularly with the young.

Riding the crest of his commercial success with both Hollywood (*Dead Again*) and Shakespeare (*Much Ado*), Branagh was tempted into blockbuster territory by accepting Francis Ford Coppola's offer to direct a remake of *Frankenstein*. The *Frankenstein* project provided Branagh with the largest cinematic canvas of his career and he did not hesitate to

Branagh, in costume as Victor Frankenstein, looks up at the garret in Ingolstadt where Victor will establish his laboratory that will lead to the making of the Creature in *Mary Shelley's Frankenstein*.   [Photographer: David Appleby, Courtesy of Photofest]

splatter it with the boldest colors in his palette. The film was Marlovian, rather than Shakespearean, in its excess. Branagh wanted it all—passion, romance, big ideas, gothic horror, and more fire and ice than Mary Shelley's ambiguous fable could safely contain. The film, despite its critical failure, remains the quintessential Branagh visual statement. He's testing his epic urges in *Mary Shelley's Frankenstein* and is willing to throw caution, and often taste, to the winds. The film has a mad energy meant to match Victor Frankenstein's racing mind and daring experiment. It tosses, turns, tumbles, and eventually goes up in flames in both Zurich and the frozen North. The film actually turned a handsome profit in worldwide box office and video rental sales, but it will always be remembered as the film that brought down Branagh's cinematic comet.

The last of Branagh's big films, *Hamlet* (1996), was the event his young career had been heading towards. In many ways it was a more daring gamble than *Mary Shelley's Frankenstein*. Only Branagh, with his credentials as a Shakespearean and film director who delivered his work on time and within budget, could have convinced Hollywood producers to finance a four hour film of the complete text of *Hamlet*. The film was a culmination of his work with Shakespeare and Renaissance and revealed his growth as a director. The film is an intelligent epic—a homage not to Hollywood but to the British Film Industry as represented by the work of David Lean and Richard Attenborough. The film is a remarkable achievement from its huge and eclectic cast (including Julie Christie, Lean's Laura in *Doctor Zhivago*), to its Blenheim setting for the exteriors then blended into a version of Versailles' Hall of Mirrors for its studio interiors, to its dazzling but subtle (a difficult trick to accomplish) cinematography by Alex Thompson (another Lean veteran), to its determined attention to delivering Shakespeare's heightened language as if it were naturalistic conversation, to presenting a romantic and heroic Hamlet in a cynical age.

Branagh's big films reveal his desire to be lushly cinematic, nowhere more obvious than in his collaboration with Patrick Doyle, the composer of the scores for all of his films. Branagh and Doyle are aware that music is an essential element in any movie's rhetoric. Shakespeareans often complain about the way film scores distract from Shakespeare's verbal music, but can one imagine Laurence Olivier's Shakespeare films without William Walton, or Gregori Kozintsev's without Dmitri Shostakovich? Iago's attempted murder of Roderigo in the Turkish bath in Welles's *Othello* is locked in our memory by the frenzy of those mandolins under the action; the bittersweet romantic yearning of Zeffirelli's *Romeo and Juliet* is carried along as much by Nino Rota's lush score, as by Leonard Whiting and Olivia Hussey's breathless speaking of the verse. For instance, in *Hamlet* Doyle's eclectic and allusive style of musical expression and his formal skill in writing for orchestra is striking. As the film unfolds he uses a variety of musical elements including conflating Latin mass and grand opera; chamber ensembles contrasted with full orchestra; orchestra sections playing in complex polyphony; chromatic as well as diatonic melodic lines; and dissonant, quasi-atonal harmonies. As with Walton's work for Olivier, Doyle identifies characters with musical motifs. Ophelia's theme, for instance, illustrates Doyle's talent for original use of melodic influences. Her theme is almost a direct quotation from Mahler in its pronounced and repeated resolution of the seventh scale degree downward. Mahlerian too is the theme's progression between the letter scene and the mad scene, from soulful yearning and naiveté to elegiac mourning, as captured by the prevalence of horn and woodwind orchestration in these scenes. The Hamlet theme, by contrast, is small in compass, virtually contained within a fifth; it is short and convoluted, the melodic equivalent of being bounded in a nutshell.[12]

Doyle's film scores are more than matched by Branagh's shooting style. Branagh loves to use the full repertory of technical devices available for handling the camera: tracking shots, dollies, zooms, steadicams, cranes. Because he trusts his actors, he is fond of shooting in long takes with the camera maneuvering in and around the characters. He likes the dizzy energy of circle shots where the camera can swirl or prowl around the edges of the action. *Mary Shelley's Frankenstein* is defined by such swirling shots meant to capture the elegant waltz (as emblem of family romance and harmony) Victor Frankenstein remembers enjoying as a boy with his mother. That dancing motif is repeated in the birth-of-the-Creature sequence where Victor attempts to defeat death (provoked by his earlier reaction to his mother's death in childbirth) by creating life. For *Hamlet*, Branagh had a special dolly built in Italy to support the heavy 65mm camera used to shoot the film. The dolly allowed him to glide about Elsinore's Hall of Mirrors, sometimes circling the actors, as in Hamlet's early meeting with Horatio and Marcellus when they bring news of the Ghost, and sometimes catching their reflections in those mirrored doors trimmed in gilt lining the great hall, as in Hamlet's "To be or not to be" soliloquy or in Ophelia's mad scene.

Branagh is, perhaps, most attached to the steadicam, which allows for even more fluid movement, coupled with the use of a crane that can move the camera from tight intimacy to deep perspective. The most famous steadicam example in his films is the final shot in *Much Ado About Nothing* where the steadicam operator had to follow the lovers from the chapel into the villa's courtyard, pivot, and continue, now backing away from the singing and the dancing throng, into the garden where he then had to find the crane's seat while still backing up, sit, and be elevated up into the sky to capture the celebration from overhead before turning for a final shot out over the distant Tuscan countryside. It took eighteen takes to finally achieve Branagh's cinematic idea. The opening, single-take sequence of *Peter's Friends* is equally remarkable, this time for accomplishing similar film magic within a cramped and constricted interior space. Branagh clearly thrives on such challenges. His cinematic imagination is fired by bold, bravura moments. It is moments such as these that leads Pierre Berthomieu, in the only single-volume study of Branagh's films yet published and available only in French, to declare: "Branagh loves the spectacular. . . in the interest of a vital energy which gives his work its coherence."[13]

Branagh is an actor's director—employing, particularly for his Shakespeare films, an extended rehearsal period where collaborative ideas about the rhythm and chemistry of individual scenes influence his directorial choices. He doesn't story board his films except for important scenes, such as the creation sequence in *Mary Shelley's Frankenstein*.[14] He does, however, come to each film with what he calls certain "anchor images" already developed in his mind.[15] These include, for example, the long tracking shot back across the Agincourt battle field at the end of the conflict in *Henry V*; the opening sequences in *Much Ado* and *Peter's Friends*; the crane shot of Hamlet's "How all occasions do inform against me" soliloquy that begins in tight close-up and ends with Hamlet just a black speck trapped against a vast expanse of winter wasteland; the helicopter shot of Victor Frankenstein tracking his creation through the frozen Alps; and the cast of *A Midwinter's Tale* gathered around Madge's model of the set which simply replicates the church where their performance of *Hamlet* is to take place. Each of these shots helps to create the signature of Branagh's film aesthetic. They are robustly cinematic and memorable as images independent of their context, but they also speak powerfully to Branagh's goal of merging text and image; actor and landscape; shot and sequence. As Sarah Hatchuel has commented on these anchor shots, "Branagh often combines the visual strategies of literal illustration and metaphoric association."[16] The bold dare of these shots and sequences always risks the charge, particularly when working with classic texts, of being banal at best, vulgar at worst. Branagh is willing to take that gamble; his films always aspire to push the envelope of broad appeal and never seek to settle for the tidy good manners and refined taste that marks the Merchant/Ivory approach to translating highbrow literature (James, Forster, Ishiguro) into film.

If Beethoven set the standard for writing big symphonies at nine, Olivier, Welles, Kurosawa, and Zeffirelli set the mark for Shakespeare films at three. Branagh's remarkable decade of achievement as a film director concluded with the release of his fourth Shakespeare film, *Love's Labour's Lost*, in 2000. He revitalized the genre and moved it in new directions. Branagh set out to make an intelligent, popular synthesis of Stratford and Hollywood and succeeded. Trevor Nunn, the former director of the Royal Shakespeare Company and the Royal National Theatre, has generously allowed, "It has become possible for many people to think in terms of filming Shakespeare almost entirely because of the achievement of Kenneth Branagh."[17] From the Hollywood side of the equation, Al Pacino has commented, "Branagh opened it all up with *Henry V*. Now you say Shakespeare on film in Hollywood and people listen."[18] What Branagh opened up was a decade that saw the release of twenty major Shakespeare films (after two decades that saw the release of four) and an equal number of spin-offs and clever adaptations. Suddenly Shakespeare was everywhere on film including starring in the Academy Award winner for Best Picture in 1998, *Shakespeare in Love*.

Kenneth Branagh began his career as a director as a novice outsider willing to take on the Shakespeare establishment and the moribund genre of Shakespeare on film. The brave little film he made took an English icon (Henry V and his heroic 1944 impersonator, Laurence Olivier) down into the messy work of imperial conquest and nation building. In the process Branagh got his mud-laden version of the character admiringly tagged as "Dirty Harry." Branagh then became the first English actor of his generation to follow the original Dirty Harry, Clint Eastwood, into becoming a film director. Branagh differed from American actors-turned-filmmakers like Redford, Beatty, Costner, and Gibson in one chief respect: Branagh saw his move into films as a way of extending and enlarging the community experience he had sought to achieve with his Renaissance Theatre Company. That experience meant sustaining a common company of actors and production associates, including designer Tim Harvey, composer Patrick Doyle, text consultant Russell Jackson, advisor Hugh Cruttwell, and producers David Parfitt, David Barron, and Stephen Evans, across the eight feature films Branagh made between 1989 and 2000. He may have begun his directing career as an anti-establishment outsider like Dirty Harry, but by the end of the decade he had created a new film dynamic and had earned, much like Eastwood himself, the respect and admiration of the global film community.

This study presents a chapter-by-chapter analysis of each of Branagh's eight commercial films, in chronological order. My previous work on Branagh was exclusively devoted to his Shakespeare films and sought to understand them in the context of the development of the Shakespeare film genre. Here I am more interested in exploring them within the landscape of Branagh's other films and in the context of his development as a filmmaker. Occasionally I have relied on previous formulations about his Shakespeare films, but I have tried to take a fresh look and approach to the way they reveal his continuing concerns about style and substance across the complete body of his film work.

Chapter 2

HENRY V

A black screen. The rasping sound of a match being struck. The sudden illumination of actor Derek Jacobi's face in close-up quietly confiding to the camera, "O for a muse of fire." That match became the cinematic muse of fire that rekindled the Shakespeare film genre that had been moribund for almost two decades.[1] Jacobi finished the Chorus's famous opening lines of Shakespeare's *Henry V*, "that would ascend / The brightest heaven of invention," as the camera slowly pulled back to reveal Jacobi's movement across a steel grid and down a set of stairs. The actor threw a large industrial light switch, literally making bright the imaginative heaven of Kenneth Branagh's cinematic invention. "A kingdom for a stage," Jacobi assured us, as he crossed over a film sound stage surrounded by props, the backs of constructed sets, kleig lights, wind machines, and a Panaflex 35 motion picture camera.

This vivid opening—words and fire emerging out of the void—announced Branagh's arrival in the world of Shakespeare on film as he became the first British Shakespearean in twenty years to translate Shakespeare into film.[2] Much like Williams's challenging Henry V on the night before the Battle of Agincourt, Branagh's film also threw down a gauntlet in front of the most important Shakespeare film ever made, Laurence Olivier's *Henry V* (1944). The success of Olivier's film was as much of a surprise as the eventual success of Branagh's, though Olivier's adaptation came from the leading British actor of his age and not an unknown Northern Irish upstart. Olivier's *Henry V*, made to bring Shakespeare to the service of the war effort as the Allied Forces were gathering for the invasion of France, was the first Shakespeare film to be considered both a commercial and an artistic triumph. The film and its Shakespearean source represented a culture and a heritage worth preserving and fighting for. Some regard it as the greatest war propaganda film ever made. It also launched what we now regard as the golden age of Shakespeare on film: the post–World War II period, extending for almost twenty-five years, that produced the great Shakespeare films of Olivier, Orson Welles, Akira Kurosawa, Grigori Kozintsev, Joseph Mankiewicz, and Franco Zeffirelli.

Branagh's impudent film brazenly challenged Olivier's and became itself a spur and inspiration to a new generation of Shakespeare films. Olivier's film was a nostalgic celebration of Shakespeare's age and stage. The film's famous opening in a restored version of the Globe Theatre established the communal harmony of the theatrical enterprise as a microcosm of the larger culture. Olivier shot his film in vivid Technicolor. With the exception of the Boar's Head Tavern scenes and the scene of Agincourt eve, the sun was always shining. Olivier cut all of the darker underside of Shakespeare's conception of Henry V by eliminating his barely controlled anger at being mocked by the Dauphin and discarding the traitors' scene, the violent threats at Harfleur, the hanging of Bardolph, and the order to "Kill all the prisoners." The film made a stunning contrast with World War II England, hammered from above by Hitler's Luftwaffe and from below by the daily deprivations of wartime existence. The film brought Shakespeare, Henry V, and Olivier to the rescue by reminding the British of their glorious cultural heritage. Olivier's Henry V was a version of the filmmaker himself: a man at the zenith of his considerable powers. Peter S. Donaldson has captured evocatively this element of Olivier's strategy:

> Laurence Olivier's film version of the play . . . aligns itself with the affirmative, heroic energies of *Henry V* . . . Olivier's conception of his role as adaptor was shaped by patriotic fervor and sanctioned by what he describes as an almost mystic or dyadic identification with Shakespeare: 'I had a mission. . . . My country was at war; I felt Shakespeare within me, I felt the cinema within him. I knew what I wanted to do, what he would have done.'[3]

Olivier gave himself a delicious double entrance in his film, first sliding into the frame from the left, backstage at the Globe, and then clearing his throat before making the star's grand entrance onto the stage itself to be greeted rapturously by the audience. Olivier, as adapter and director, thus aligned himself not only with Shakespeare but also with Richard Burbage, the leading man of Shakespeare's Company: all the stars are in conjunction here.

Branagh's film of *Henry V* emerged from a very different historical moment. Branagh was twenty-seven when he began shooting the film in the fall of 1988. He was one of a handful of younger British actors, including Antony Sher, Rupert Everett, Daniel Day Lewis, Mark Rylance, Ralph Fiennes, Juliet Stevenson, Fiona Shaw, Simon Russell Beale, and Emma Thompson, beginning to establish reputations in London's West End and the major repertory companies. Branagh had directed studio productions of *Romeo and Juliet* and *Twelfth Night* and had led the Renaissance Theatre Company, which he created, in its first season of three Shakespeare plays: *Hamlet*, *Much Ado About Nothing*, and *As You Like It*. He was most widely known for playing Guy Pringle in the BBC's adaptation of Olivia Manning's novel *Fortunes of War* (1987). He was virtually unknown in the world of film.[4]

Branagh had played Henry V in Adrian Noble's highly praised production for the Royal Shakespeare Company (RSC) in 1984. In a move that was typical of Branagh's imagination and ambition but atypical for a twenty-three-year-old Brit in any occupation, he arranged a meeting with Prince Charles as one part of his research for the role. For generations it has been perfectly legitimate for actors to head to the prisons or asylums or, even more famously, to the zoo to find inspiration for playing knotty Shakespearean roles, but no actor had ever before prepped for playing a king by visiting the palace. Branagh was clearly different. Perhaps being a double outsider, a protestant Irishman from Belfast, led him to break the rules he had never known, but the chutzpah involved in his decision to seek out Prince Charles became emblematic of his young career. It was also the beginning of his long and contentious relationship with the British press that pounces on those who seek the limelight even in a culture famed for championing and cherishing the offbeat. Ambition is only tolerated in London if it is clothed in eccentricity.

Branagh's decision to leave the RSC after a single season to strike out on his own, his determination to juggle work on stage with film and television productions, his creation of his own repertory company without a permanent home, and his unavoidably public courtship and marriage to Emma Thompson all revealed the same sense of iconoclastic energy that had induced him to seek out the prince for lessons in royal responsibility. But his decision to make a film of *Henry V* was the biggest dare and gamble of them all.

Fittingly, Olivier's Henry V is an established star, Branagh's a cheeky pretender. When he made his *Henry V*, Olivier had already appeared in twenty-one films, including such popular Hollywood fare as *Wuthering Heights* (1939), *Rebecca* (1940), and *Pride and Prejudice* (1940);

Ian Holm as Fluellen passes the torch to a new generation of English Shakespeareans led by Kenneth Branagh in Branagh's film of *Henry V.* [Photographer: Sophie Baker, Courtesy of Photofest]

Branagh, at the time of his adaptation, had appeared in but two small and quickly forgotten ones: *High Season* (1987), and *A Month in the Country* (1987). Accordingly, Olivier's film begins in daylight dazzle as his camera pans over a model of Elizabethan London, down the South Bank from London Bridge to Southwark Cathedral and on to the Globe. The Thames was never so blue (courtesy of the motor oil Olivier's set designer used). Branagh's film, in contrast, begins in darkness until Jacobi strikes that match and throws that power switch, but even then, Branagh's film of *Henry V* remains shrouded in shadows and mystery. The interiors are dominated by the amber hues and dusky tones created by candlelight and torchlight and the reflections cast by roaring fires. When the film ventures outside to Harfleur and Agincourt, it's often raining, and Branagh's cinematographer, Kenneth MacMillan, shot the night scenes through a cold blue filter. It's as though the entire film flashes through Henry's mind as he discovers that the king must "bear all" on the night before Agincourt. The only relief from the somber tones and bad weather comes when the Chorus walks along the cliffs of Dover announcing England's "dreadful preparation" for the invasion and the subsequent English lesson scene between Katherine and Alice.

The cut to this scene comes after the conclusion of the nighttime siege of Harfleur, punctuated by the gigantic explosions (no giving over of the mines here) creating the breach in the town's walls. Suddenly we are in a white room; Katherine is all in white; and momentarily the film's claustrophobia is lifted as light streams in through the first use of windows in the film. Windows will not reappear until the film's final scene, in which the windows signal the peace accord that seals Henry's personal and political triumph.

The film's intense, claustrophobic atmosphere is established at the outset in Branagh's handling of the scene between the Archbishop of Canterbury and the Bishop of Ely as they plot the church's advantages in sending the king on his French adventure. Olivier played the scene for comedy, but Branagh treated it with conspiratorial seriousness: a door creaks open; Canterbury (Charles Kay) peeks out and sees the shadows of figures moving down a corridor. Canterbury shuts the door and begins to confide to Ely (Alec McGowen) the political realities of the bill the king has introduced, a bill that would erode the church's land holdings. There is no establishing shot. Branagh's camera is in tight; Kay and McGowen are captured in close-up with quick cuts for reaction shots. The film then cuts to a smoky room and the camera pans down a line of young, attentive faces and turns with them to see a figure, backlit, standing in a huge doorway. This shot is the beginning of the remarkable double entrance Branagh gave his Henry V. It may well be the most dramatic first entrance any actor-filmmaker has given himself in the history of the movies. Pauline Kael was the first to recognize the shot's debt to George Lucas's treatment of Darth Vader.[5] As the figure enters the council room and makes his way down the line of courtiers, we see only the courtiers' reactions to his progress. We finally first see this mystery man's face when he reaches the throne, turns, sits, and slides off his cloak to reveal a tousle-headed boy dressed in a powder blue tunic, completely dwarfed by the size of the throne chair in which he is decidedly uncomfortable. Darth Vader has morphed in front of our eyes into Luke Skywalker.

The shot works not only because it employs cinematic humor, but also because it silently conveys Branagh's approach to Henry V. His king is a work-in-progress rather than Olivier's fully formed "star of England." Branagh's Henry is too young to be a master manipulator, and the filmmaker gives his full attention to Canterbury's Salique Law justification for Henry's claim to the French throne. Henry darts a quick glance that says "Is Canterbury on the level?" at Exeter (Brian Blessed) who nods affirmatively before quietly and cautiously responding, "May I with right and conscience make this claim?" (1.2.16).[6] Branagh expresses himself in the council sequence, featuring Canterbury's speech and the Dauphin's mock with the tennis balls, with a quiet determination as though he is finding the character through a restrained release of his rhetorical voice. An important aspect of Branagh's style in speaking Shakespeare's verse first emerges in this scene. The actor speaks with a confidential tone, recognizing that the camera is an auditor equal to those fellow actors who share the frame with him. He never rushes, and he strikes his consonants with a telling force that maintains a steady beat. Branagh's lung power is remarkable; he negotiates a Shakespearean sentence of four or five iambic pentameter lines without ever appearing to breathe. Later, before Harfleur and Agincourt, Branagh lets Shakespeare's rhetoric rip and soar, underlined by Patrick Doyle's score, but it always takes off from a quiet moment grounded in the reaction shots of the familiar faces of his troops. Branagh expresses Shakespeare's music in a lean and muscular tone. This approach extends to the other members of his cast as well. Geoffrey O'Brien has tried to capture this effect in his review of *Henry V*:

> The job of the actor was to clarify, line by line and word by word, not just the general purport of what the character was feeling, but the exact function of every remark . . . the result was a more pointed, even jabbing style, a tendency to deflate sonority in favor of exact meaning, while at the same time giving the meter of the verse a musician's respect and the rhetorical substructure of the lawyer's questioning eye.[7]

Though Branagh has a well-trained ear for communicating Shakespeare's richly evocative language, he also has an instinctive understanding of the significant role the musical score plays in cinematic rhetoric. All of his films, even those such as *Peter's Friends* and *Love's Labour's Lost* that rely on twentieth-century popular songs for their musical language, have been scored by Patrick Doyle. Their collaboration is one signature of Branagh's film style. Doyle's musical aims are clearly in concord with Branagh's dramatic genius for accessibility and clarity in performing Shakespeare's texts. Together in *Henry V*, Branagh and Doyle synchronize sound, image, and language, achieving an immediacy of aural and visual experience that renders the play's distillation of history, the range of its scenes, and the complexities of Henry's character coherent and compelling. Doyle, as he indicates in his liner notes for the CD of *Henry V*, attempts to "hold a mirror up to the dialogue and action; my approach was in many ways operatic."

Doyle holds his mirror up to drama in several clear and quite effective ways, sometimes quite literally. Henry's overreaching character is literally depicted, for instance, in a musical motif emphasizing and repeating a leap of a sixth. This musical convention is familiar in baroque music, in which reference to the almighty, for instance, is often set to a noticeably high pitch. Doyle is not a conscious borrower; he is a synthesist and an assimilator of musical allusions and traditions. In no sense is the Henry theme an allusion to anything, but the device works to essentialize a feature of the character, which then ties the action together and drives it forward. When the same musical theme plays slowed and muted in Henry's introspective night among the soldiers before Agincourt, it coordinates, complicates, and explains the action. Then when it is transformed again in the *Non Nobis* chorale after the battle, the music further underscores and embellishes character and action, contributing finally to the sacred dimension of Henry's kingship and fulfilling the opening invocation of "the brightest heaven of invention."

In general Doyle shows himself to be an adroit borrower and synthesist of musical traditions, devices, and references. He invokes class and period contexts deftly in *Henry V* by using mock period instruments—drums and woodwinds—in simple rhythmic patterns, combining these effects in the tavern scenes with the unyoked humor of a rapid scherzo theme in the strings. Inventively, the string scherzo theme returns full volume, traded by all sections of the orchestra in turn as the battle of Agincourt ends triumphantly, thereby underscoring again the play's reconciliation of class issues and national ideology.

At first glance it seems that *Henry V* is one of Shakespeare's less congenial plays for translation into film. Because of the play's use of the Chorus, it is Shakespeare's most metatheatrical work, rivaled only by *Hamlet* and *A Midsummer Night's Dream*. How does the film adaptor incorporate a character apologizing for the limitations of theatrical representation in a medium that can potentially show anything, including those vasty fields of France and casques that did "affright the air at Agincourt"? The Chorus is also a highly rhetorical character; he gives the palace's version of Henry's character ("a little touch of Harry in the night" [4.1.47]) and of the invasion of France ("Now all the youth of England are on fire" [2.1.1]). His presence and his rhetoric seem inimical to the film experience. Olivier solved the problem by opening in the Globe and allowing Leslie Banks's wonderful chorus a broad theatrical style of language and gesture that placed him in his originating landscape. Later, when the film moved out of the Globe into a more recognizable cinematic territory, Banks became a figure disappearing into the sky and clouds as he urged the "mirror of all Christian kings" and his men on to France, and finally he became just a disembodied voice setting the scene the night before Agincourt.

Branagh explored another option. Jacobi's casual Chorus, dressed in a dark crew neck sweater and wrapped up in a scarf and black greatcoat, is a resolutely contemporary figure. He provides a Brechtian edge to the narrative, just as Branagh's treatment of Shakespeare's material is meant to be as unsettling as it is ultimately heroic. Jacobi is less a press agent and more an embedded reporter. He crouches down in the fiery chaos at Harfleur to give us a report on the siege as explosions burst in the background; he reappears at the end of the Bardolph hanging scene, with Bardolph's feet still dangling at the top of the frame, and casts a cold eye up at the body before pulling his coat tighter around his shoulders as he launches into the Agincourt eve speech; as soldiers rush past him to the battle, he moves across a row of sharpened stakes the English have hammered into the ground, and he breathlessly announces, "And so our scene must to the battle fly." The Chorus is then banished from the film as Henry and Agincourt completely co-opt the narrative, and he is only restored for the epilogue. As Jacobi had flung open a huge set of medieval double doors to usher us into the action at the end of his prologue (on "kindly to judge our play"), so now he shuts those doors, closes the narrative, and the screen returns to the black void with which the film began.

Jacobi's Chorus is a decidedly modern figure; and he shares modern criticism's divided response to Shakespeare's Henry V: Hero or Machiavel? Tyrant or Christian king? Ruthless warrior or gentle gamester? The Chorus is one means by which Branagh's film distances itself from Olivier's untarnished portrait of Henry. Another is intimacy.[8] As previously mentioned, the opening moments of the film are shot largely in tight close-ups. The only long shot is not a traditional establishing shot meant to familiarize us with the landscape, but that mysterious entrance of Henry V framed in the huge doorway and shrouded from our view by backlighting. Branagh's camera repeatedly focuses on the faces of Gloucester, Bedford, York, Scroop, and the other members of Henry's Court. With the exception of the church figures, Exeter, and "good old" Sir Thomas Erpingham, the faces are all young ones. The court is largely composed of Henry's contemporaries. This bond of age is driven home by its rupture in Henry's exposure of the traitors: Cambridge, Scroop, and Grey. The scene is set in a small timbered room with a low-beamed ceiling adding to the claustrophobic atmosphere. The tension builds as Henry toys with the trio about what to do about the "man who railed against our person" and then hands them their commissions that, rather than revealing their military assignments, list their crimes against the king. When the three reach for their swords, Branagh's Henry explodes by grabbing Scroop by the throat and pinning his back down on a small table. The king's face is pressed, again in tight close-up, against the traitor's as Henry vents his anger and then softens with "I will weep for thee; / For this revolt of thine, methinks, is like / Another fall of man" (2.2.140–142). Branagh's Henry feels Scroop's betrayal; his response indicates it has the sting of a personal as well as political rejection and the consequences are lethal. Branagh's Henry does not ride above the fray as does Olivier's; he has intense homosocial yearnings, and his plunge into battle at Harfleur and Agincourt is his way of regaining the respect of his men stained by his betrayal by Cambridge, Scroop, and Grey.

Peter Donaldson, in the best essay written on the film, notes the interesting compositional connection between the shot of Henry's face pressed against Scroop's and the shot of Mistress Quickly's (Judi Dench) face hovering over the dying Falstaff (Robbie Coltrane) in the next scene. Donaldson sees that Branagh, picking up on the resonances in Shakespeare's text, is making a cinematic link between Hal's past tavern life and Henry's political situation: "The king's relationships to early friends and companions are intense and mistrustful, charged with the emotional weight of tangled family dynamics."[9] Donaldson sees that in the rejection of Falstaff and the sentencing of the traitors, Branagh's Henry is jettisoning one family (his father's death in *2 Henry IV* looms behind both moments) only to attempt to build another in France through "his successful transformation of his army into a 'band of brothers' and then his winning of Katherine."[10]

Branagh carries this sense of intimacy into the film's battle scenes where we might have expected a more epic tone to dominate. He does give us one heroic shot at Harfleur of Henry urging his troops into the fray while mounted on his rearing white charger. This is pure Olivier, and Branagh abandons the scene's visual romanticism immediately and replaces it with something far more earthy and grounded: mud. Adrian Noble's stage production, picking up on Henry's remark before Agincourt that the English's "gayness and our gilt are all besmirched / With rainy marching in the painful field" (4.3.110–111), had dumped buckets of rain down upon Henry's tiny army huddled under make-shift tarpaulins.[11] Branagh takes Shakespeare and Noble's bad weather and extends it into the heart of his film's actual and symbolic landscape. Gloomy skies, rain, and mud define Branagh's film from the hanging of Bardolph through to the end of Agincourt.

Branagh's Henry V is not a sleek greyhound like Olivier's, but a solid English bulldog built close to the ground. His leadership genius is to get down in the muck and scrum of historical conflict with his men rather than to glide above it wafted on the clarion call of his rhetoric. Branagh's camera helps to create this effect by remaining in tight focus on Henry V for the Saint Crispin's Day Speech, cutting away three or four times for reaction shots from the soldiers gathered around him, and by filming the Agincourt battle scene with the same tight focus, repeatedly cutting from the action to the by-now familiar faces of his men: Exeter, York, Glouces-ter, Bedford, Fluellen, Nym, and Pistol. Branagh's Henry charges through the rain and mud with the men in slow motion, emphasizing the physical labor and struggle of battle they share: it is as though the very "air at Agincourt" is thick with resistance. Branagh becomes smeared with the blood and grime of war.

The film creates this homosocial experience and its effect on Henry by concentrating on four figures: Falstaff, Exeter, Williams, and Fluellen. Branagh includes two flashbacks to very abbreviated Falstaff moments: the first comes early on as Falstaff lies dying at the Boar's Head, and the second occurs when Branagh's Henry presides over the hanging of Bar-dolph in France. The brief scenes are more interesting in their visual details than in the awkward way Branagh's screenplay collapses, rear-ranges, and even reassigns scraps of Shakespeare's dialogue. The shots, dominated by ambers, reds, and oranges, are the warmest in the film. Rob-bie Coltrane's Falstaff is remarkably young and looks to have stepped out of a Rembrandt self-portrait. His face is soft, fleshy, and sweet, revealing none of the ravage captured in Bardolph's (Richard Briers) and Pistol's (Robert Stephens) countenances. Branagh's Hal is clean-cut and clean-shaven with no touch of decadence or dissipation marked on his cherubic face. The film does not find in the Boar's Head a subversive parallel to the events at Agincourt. The Hal who here dismisses Falstaff, not directly but in voice-over ("I do. I will"), is a callow youth rather than an already heady politician. His lessons are still to be learned, and his teachers will be Exeter, Williams, and Fluellen rather than Falstaff.

Branagh's film positions Brian Blessed's Exeter as the young king's guide and protector. Blessed, along with Derek Jacobi and Richard Briers, is one of a trio of older actors Branagh gathered into his Renaissance Company, and they all came to occupy separate but pivotal roles in Branagh's development as an actor and director. Blessed was the unruly friend urging him to take on challenging assignments (the film of *Henry V*) and then humorously challenging his authority ("You can't direct for toffee, you big pouf").[12] Blessed's role transcended his artistic collaboration with Branagh; for Blessed also served as the best man in Branagh's wedding to Emma Thompson.

Blessed is a big man. His burly, bearded Exeter is a powerful physical presence, especially among the predominantly young nobles of Henry's Court. He nods the king into the invasion of France; stage-manages the unmasking of the traitors; supports Henry V when he collapses in weariness and relief when Harfleur capitulates; and is positioned directly behind Henry in his final peace negotiations with the King of France. Most interestingly, in a film heavily indebted in its handling of the Battle of Agincourt to Orson Welles's *Chimes at Midnight*, when Blessed's Exeter, dressed in his full armor, swaggers into the French Court to present Henry's demands, he greatly resembles Welles's Falstaff in his Shrewsbury battle gear. There is a sense that Branagh visually has reimagined Falstaff as Exeter: the Prince's dog (*2HIV*, 1.2.150) transformed into the king's bully.

If Exeter is the older uncle who encourages Henry's imperial adventure, Williams (Michael Williams) is the anonymous foot-soldier who challenges the king's conscience on the night before Agincourt. Michael Williams was one of a number of lesser-known actors (overshadowed by his more famous wife, Judi Dench) who contributed to the great success of the Royal Shakespeare Company in the 1960s and 1970s. Unlike fellow company member Ian Holm, he never had a second career in the movies.[13] Branagh had a keen appreciation for such older actors and was responsible, for example, for rescuing Richard Briers from British television situation comedies and restoring him to major Shakespearean roles (Malvolio, King Lear, Polonius) on stage and in film.

Michael Williams was an actor who worked in the theatrical trenches developing a reputation for good, honest work while the limelight and glory were directed to others. There is a poignant autobiographical resonance in the exchange between Branagh's Henry and Williams's Williams in the film. The young hero (king, actor, director) is being confronted by the gruff old pro who isn't afraid to raise the questions about the king's authority and about the legitimacy of his enterprise that remain unspoken by Henry's peers. In the scene with Williams, Court, and Bates, as well as in his handling of the exchanges between Fluellen, MacMorris, and Captain Jamy, Branagh is aware that Shakespeare is anticipating a convention of the American World War II and Vietnam war film: the symbolic bonding of soldiers from different national and ethnic backgrounds.

Finally, the actor and character Branagh positions his Henry to most identify with is Ian Holm's Fluellen. Holm, himself, was a famed anti-heroic Henry V in Peter Hall's staging of Shakespeare's two tetrologies of

English history plays, under the title *The War of the Roses*, early in his tenure as the founding director of the RSC. Holm, like Branagh, was not physically cut in the heroic mold of previous Henry V's like those of Laurence Olivier and Richard Burton. Holm's Henry was even darker than Branagh's, in keeping with the skeptical, even cynical, atmosphere about politics and politicians at the core of Hall's interpretation of Shakespeare's cycle of history plays. Holm was an ideal model for Branagh, for when his stage career waned (he developed a disabling case of stagefright in his mid-40s), he found a second life in film. Holm knew how to lower the volume for communicating Shakespeare on film and had developed a naturalistic style for film acting that Branagh admired and sought to emulate in the work of his Renaissance Company on stage as well as screen. As Branagh jokingly remarked on the set of Henry V, "I'd heard the Ian Holm School of Acting described as follows: 'Anything you can do, I can do less of.'"[14]

Fluellen is conceived as a fussy, pedantic, comic Welshman, and Shakespeare has almost as much fun with his accent and locutions as he does with Alice and Kate in their English lesson. But Holm ignores

Henry V (Kenneth Branagh) negotiates a peace and a romance with Princess Katherine of France (Emma Thompson) in *Henry V.* [Photographer: Sophie Baker, Courtesy of Photofest]

almost all the invitations for comedy contained in the character. His Fluellen is serious, self-contained, and deeply moved by Henry's willingness to make tough choices (the hanging of Bardolph) and join his infantry down in the rain and mud at Agincourt. In many ways, Branagh's film moves as resolutely toward the blood-stained embrace of Henry and Fluellen at the miraculous ending of the struggle at Agincourt as it does to the more obvious, and also comically awkward, kiss between Henry and Kate that seals the king's triumph at the peace table. Fluellen also displaces Exeter (as the king's physical and emotional support) at this moment as the embrace between Henry and Fluellen echoes Exeter's helping Henry regain his feet and balance after his collapse at Harfleur's gates. Peter Donaldson is right to read this moment as "the emotional climax to the film" and to see that Branagh's consciousness of his own Irish heritage is at work here:

> Branagh's Irish working-class identity shows through his stage English royal persona at strategic moments, giving depth to the king's identification with the common soldiers, lending credence to his claim to be a work-a-day, plain-style king. Branagh's partly suppressed Irishness—which breaks through as catharsis in the scene with Fluellen—also adds a dimension to his exploration of the king's ambivalence toward his past self. Henry's emotional range, along with his deep, slightly mad, 'Welshness,' can only be fully expressed when he has achieved success in his more self-controlled role as English warrior-king.[15]

The king's relationship with Fluellen reflects and reaffirms Branagh's relationship with Ian Holm and the rest of his largely male cast. A community is being established both inside and outside the textual narrative, a community of actors and Shakespeareans as well as Henry's "band of brothers."

The other group of characters central to Shakespeare's extended concerns in *1 and 2 Henry IV* and *Henry V* are the denizens of The Boar's Head Tavern: Falstaff, Pistol, Bardolph, Nym, Mistress Quickly, and Falstaff's Page. I have already written of the rich amber glow that Branagh's cinematographer, Kenneth MacMillan, provided for the two flashback scenes with Falstaff. MacMillan and Branagh make it evident that the warmth and spark of the first flashback scene emanates from Robbie Coltrane's Falstaff (if Rembrandt painted cherubs, Coltrane's face is what they would look like). The Boar's Head scenes without Falstaff are drained of life and color. The tavern is a mess with cats picking over the capon carcasses still resting on the uncleaned plates from the night before. There's no vitality or energy here: Robert Stephen's Pistol is a haggard burnt-out case and Judi Dench's Mistress Quickly is grey and wan. All the lads of England, as the Chorus proclaims, may be on fire, but the fire that once illuminated the Boar's Head world is out.

This bitter, wasted image extends to Branagh's treatment of the crew in France from the hanging of Bardolph to the death of Nym as he loots the body of a fallen French soldier at Agincourt to Pistol's ravaged post-Agincourt promise to turn cutpurse and bawd. The sustaining camaraderie that once distinguished the Boar's Head crowd has all been transferred by Branagh to the king's relationship with his soldiers. Something like this transfer is symbolically taking place in one of the film's most ingenious segues. Branagh's camera closes in on Judi Dench's drained face as she reaches the climax of Mistress Quickley's famous description of Falstaff's death, and then that face fades into a map of France showing the progress of Henry's army, followed by a further fade into a close-up of Paul Scofield's sad and weary face as our first encounter with the French Court. The French are thus linked with Pistol, Quickly, and company: mutual elements in Henry's transformation from gentle gamester to warrior-king. Branagh, in his use of Dench and Scofield here, is also acknowledging his debt to the English performance history of Shakespeare on stage and screen even as he places his own stamp on that tradition.[16]

The last member of The Boar's Head landscape to be included in the film's Agincourt sequence is also perhaps the most significant in establishing Branagh's revisionist claim to Olivier's legacy as the premier English Shakespearean actor-filmmaker. The energy of Olivier's approach to filming Agincourt was established in the famous long tracking shot of the French charge, backed by William Walton's glorious score, building to the moment when the music suddenly stopped and Olivier cut to the English longbow archers launching an epic flight of arrows at the French with the soundtrack now filled only with the sound of the arrows's release and flight (thawap, thawap, thawap, swooosh). The shot of those arrows filling the sky, peaking in their trajectory, and then heading down toward the French remains the film's most vivid image.

Branagh's handling of Agincourt reverses Olivier's heroic clash. Olivier's film, made as the Allies were about to launch the invasion of France to reclaim Europe from Hitler, was all about going over. Branagh's film, made in the shadows of Vietnam and The Falklands War, was all about coming home. As a result, he treats Agincourt as a muddy quagmire and saves his great tracking shot for the end of the battle. One of the boys killed by the French when they raid the English tents is Falstaff's page (Christian Bale). After the victory has been secured and confirmed and the King has called for the singing of "Te Deum" and "Non Nobis,"

Branagh picks up Bale's body, swings it over his shoulder, and carries it back across the battlefield laden with the carnage of war. A remarkable four-minute tracking shot follows as Branagh moves through the mud and the bodies of fallen men and horses, while on the soundtrack a "Non Nobis" swells from the voice of a single soldier (Patrick Doyle) to a full male choir as the camera crane elevates to give us a picture of the full field. In a brilliant stroke, Branagh has the French woman try to attack the king in outrage for the slaughter of the French men. The shot ends with Henry—face caked with mud and blood—mounting a cart piled with the bodies of the murdered boys, thus making a circle with the battle's beginning sequence put in motion by the St. Crispin's Day speech delivered from a similar cart.

Olivier glides through his Agincourt with a stunning grace, while for Branagh it is a far less glamourous rite of passage. Branagh gives us neither the confident hero nor the short-tempered tyrant, but rather a worker-king who puts his shoulder and body into the messy scrum of history and emerges, in Donaldson's fine formulation, ritually cleansed, receiving his final and most miraculous transformation as the film cuts from his battle-stained face at Agincourt to his freshly scrubbed one come to claim (and woo) his prize at the French court.[17]

Shakespeare makes a radical change in tone in the play's final scene as he attempts to wrench his tough-minded assessment of war and Henry's imperial campaign into the structure of the romantic comedies he has been producing at this stage of his career. Olivier and his Kate (Renee Asherson) played the wooing scene stressing its charm: Asherson is sweetly coquettish and Olivier plays as much to the camera as he does to Kate. Branagh and Thompson, in their first appearance together in a film, allow more of the uncertain subtext of the scene to emerge.[18] Thompson's Kate is skeptical and resists all temptation to flirt by playing hard-to-get. Branagh's camera lets her intelligent, quizzical face dominate her exchanges with Henry. She makes him work at the wooing even though she realizes her options are limited. Branagh is more earnest than playful (the "plain soldier" in wooing as in war), and Thompson's Katherine only begins to melt when Henry's awkward schoolboy French moves her to laughter. The schoolboy nervousness is sustained as the French King and the peace negotiators re-enter the room, and Henry breaks off the kiss that seals their bond on the line "Here comes your father." The gesture gets its intended laugh but also undercuts the confidence of Henry's response to Kate's first refusal of his invitation to kiss: "Nice customs curtsey to great kings . . . we are the makers of manners, Kate" (5.2.293–94).

As the peace and the marriage are sealed, Branagh's camera pulls back to discover Jacobi's Chorus standing next to the partially open double doors leading into the council chamber. Jacobi delivers the play's Epilogue with Shakespeare's apology for being forced to confine mighty men in a little room and thus mangling "the full course of their glory." The Chorus then closes the door on the action just as he had invited us into in the film's opening sequence.

Though Branagh opens up Shakespeare's play to the world of film, his claustrophobic camera technique makes it a closed universe. His visual imagination rightly understands that *Henry V*, for our age, is as much about impasse as expanse. Henry's options are always being closed off or hemmed in: by his tavern past, by his father's legacy, by his youth, by the traitors, by the weather, by his depleted and weary troops, by his own ruthlessness, by dynastic marriage. Branagh's cinematic technique is always to move in rather than open out—he's trying to capture intimate rather than epic impulses suggested by his Shakespearean material. Such an intimate atmosphere began with Jacobi's face illumined by that match and extended back to Branagh's attempt to capture Henry in his own age: "I wanted a smoky, firelit, medieval darkness in which we could still see people's faces and which was not too dour."[19]

Branagh manages to straddle the medieval and the modern through his own powerfully naturalistic performance as Henry; through the creation of a sense of mystery surrounding the king; through a series of landscapes dominated by fires, torches, shadows, doorways, mud, and rain rather than fully representational movie sets; by a camera style that constantly moves in on the action and concentrates on the contours and secrets of the face rather than pulling back to overwhelm us with the distancing power of spectacle; by providing that missing visual sweep and spectacle musically through Patrick Doyle's rousing score; and finally by instinctively drawing upon, as Sarah Hatchuel has convincingly detailed, the codes and conventions of popular Hollywood movies.[20]

Branagh's genius was to mix these elements in a manner that seemed fresh and new as an approach to translating Shakespeare into film. These qualities were all sensed by the film's initial reviewers. As Stanley Kauffmann noted, Branagh "is a genuinely gifted film director. He has a good eye for cinematic flow that seems to bear the language along, as in the scene with the three traitors, and he has an equally good eye for composition that underscores the moment."[21] Richard Corliss, writing in *Time*, found that Branagh had created a "*Henry* for a decade poised between belligerence and exhaustion. He found a camera style that illuminates actors with torch power and Rembrandt lighting."[22] And, perhaps most tellingly, in one of her last reviews for *The New Yorker*, Pauline Kael was knocked out by Branagh's performance, calling his weeping embrace of Ian Holm's Fluellen at the end of Agincourt a "daring release" that "feels like pure, spontaneous Branagh."[23] Kael went on to comment about the range and suggestive power of Branagh's voice:

> This actor's earthy, doughy presence is the wrapping for his beautiful, expressive voice. Emotion pours out of it with surprising ease; he's conversational without sacrificing the poetry. His readings are a source of true pleasure. Listening to him, you think, with an instrument like that, he can play anything.[24]

The enthusiasm shown by Kauffmann, Corliss, and Kael for Branagh and his film was shared by both American and British film reviewers. Amazingly, Branagh's film, made on a budget that would not have paid for the catering on *Titanic* or *Gladiator*, was eventually nominated for three Academy Awards, including a remarkable double nomination for Branagh as Best Actor and Best Director. Such attention to a low-budget, first film from a virtually unknown actor and director was rare in Oscar and Hollywood history. It was certainly not surprising, given the basis in Shakespeare's *Henry V*, that Branagh drew immediate comparison to Laurence Olivier and his famous film of the play. None of the film's initial reviewers associated Branagh with Orson Welles (except for the always perceptive Kael), but once *Henry V* garnered its multiple Oscar nominations, film historians immediately reached back to *Citizen Kane* to find a film from a first-time director that had made such an impact. Welles, however, was already a well-known theatrical figure famed for his Mercury Theater productions in New York for the Works Progress Administration (WPA) and his long-running radio program that scared the pants off the nation with its broadcast of H. G. Welles's *The War of the Worlds* in 1938. Branagh was suddenly Citizen Ken, linked in the press with the transatlantic theater-film-Shakespeare legacy shared by Olivier and Welles.

By the age of twenty-eight, Branagh had succeeded in establishing himself as an actor comfortable working in the commercial West End Theatre, with a classical repertory company, and in television and film. He had demonstrated his administrative and organizational skills in the founding of the Renaissance Theatre Company where the actor's art and energy were paramount. The world of the English classical theater had been dominated since the 1960s by university-educated directors (largely from Cambridge), replacing a tradition of theaters led by actor-managers, a tradition as deep as Burbage and the Globe. Branagh's Renaissance Company restored the actor to the managerial and directorial role. He directed the company's first productions of *Romeo and Juliet* and *Twelfth Night* and then enlisted three major English actors, Judi Dench, Geraldine McEwan, and Derek Jacobi, to direct for the first time in their careers.

By the conclusion of Renaissance's most ambitious season in 1988, Branagh was convinced that he had the imagination and daring to make the leap into the world of film. He had established a reputation for taking bold theatrical chances and succeeding. He had gathered a nucleus of younger actors around him who believed in his naturalistic approach to staging and speaking Shakespeare, and he had wisely reached out to include older, more famous English actors in his company. He had ideas and energy and ambition. Most importantly, he had momentum. And luck. Though all the members of the small and struggling British film industry he approached, including David Putnam, who had once led a major Holly-wood studio (Columbia), thought his idea of making a film of *Henry V* sheer folly, a financier from the City (London's Wall Street), Stephen Evans, became attracted to Branagh's stage work and eventually became sold on Branagh's idea for making a new Shakespeare film. Evans managed to raise the shooting budget of 4.5 million pounds (then about 6.5 million dollars) from independent sources, allowing Branagh to make his first film without any "suggestions" or more direct demands (particularly about casting) from studio producers. The filmmaker was never to experience such total freedom (on a Shakespeare film) again. In talking with me about the making of *Henry V* more than a decade later, Branagh became, quite naturally, nostalgic about the innocence of the experience: "Everything about it was singular: the money coming from the City of London through Stephen Evans's efforts; no pressure; no influence from an existing film production company; and no pressure on casting. . . . So there was a freedom."[25]

The result was a minor miracle: the first Shakespeare film in almost two decades (since Zeffirelli's *Romeo and Juliet* in 1968) to become both a critical and a commercial success. Branagh's film career as a director was launched with, of course, little understanding that his *Henry V* would inspire the greatest decade of Shakespeare filmmaking in the one-hundred-year history of the genre. Equally unknown, as well, was Branagh's next step. He was suddenly a hot property as an actor and director. Hollywood thrives on such fresh faces and commodities since it often chews them up, spits them out, and moves on to the next wunderkind. Given Branagh's background as a Shakespearean, his next film would prove to be, in its own fashion, as much of a surprise as his first.

Chapter 3

DEAD AGAIN

The release of his film *Henry V* in 1989 brought the first beat, or phase, in Branagh's career to a close. The decade of the 1980s had been miraculously productive for the young actor since his graduation from The Royal Academy of Dramatic Arts in 1981. The range of his work was startling: an award-winning role in a West End hit play (*Another Country*); the lead in a BBC Play for the Day (*Too Late to Talk to Billy*) that would inspire three sequels; a season with the Royal Shakespeare Company at Stratford in leading roles (Henry V, Laertes, the King of Navarre, and Mike in *The Golden Girls*); parts in several films (*High Season, A Month in the Country*); a starring role in a major BBC television series (*Fortunes of War*); writing and playing the lead role in his first play (*Public Enemy*); directing and playing Romeo in a production of *Romeo and Juliet*; directing *Twelfth Night*; and creating and leading a new, actor-centered theatrical company (Renaissance) in an ambitious repertory of three Shakespeares—*Much Ado About Nothing, As You Like It*, and *Hamlet*—in which he played Benedick, Touchstone, and Hamlet. The Renaissance season closed its sold-out London run in October, and two weeks later Branagh gathered his *Henry V* cast at Shepperton Studios to begin shooting his film. Six weeks later he celebrated his twenty-eighth birthday on the set as the film entered its final week of shooting. Few actors can claim such a range of achievement in the first decade of their professional careers.

Branagh's early career gave him exposure as an actor to the major modes of contemporary entertainment: theater, television, and film. He experienced working in the West End, acting in the leading Shakespearean company in the world, performing in small-scale fringe theater, and shooting film and television scripts in studio and on location. Four major elements in his artistic energies emerged from this early work: a commitment to Shakespeare and the repertory company ideal, a fascination with film, a huge capacity for work, and a willingness to take risks. When reading *Beginning*, written to help finance the administrative structure of Renaissance as Branagh was finishing *Henry V*, one is struck repeatedly by the ways in which Branagh's creative energies are fired and nourished by a constant flurry of activity generally conceived by having two or more projects going at once. There's ambition at work here, for sure, but also some deeper drive to seize the moment when his career is hot and his star is in ascendancy and a lingering sense (which he calls his "Irish guilt") that he has to constantly prove himself (and his profession) by being in the business of creating not only art but also a community of artists.

This first phase of Branagh's career was very much London-centered with work for the major institutions in British theatrical life: The West End, The RSC, The BBC, and the modest British film industry. The second phase would be dominated by America and Hollywood and exposure to larger film and stage audiences. Renaissance's second season, featuring productions of *A Midsummer Night's Dream* and *King Lear*, was conceived not for local but for international audiences. In a typical instance of Branagh's ability to combine cunning and luck, the company was in residence in Los Angeles at the Mark Taber Forum when the Academy Award nominations for 1990 were announced, and *Henry V*'s three nominations included Best Director and Best Actor nominations for Branagh. Suddenly Branagh was hot and he was in town. As he recounted to Bruce Weber of *The New York Times*:

> The studios were all keen to meet me . . . I was in town and, you know, at my most flavorsome. I was sent lots of scripts. All the Vietnam pictures that never got made. Anything with fighting and rain. Next to those were all the worthy pictures that never got made. The Life of Tolstoy. The Life of Chekhov. The Three Lives of William Shakespeare. They didn't appeal to me.[1]

Branagh, here and elsewhere, resists the temptation to be defined by others; he's British and he's made a stirring *Henry V*, so Hollywood figures he's ripe for battle pictures or the Merchant-Ivory film. What Hollywood can't read about Branagh is right before its eyes on the stage of the Mark Taber Forum where Branagh is gently sending up Peter Quince, in *A Midsummer Night's Dream*, by playing him as a version of Cecile B. DeMille complete with jodhpurs and a snap-brim driving cap worn back-

Mike Church (Kenneth Branagh), Franklyn Madson (Derek Jacobi), and Amanda Sharp (Emma Thompson) examine an old copy of *Life* magazine that contains details of the relationship between Roman and Margaret Strauss in Branagh's film *Dead Again*.
[Photographer: Peter Sorel, Courtesy of Photofest)

wards. As his early career attests, Branagh isn't interested in repeating himself or in making tasteful, restrained "British" films. He's in love with American movies and the men who made them. When he was sent Scott Frank's script for *Dead Again*, his movie meter began to tick: "this script arrived out of the blue, and I couldn't put it down. Immediately I was thinking of *Dial M for Murder*, all those Hitchcock movies. The Welles pictures I grew up watching on television."[2]

Branagh quickly saw that Frank's script allowed him the opportunity to explore his fascination with a classic Hollywood genre and style, the 1940s romantic thriller; to provide a pair of lush roles for both himself and Emma Thompson; and to do so by building upon, rather than abandoning, his vision of Shakespeare's essence as a popular writer: "When I read [*Dead Again*], I was astonished how my disbelief was completely suspended and I was reminded once again of the power of a good narrative, which was Shakespeare's supreme strength."[3]

Shakespeare took Branagh to Hollywood and helped to sustain him as he moved into another tradition and another production language. Most plays open slowly like petals on a flower allowing the audience to gradually

absorb setting, character, and circumstance. Films typically start more
suddenly relying on a montage of visual images underlined by the film
score to establish landscape and atmosphere. Our eyes can absorb information more quickly than our ears. The openings of some films, the
Bond films for example, are so powerful that they are over almost
before they have begun. Much of what was new about Branagh's
approach to filming Shakespeare in *Henry V* was established in his
treatment of the opening credits—blood red letters on a black background with Patrick Doyle's vivid film score underlining title and credits as if we were already deep in a mysterious, insistent, powerful
world—followed by the rasp of a match striking and Derek Jacobi's face
suddenly illuminated by its flare.

Branagh's film style, in *Henry V,* was bold and brazen, the work of a
director determined to make Shakespeare fresh and popular. The film had
parallel narratives. For the young, with little or no exposure to Shakespeare and the tradition of Shakespeare on film, Branagh provided an
intense, gripping narrative, performances distinguished by a conversational rather than rhetorical approach to Shakespeare's language, tight
shots and quick cuts, and Doyle's pounding (and sometimes soaring)
score. Young audiences were swept up by a Shakespeare and Shakespearean who seemed of their generation. For older Shakespeareans, academ-
ics, and film buffs—with memories of Olivier and Welles and Zeffirelli
dancing in their heads—the experience of Branagh's achievement was
bound up with the film's debts to the great Shakespeare films of the
1940s, 1950s, and 1960s. This played out in the press where Branagh was
hailed as the new Olivier or Welles.

Dead Again, though working a seemingly different tradition and territory, provided some of the same pleasures and anxieties. As with *Henry V,*
Branagh seized upon a compelling narrative stocked with ambiguities and
a genre that would allow him, again, to develop parallel pleasures in the
unfolding of content, form, and context. In the case of *Henry V,* Branagh
was clearly competing with Olivier rather than providing an act of homage. Welles and Zeffirelli became his coconspirators in his project as he
smuggled in key elements of their cinematic styles as his way of moving
beyond the clever but wooden structure (built on the foundation of a
reconstructed Globe) of Olivier's film. In *Dead Again* Branagh does offer
a playful (and sometimes witty) homage to Hitchcock and Welles as a
means of generating an important dynamic to his film's achievement and
its cinematic pleasures. What excited Branagh about the script for *Dead
Again* was not only its narrative but also the way that narrative immediately evoked for Branagh a specific cinematic style and pace. *Dead Again*

became the perfect vehicle for this upstart Shakespearean to exercise his education in the Hollywood films he watched on television as a boy in Belfast. Branagh's only modification to the script was to insist that he and Emma Thompson play the dual roles of the film's central couples, Roman and Margaret Strauss and Mike Church and Amanda Sharp. The film's plot explored the uncanny connections between Strauss's apparent murder of Margaret in 1949 and Mike Church's efforts to help the amnesiac Amanda discover her true identity in the Los Angeles of the 1990s.

Branagh's indebtedness to studio Hollywood begins with the first notes of Patrick Doyle's Bernard Herrmann–inspired film score beating up a frenzy underneath a montage of newspaper headlines screaming, "Murder. Scissors. Trial. Guilty." Branagh interweaves this montage, which tells the story of Roman Strauss's brutal 1949 murder of his wife, Margaret, as written by the newspaper reporter Clay Baker, with his title sequence. Branagh again opens a film by reaching out and grabbing the viewer's attention.

Branagh leads us into the narrative through the interaction of music (Prisoner Strauss singing snatches of Billy Strayhorn's "Lush Life"), printed word (the newspaper clippings), image (Strauss shot in medium close-up in black and white with his eyes in the shadows), and sound effects: the "snip . . . snip . . . snip" of barber scissors as Strauss is given a final haircut before being led to his execution. Branagh shot this opening sequence in black and white, evoking the cinematic worlds of Orson Welles and the early Hitchcock (especially *Rebecca*), and he invitingly— even humorously—laid almost all of his cinematic cards on the table. For Shakespearean insiders the best joke is the prisoner's number on Strauss's uniform: 25101415. This happens to be the date (October 25, 1415) of the Battle of Agincourt, where Henry V and his band of brothers prevailed over the superior French forces. Yet before we can relax into the flow of the film, Branagh turns out to have another trick up his sleeve.

As Strauss rises to begin the journey to his execution, he slips the barber sheers up his sleeve. As he walks down the cellblock, quietly murmuring the opening refrain of "Lush Life" to himself, he moves toward a small group of reporters and photographers at the row's end. When he arrives, he confronts a woman resembling Emma Thompson, slips the scissors down from his sleeve, and raises them to attack her while muttering in a thick German accent, "Theeze are for you." The scene slam-cuts to a Technicolor close-up of Thompson screaming awake from a nightmare. Are we in Kansas or Oz? We're in the present and at St. Audrey's orphanage in Los Angeles (housed in Roman Strauss's former mansion).

Thompson is an amnesiac caught trying to climb over the gates into St. Audrey's. The film then sweeps us up into trying to solve the mystery of her identity, her relationship to the events of Strauss's life, and her relationship with Mike Church, the young wisecracking private investigator summoned by the orphanage to take Thompson off its hands because he is one of St. Audrey's boys. Branagh intends our plunge into the woman's nightmare to complicate a crucial paradox of the film: who's story is this? And who's telling it? Was the entire opening montage and sequence in the cellblock in 1949 an omniscient narrator's recounting of Roman Strauss's murder of his wife, Margaret? Or was it the dream of Thompson's character living in the present but curiously linked to the Straussian past? This is just one of a series of slippery narrative perspectives that would come to define Branagh's way of keeping the viewer off balance even as the film appears to increasingly give the story a solid structure.

That solid structure is provided by the entrance of Franklyn Madson (Derek Jacobi) into the story. Madson is an antiques dealer with a talent for tracking "pieces" from the past by hypnotizing his clients, and he surfaces after Mike's newspaper, seeking information about the woman's identity, publishes the mystery woman's photo. Madson offers to hypnotize her as an aid to recovering her memory. Hypnotism, like her nightmare, takes the woman into the past and back into Roman Strauss's world. As she regresses into the world of post-war Hollywood, where composer Strauss has landed in his flight from Nazi Germany, the style and structure of Branagh's film emerges. In the past our mystery woman appears to have been a concert pianist, Margaret, who became romantically involved with composer and conductor Strauss. Since Thompson and Branagh play both parts (amnesiac and Margaret; Mike and Roman), we assume the fates of both couples are linked. Director Branagh captures the past in black and white footage with the use of a romantic chiaroscuro. Welles and *Citizen Kane* are also evoked by the presence of Clay Baker (Andy Garcia), who is a Jed Leland figure and a cynical newspaper reporter who becomes infatuated with Margaret Strauss. Branagh's romantic European bearing as Roman Strauss is meant to remind us of Laurence Olivier's Maxim deWinter in Hitchcock's *Rebecca* even as Strauss's mansion is meant to recall Manderley. Thompson's Margaret is a stronger, more intelligent and lively version of Joan Fontaine's second Mrs. deWinter, but, like Fontaine, she has to compete with a powerful and mysterious housekeeper for control of Strauss's life. In typical Branagh fashion the filmmaker complicates the range of film associations being evoked here by casting Hanna Schygulla, the star of many Warner Fassbinder films, as the housekeeper.

Dead Again wants to present a many-sided contrast, in setting, technique, and acting styles between the film's past and present. The past is formal, dense, studio driven, and full of shadows. The present is zany, colorful, and spontaneous, with lots of location shooting. The link between the two worlds is provided not just by Thompson's character but also by Franklyn Madson and Cozy Carlisle (Robin Williams). The film deftly sets these two eccentrics against each other. Madson, in a polished turn by Derek Jacobi, appears to be a concerned European Samaritan offering his special services (and unctious charm) to uncover the amnesiac's identity. Carlisle is a defrocked psychiatrist suspended from practice for becoming intimate with his patients. Mike and Grace (as Thompson's character is temporarily named) seek their advice to help understand her puzzling connection to the events of 1948–1949.

Williams's Carlisle is Madson's opposite. His habitat is the meat locker of a Salvadorean grocery store—about as contemporary L.A. as possible— in contrast to Madson's past-encrusted Laughing Duke antiques store. Carlisle is a typical Williams creation: bright, edgy, and rattling off New Age aphorisms in a staccato fashion while blinking back an essential shyness behind wire-rimmed spectacles. Branagh's use of the Jacobi– Williams pairing is the first example of what would become one of his trademarks as a director (particularly revealing in his subsequent Shakespeare films): incorporating actors from two drastically different traditions (the London stage and the American film) into his movies. Branagh is powerfully drawn (some would argue fatally in the case of Michael Keaton) to using American comedians and comic actors to play Shakespeare's clowns. His use of Williams is the first instance of his desire to bridge those two worlds.

Henry V featured an entirely British cast, and all, with the exception of Robbie Coltrane's cameo appearance as Falstaff, were Royal Shakespeare Company or Royal National Theatre veterans. As *Dead Again* gathers its energies from contrasting past with present, from placing a style from the Hollywood 1940s in conjunction with the Los Angeles of the 1990s, from playing with fanciful ideas about past lives and reincarnation, so it mirrors these concerns in its casting. Jacobi and Williams came to represent the powerful competing strands in Branagh's cinematic imagination: Stratford and Hollywood. Jacobi represents the historical tradition and training of the British classical actor; he is Branagh's personal symbol for the line that runs from Burbage to Garrick to Irving to Olivier, for it was Jacobi's Hamlet that first thrilled Branagh when he was a teenager. Jacobi became central to Branagh's Renaissance Company by directing Branagh as Hamlet in the company's first season and then by playing the Chorus and

Claudius in Branagh's films of *Henry V* and *Hamlet*. There's an acknowledged Freudian joke running in their relationship as it becomes playfully obvious that Branagh repeatedly tries to make Jacobi dead again first by impaling him on a giant set of scissors in this film and then by hurling his rapier into Jacobi's chest in *Hamlet*. As Branagh said to me with a grin, "I keep killing Derek Jacobi on screen. . . . I don't know how I'm going to kill him next. But he keeps bouncing back."[4]

Though Branagh enhances his Shakespeare films by his willingness to cast American actors with little or no classical experience, he swerved in the other direction by insisting on including Jacobi in his first American film. Jacobi was a name known in Hollywood only for his television performances, especially in the Masterpiece Theater toga-drama hit *I Claudius*. Branagh's insistence on cross-Atlantic casting is one element of his risk-taking. Jacobi was not (and has not become) a film star, and Emma Thompson, in 1991, was still a relative film novice (*Henry V* and *The Tall Guy*). Her Academy Award–winning performance in *Howard's End* was still a year away. Because of the popular appeal (and even notoriety) that Hollywood actors like Denzel Washington, Michael Keaton, Jack Lemmon, Alicia Silverstone, Natasha McElhone, and Billy Crystal brought to Branagh's Shakespeare films, some have argued that Branagh was just cashing in on their commercial appeal, but his practice was first revealed in *Dead Again* where it was much more of a gamble than a safe bet.[5]

Robin Williams is the key representative of the Hollywood end of Branagh's transatlantic connection. Like Branagh, he's adventuresome in his career choices, and he represents a contemporary generation of Hollywood stars willing to play bit parts or supporting roles in films when the material (or the director) is of interest. Williams exhibited his own generosity as an actor by working uncredited in *Dead Again* and by playing Osric in Branagh's *Hamlet* when his eye might well have been fixed on the even more attractive clown, the first gravedigger.

The structure of *Dead Again* is based on Branagh's manipulation of past and present through Hollywood genre history. The performances that propel the narrative are based on a similar contrast, this time widened to include Hollywood's transatlantic connections in past and present. Not only do Branagh, Thompson, and Jacobi bring their own British theatrical credentials to the film, but they also become contemporary stand-ins for British-trained performers like Laurence Olivier, Vivien Leigh, and George Sanders who had their Hollywood moments in the 1930s and 1940s. The Hollywood balance is provided by Williams, Andy Garcia, and Campbell Scott as Branagh begins to develop the casting mix that becomes one of the chief ingredients of his film style.

Though much of *Dead Again's* energy, style, and narrative mystery are generated by the film's cutting back and forth between the interrelated lives and tales of Roman and Margaret and Mike and Grace, Branagh's handling of individual scenes shot within the past or present deserves some scrutiny. Particularly representative and effective is the complicated shot in the Laughing Duke antiques store the first time Madson hypnotizes Grace and she regresses to the events of 1948. Madson's shop is crammed with antiques, creating, quite intentionally, the claustrophobic feeling of the past pressing relentlessly in on the present. Madson and Grace are seated at a small table with Mike standing in the background. As a single candle flickers on the table within this cramped, tightly packed space, Branagh's camera begins to circle Madson and Grace, holding them in a tight two-shot while also, through deep-focus, keeping Mike visible at the rear of the frame. The scene is played without a cut until Grace has fully regressed and the camera cuts from the hypnotist's candle to a gleaming chandelier in a symphony hall in 1948 where Roman Strauss is conducting Margaret in the Rachmaninoff Piano Concerto.

The shot is significant because it reveals Branagh's stylistic fondness for keeping his camera in motion (the long post-Agincourt tracking shot back across the battlefield in *Henry V* is the most obvious early example of this practice), his trust in his actors to be able to work in long takes, and his desire to keep the focus on the three principal figures in his tale even as the film moves deeper into Grace's imagination, memory, nightmare, or fantasy. The circle shot will also become a feature of Branagh's repertory, made central to the swirling passion of *Mary Shelley's Frankenstein* and the intense entrapment of being bounded in Hamlet's nutshell. Branagh's natural way of working—emanating from the repertory ideal—demands the close interaction of cast and crew. Being a relative novice, Branagh had the temerity to insist on trying to shoot in some unconventional ways. As Emma Thompson has said, "Ken works fast and wants other people to keep up."[6] When the first crew members on *Dead Again* were too sluggish for Branagh's pace, he had them replaced. When filming the murder scene where young Frankie goes after Margaret with a pair of scissors as she sleeps in her bed, Branagh quickened to the intimate involvement and cooperation of the entire crew. The complicated scene involved the use of huge shadows, a moving wall, and special-effects people under the bed flicking blood onto gauze-like curtains; the murder is captured as shadow-play while the opera Strauss has been composing swells on the soundtrack. "Literally every single member of the crew was working," Branagh said. "We eventually got it, and there was an enormous cheer and camaraderie. That felt like *making movies*."[7]

Camaraderie and the company atmosphere are central to the Branagh experience. Obviously, he's a director who relishes in the give and take with fellow professionals. From his initial partnership with RADA contemporary David Parfitt, Branagh slowly put together the team of actors, designers, and administrators who would become the nucleus of his Renaissance Company, most of whom have remained with him throughout his theater and film career. Most importantly, they include Parfitt, who became the administrative head of Renaissance; Stephen Evans, who raised the money for Renaissance's early seasons and was the key to unlocking unconventional backers for Branagh's film of *Henry V* after British film producers like David Putnam turned their backs on the project; Tim Harvey, the designer; Phyllis Daulton, whose costume designs for *Henry V* won an Oscar; Patrick Doyle, who has done the scores for all of Branagh's films; Russell Jackson, who has served as text and script consultant for all of Branagh's Shakespeare films; and the late Hugh Cruttwell, the head of RADA, who monitored Branagh's own performances as Branagh juggled his responsibilities as lead actor and director. Among the actors, the key contributors have included Derek Jacobi, Richard Briers, Emma Thompson, Michael Maloney, Brian Blessed, and Geraldine McEwan.

Branagh's dream, expressed early in his film career, was to create a more commercial version of Ingmar Bergman's experience (and Welles's too when he took many of his Mercury Players with him to Hollywood to make *Citizen Kane* and *The Magnificent Ambersons*) of directing plays and making movies with the same company of actors. Branagh's fantasy was to find a fairy godmother who would "wave her wand over our coffers and say 'Look, we'll give you this amount of money every year; do a play, do a film. You are not forced to make a profit. Just do things to entertain people.'" "That's my idea of heaven," Branagh said.[8] Branagh's vision, expressed in 1991, combined a small-scale version of The Royal Shakespeare Company and a film studio. He has not yet found such a fairy godmother. When Adrian Noble, a decade later, proposed a similar new direction for The Royal Shakespeare Company, his own fairy godmother (the RSC Board and the Arts Council) promptly threatened to break Noble's wand, leading to Noble's resignation as director of the company. Branagh's idea and Bergman's example make sense, but the worlds of theater and film still eye each other with a fatal combination of envy and suspicion, and film remains almost prohibitively expensive in the context of multiple demands upon national arts funding boards. Branagh's inability to attract the funding necessary to allow him to move his company with ease back and forth between stage and film projects led him, for most of the 1990s, to concentrate on making movies.

In many ways, personally and professionally, the key member of Branagh's core group of actors was Emma Thompson. Their relationship began during the long year they spent making the many installments of *Fortunes of War*. She galvanized his thinking about Renaissance and encouraged him to take the gamble to make his idea a reality. They made an impressive pair: young, smart, determined, and clever. He was the plucky Irish outsider, with his family roots in the Belfast docks, with the drive and ambition that had brought him success at RADA, in The West End, and at the RSC. She was the cool, intelligent, English classic beauty with a strong theatrical pedigree and a Cambridge degree. They made a fine mix of passion and irony, fire and ice. Their relationship was too good to last, but Thompson was a central ingredient in Branagh's early film successes with *Henry V*, *Dead Again*, and *Much Ado About Nothing*.

Thompson is one of those rare film actresses, like Katharine Hepburn and Meryl Streep, who make intelligence sexy. Branagh brought her into the movies, but she quickly eclipsed his standing as a film actor with her work in *Howard's End* (for which she won the Oscar for Best Actress), *The Remains of the Day*, and *Sense and Sensibility* (where she picked up a second Oscar for Best Screenplay). But they made a powerful and unusual team in the three films they made together. Branagh is an unconventional leading man. He lacks the traditional romantic good looks of Englishmen like Douglas Fairbanks Jr., Laurence Olivier, Cary Grant, or Ralph Fiennes. Nor does he have the ironic, understated tough-guy appeal of a Humphrey Bogart or George Raft. He can best be described as possessing a combination of qualities of the young Albert Finney and Jimmy Cagney. He's got Finney's boyish charm coupled with Cagney's determined body language and drive.

In *Dead Again* he assigned himself the tough task of taking on two widely opposite film types: the cultivated 1940s European refugee and the brash 1990s American private eye. When Branagh pitched his idea not only to direct the film but also to play both Roman and Mike to producer Lindsay Doran and screenwriter Frank, he brashly declared, "Let me be your Lon Chaney."[9] Part of the film's pleasure is in watching Branagh walk the fine line between playing stereotype and finding genuine character in both roles. He's having disciplined fun and showing off at the same time: a little like Welles's obvious joy in capturing Charles Foster Kane's decline from young maverick to middle-aged tycoon to dying icon stripped of his charisma and power.

Branagh's best moment, as Mike Church, comes in the scene when he creates the name "Grace" for Thompson. Mike has taken her out for a romantic evening at the Echo Park Café expecting a little wine, a little

Roman Strauss (Kenneth Branagh) and Margaret Strauss (Emma Thompson) dance at a Hollywood party as their relationship begins to fray in *Dead Again*.   [Photographer: Peter Sorel, Courtesy of Photofest]

music, and a little romantic chat as the café lights sparkle off the small pond by which the café sits. All is dashed and expectations are deflated when the café proprietor reveals he's lost his liquor license, there's no music tonight, and he's closing early because of the threat of rain. Mike and Thompson make do with Styrofoam cups of tea, and trying to keep the conversation from turning as soggy as the weather, Mike declares with a twinkle that he can read tea bags. This scene, like many in the film, has its parallel moment in the past when Roman, entertaining Margaret in an opulent restaurant, insists on reading her palm. Branagh's camera cuts, in medium close-up, back and forth between Mike and Grace as they make uncomfortable small-talk about her condition. When Mike begins his tea-bag reading routine, Branagh reverses to a long two-shot, and slowly the camera moves in on them as Mike creates a funny yet tender past for Thompson as a bungee-jumping Westerner married to the Idaho Potato Prince. Branagh's eyes dance and that slit of a mouth breaks into a smile as he delights in the way his tale amuses Thompson and moves her out of her melancholy and into a momentary state of grace. The speech is Branagh's longest in the film, and it gives him something to work with when he's at his best: combining words with camera work. The scene is quiet and much less complicated technically than many others in the film, but effective because of the way it reveals Branagh's talents as actor and director.

As already noted, much of the power and energy Branagh generates in his film of *Henry V* is underlined and enhanced by Patrick Doyle's film score. *Dead Again* provides Doyle with another rich text and set of images to score. He's working with a film featuring—in the events of 1948–1949—the relationship between a conductor and composer and a pianist. When we first meet them, Strauss is conducting the Los Angeles Philharmonic with Margaret as soloist in Rachmaninoff's First Piano Concerto. Strauss is also working on an opera, so Doyle has access to the nineteenth-century classical tradition as a source for the Roman–Margaret sections of the film. But he also, like Branagh's narrative style itself, raids the great Hollywood film composers of the 1930s, 1940s, and 1950s like Bernard Herrmann, Alex North, and Alfred Newman to create the suspenseful atmosphere reminiscent of Hitchcock's *Rebecca* (1940) and *Dial M for Murder* (1954). Doyle's music becomes a central ingredient in Branagh's aesthetic. Doyle prefers the bold attack and the jagged crackling edge, and Branagh understands, not always common for stage actors turned film directors, the importance of music in film to create atmosphere and heighten emotions. In his Shakespeare films he's not shy about bringing the score in under the verse even when, to the purist's ear, the natural rhythm of Shakespeare's music seems at odds with Doyle's score. On the other hand, in *Dead Again*, Branagh refrains from introducing the film score in the tea-bag reading scene until the scene reaches its climax as Mike conjures the name of "Grace" for Thompson's character.

In its past versus present structure, in the theories of past lives and future consequences spun out by Madson and Carlisle, in the seemingly parallel relationships between Roman and Margaret and between Mike and Grace, and in its very title, the movie suggests that we are moving toward a repeat of Margaret's murder in the present, with Mike replacing Roman as the murderer and Grace Margaret as the victim. Frank's screenplay provides one final confusing twist to the mystery that I think Branagh's film decided to confront by blazing past it in such a rush that it gets lost in the dash to the final catastrophe. Mike is literally (as an orphan) a man without a past, and when he, under pressure from Madson and Grace, makes his own regression into the Roman–Margaret past and is forced to confront himself in a mirror, the image that stares back at him is not Roman's but Margaret's! The film almost trips over the screenplay's final clever gender-bending twist because it has not been prepared for; nor is it explored with the attention it deserves. There has been much fuzzy talk between Roman and Margaret about their being two halves of the same soul, and Roman has given her an antique anklet saying that the man who sold it to him said that the two people who share it "become two halves of the same person. Nothing can separate them. Not even death." The anklet becomes a fetishized object reminiscent of Othello's spotted handkerchief and plays a key role in the development of Roman's jealousy. The anklet is a red herring,of course, and Branagh is probably right to propel his film forward as fast as he can so that his audience has little time to absorb this final turn of the plot.

Once Mike has visited Clay Baker, now holed up in a nursing home in the valley, where he cadges cigarettes and puts them to mock-revolting use, Mike realizes who Margaret's killer is and that Grace's danger is not in reincarnation but in a segment of the past that remains vitally alive. Branagh has played the *Dial M for Murder* scissors parallel for all its worth from the initial "snip . . . snip" on the sound track to the mysterious word "dyshear" that Thompson's amnesiac utters when she awakes from a nightmare, to the scissors that litter Mike's apartment to the giant scissor sculptures that Grace has made when we discover her true identity as the artist Amanda Sharp. And, of course, the *Die Shears* used by Margaret's killer.

In the climactic scene in Grace/Amanda's studio, the fatal trio of Grace, Madson, and Mike are reunited. Grace/Amanda thinks Mike is

Roman reincarnated come to murder Margaret again. Mike, whether Margaret's reincarnated soul or not, has discovered that Madson is out to kill them both, in the same way he, as young Frankie, the housekeeper's son, had murdered Margaret because Margaret had come between Strauss and Frankie Madson's mother. In the cathartic conclusion, Grace/Amanda, urged by Madson, shoots and wounds Mike, who recovers just in time to position Amanda's giant scissor sculpture to impale Madson on the scissors (hoist, so to speak, on his own petard) as he hurls himself toward Mike to finish him off. Scissors, scissors everywhere and not an ounce to sheer. All this mayhem is underlined by the insistent percussive beat of Doyle's score working itself into a classical frenzy. As Cozy Carlisle observes when trying to convince Mike and Grace of the mysterious connections across lives and generations, "Fate is the only cosmic source with a tragic sense of humor."

Branagh's film dances gingerly with its cosmic karma without ever turning to outright parody. The film has fun with its cinematic sources without ever mocking them. Branagh doesn't take the genre of the mystery/romance thriller in bold new directions, but he doesn't trash it either. Branagh, as I think is typical of his artistic intelligence, comes close to capturing the tension between respect and play that his film attempts to achieve in evoking and updating a slice of film tradition when he remarks,

> The key tricks are sleights of hand. You mustn't give people too much time to think. They must be carried along by the excitement, by familiar images which we've hopefully reinvented with the power that they require. The detective. The woman without a name. The murder mystery. The sort of Joseph Cotten protagonist in grave danger. I wanted to go for the style of those pictures. A feeling of period, a strong sense of fine verve and style, the audacity of late '40s movies . . . A certain mystery and heightened strangeness are, to me, a necessary backdrop for such a piece—especially when you are asking people to believe in the notion of reincarnation.[10]

When Branagh first read Frank's script, the story reminded him of his first experiences "watching black-and-white American films such as *Rebecca* and *Spellbound* . . . my cinematic vocabulary was established in those movies and to this day when I direct Shakespeare in the theater, many of the references I give are to these movies."[11]

Remarks like these and the nature of Branagh's early films, especially *Henry V, Dead Again*, and *Peter's Friends*, have tempted film scholars such as Marcia Landy and Lucy Fischer and Shakespeareans such as Courtney Lehmann and Kathy Howlett to place Branagh's work within the context of the postmodern political and social aesthetic.[12] Though their work is among the most serious and compelling written about Branagh's films, it finally faults Branagh for failing to fully embody the postmodern ideology. Branagh is tough to categorize, and though his work clearly flirts with postmodernism, it never embraces it. He does make his art while drawing upon the cultural capital of his own past. He is part of a generation of British Shakespeareans, including Trevor Nunn, Adrian Noble, and Edward Hall, who treat Shakespeare as a great popular dramatist and are happy to link him to the popular art forms of our own time, especially movies and musical comedies. Branagh plunders the popular film tradition from Hitchcock to Spielberg for inspiration for his own cinematic vocabulary. Because Branagh's film debts are so obvious and brazen, it is tempting to regard him, as I initially did, as a postmodern parodist recycling the shards and fragments of modernism, as another example of Fredrick Jameson's Marxist analysis of the exhaustion of contemporary culture doomed to speak only in "a dead language" of the past.[13] Branagh's work, however, resists such a reading. The past is palpably alive for Branagh. Shakespeare is, of course, his work's central figure, and Branagh's way of making him fresh, rather than dead again, for contemporary audiences—especially the young—is leading the movement of contemporary filmmakers, such as Baz Luhrmann and Richard Loncraine, who have been uninhibited in translating screen Shakespeare into the grammar and rhetoric of popular film conventions.

Branagh is energized rather than enervated by the past. Part of his immediate attraction to the screenplay for *Dead Again* was the way the past didn't just haunt the present but was vitally alive within it. Branagh's film, for all its Hitchcockian resonances, is neither moody nor melancholy. Scott Frank gets at this quality in Branagh's style when he observes, "It's the strangest thing. Ken shot the script word for word—he didn't deviate from it by so much as a line—and yet when he assembled the first cut, it was different from what I'd pictured. Not bad—just different. He brought a view, a take on it, that had a real power apart from the writing. The look and feel of it is very magical now, very offbeat, whereas I'd pictured something darker."[14] Branagh, as he did in *Henry V*, mixes the dark with the light in tone as well as atmosphere. It's part of his own struggle with his complicated past: part Celtic melancholy, part Irish charm, part Protestant work ethic. Jameson's gloomy sense of the exhaustion of late postmodern capitalism finally doesn't seem the appropriate theoretical engine for unpacking and decoding Branagh's world, however inviting a title like *Dead Again* is for witty Jamesonian speculation.

If the tracking shot, especially in Henry's first entrance into his court and again after Agincourt, was the primary element of film vocabulary in *Henry V*, then cutting—vividly appropriate for a film about scissors—is the prime technique Branagh uses to compose *Dead Again*. As I have mentioned, the first sounds we hear in the film are the "snip . . . snip" of the prison guard's scissors cutting Roman Strauss's hair prior to his execution. Strauss's cell walls are decorated with newspaper "clippings" of Clay Baker's news stories about Margaret's murder and Strauss's subsequent trial. A montage of similar clippings is interspersed with the opening credits both to engage us with the relationship between Roman and Margaret and to introduce us to the film's style and technique. As my description of the film's sleight-of-hand in the opening sequence indicated—where the scene cuts from Strauss's walk down death row to Amanda's scream—Branagh favors the jagged, abrupt cut between past and present rather than the less jarring fade or dissolve.

This technique is most pronounced in the climactic murder scene in Amanda's studio. Appropriately, this is the moment when scissors reappear in the film as a lethal weapon. There are one hundred and fifty cuts in a scene lasting just under eight minutes. The pace is appropriately frantic and hurtles back and forth between Amanda confronting and then shooting Mike and the separate struggles of Mike and Amanda with Madson. The scissors, in the mad scramble, move from person to person, with both Mike and Grace having the opportunity to wound Madson with them. Also, in a sequence between the thirtieth and sixtieth cuts, the film jolts us back into the past to young Frankie's murder of Margaret in her bed while in the living room below, Roman's opera reaches a crescendo. Music, mystery, murder, mayhem, and madness all converge in a powerfully edited scene, capped by the hyperbolic horror of Jacobi's Madson being impaled on Amanda's giant scissor sculpture. The structure, pace, and cheeky wit of *Dead Again* are achieved and sustained by Branagh's deft ability to snip and cut and even slash his film. In *Dead Again,* form deftly shapes and mirrors content.

Filmmakers like to say that there are three versions of every film: the one created in the screenplay, the one that is shot, and the one that is assembled in the editing room. Branagh's final cut of *Dead Again* is remarkable for the way in which it incorporates all three versions: Frank's screenplay is shot word for word as written; Branagh's actors—particularly Jacobi and Robin Williams—are allowed to develop their major scenes in continuous long takes; and the pulse and power of the film's narrative images are ultimately created by the way in which they are cut and then spliced together in the editing room. The film is actually a remarkable achievement for a young, unknown British actor with a single low-budget Shakespeare film to his credit. Shot for fifteen million dollars, the film went on to gross over fifty million dollars in domestic and world-wide distribution.[15] Most significantly, the film only earned about 10 percent of its total gross on its opening weekend, indicating that strong word-of-mouth was responsible for its eventual financial success.

Not everything in the film, of course, works or hits the right note. It stretches credulity that Roman Strauss, a European-educated composer in the romantic tradition, would (in 1949) be singing Billy Strayhorn's "Lush Life"—that's simply a sweet whim of Frank's screenplay. At the big Hollywood party celebrating the release of a new film, where Strauss first is deflated by being called a "nobody" by a young starlet and then comes upon his wife and Clay Baker in a compromising situation, there's a poster for the baseball film being honored—"The Lefty Liebrandt Story." But unfortunately, in the poster Lefty is a right-hander. As Mike, knowing Amanda's danger, races in his red Corvette from his interview with Clay Baker to Amanda's studio, his car runs out of gas, but Mike's resulting panic and eventual arrival (ahead of Madson anyway) got left on the cutting room floor, making the empty gas tank business extraneous. Most significantly, Branagh just isn't interested in exploring the gender twist in Frank's screenplay, where it is Margaret's image Mike sees when he looks into the mirror upon regressing into the film's past.

These rough edges or potentially interesting paths not taken did not detract from the film's commercial success or from the growing legend of Branagh's precocious prowess. In less than a decade, Branagh managed to move in status from a neophyte classical actor to the most promising Shakespearean of his generation to the successful reviver of the moribund genre of the Shakespeare film to the leader of his own acting company to a modestly successful Hollywood film director. Suddenly a much wider cultural audience was awaiting his next move: Back to Stratford? A London season at the National? A return to touring with his Renaissance Company? A bigger Hollywood film? None of the above? His choices appeared to be infinite.

Chapter 4

PETER'S FRIENDS

Branagh's four Shakespeares are the anchor of his film career, but his other choices have been unexpected and quirky. *Dead Again* was certainly a surprise successor to *Henry V*, though it did have the plucky air of Branagh taking on Hitchcock and the Hollywood noir thriller. In *Dead Again* we could see Branagh's attempt to extend the base of his Renaissance Company into Hollywood and the world of conventional films. Following the unpredictable path that led him from *Henry V* to *Dead Again*, he swerved again and returned to England to make *Peter's Friends*.

The return to England was perhaps understandable—a strong signal that his Hollywood success had not gone to his head. He came home to London not only to make a very English film but also to return to the stage and play his third Hamlet in a decade, this time for The Royal Shakespeare Company. What was curious about his next film choice was that *Peter's Friends* made a break with the Renaissance Company Branagh had been building through his work on stage and film. The film featured none of the Renaissance regulars except Branagh and Thompson and a fleeting appearance by Richard Briers that largely ended up (like Kevin Costner's in one of the film's progenitors, *The Big Chill*) on the cutting room floor.[1] In fact the film might well have been called *Emma's Friends* because it explores the lives of her Cambridge University pals, especially those associated with the Cambridge Footlights Drama Club, in the decade after their graduation. Emma's world consisted of witty, ironic, and sometimes politically engaged university types light years removed from Branagh's own gritty beginnings in Belfast, Reading, and London.

Perhaps Branagh was trying to extend his synthesizing reach into Thompson's Cambridge territory as he had previously done with the worlds of Shakespeare and Hollywood.

Almost everyone in the film was with Thompson at Cambridge and was actively associated with Footlights. Footlights and Cambridge have a long and distinguished history in shaping English comedy in the second half of the twentieth century. In the 1960s Jonathon Miller and Peter Cook came out of Footlights to join with Alan Bennett and Dudley Moore in creating *Beyond the Fringe*, and several years later John Cleese and Michael Palin similarly emerged to help create the beginnings of *Monty Python*. *Python* was instrumental in creating the type of comedy that most influenced Emma Thompson and her generation. When I first saw the film, I imagined that Rita Rudner, the American comedienne who plays Branagh's wife in the film and who coauthored the screenplay, was a relic of Branagh's Hollywood experience mixed into this English sticky-toffee pudding to provide some crass American spice. Not so. Rudner turned out to be the wife of Martin Bergman, Cambridge graduate, Footlights alum, and the screenplay's coauthor, someone Emma knew even before she went to Cambridge. Stephen Fry, Hugh Laurie, and Tony Slattery were all in Footlights with Thompson, and Imelda Staunton was her friend at Cambridge. Of the principal members of the cast, only Branagh, Alphonsia Emmanuel, and Phyllida Law, don't have Cambridge connections, and Law is Emma Thompson's mother.

Though the film seemingly abandons Renaissance, it remains determinedly Branagh-esque. It takes a familiar model, the weekend-at-the-country-estate film—bringing together an interesting assortment of eccentrics—with roots on both sides of the Atlantic. Most reviewers were quick to seize the parallel with Lawrence Kasdan's *The Big Chill* (1983) (itself an appropriation of John Sayles's *The Return of the Secaucus Seven* [1980]), forgetting that the genre has an even longer history in English films than in Hollywood.

The film brings together six friends, Peter (Fry), Maggie (Thompson), Sarah (Emmanuel), Roger (Laurie), Mary (Staunton), and Andrew (Branagh), at Peter's father's country estate—actually Wrotham Park in North London, which was also used as the location for Robert Altman's *Gosford Park*. Peter's father has recently died; Peter has inherited the grand country house and has invited his old college friends to celebrate New Year's Eve with him. The group is augmented by two outsiders, Andrew's wife, Carol (Rudner), and Sarah's new lover (Slattery). The estate is run by its longtime housekeeper Vera (Law) with help from her son Paul (Alex Lowe). The premise is that, surprisingly, these great col-

lege pals have not seen much of each other in the decade since they graduated in 1982, so the weekend constitutes something like a grand tenth
reunion—mingling an American tradition of the college reunion with the
country-weekend-film convention.

The genre's attraction is that it allows for several stories to be told con-
currently, for a mingling of past and present, and for a focus on both the
group and the individual. Particularly, in director Branagh's actor-
centered universe, the genre allows for intimate moments for each
individual actor as well as larger scenes of ensemble work. Branagh is
naturally drawn to such forms, Shakespeare and Chekhov's plays being
the classic examples, because of his strong notion of community as the
basis for his work on stage and film. The film, for all the conventionality
of its form, does offer, in Branagh's hands, some wonderful moments
where the camera allows a scene to build, as in *Dead Again*, relying primarily on the actor's art rather than the editor's.

The sheer theatricality of the film's opening shot is remarkable. It joins
Branagh's long tracking shot after the battle of Agincourt and the circle
shot in *Dead Again* when Derek Jacobi first regresses Emma Thompson,
creating a growing list of signature shots that come to define his cinematic
style. This opening sequence also anticipates the hyperbolic final steadicam shot in *Much Ado About Nothing* in which the entire community of
the film—minus Don Pedro—is captured dancing in festive celebration
and singing a refrain of Balthazar's song "Sigh no More."

The time is New Year's Eve 1982. The setting is the dining room at
Peter's father's estate, where a makeshift stage has been created across
one side of the room. In a single cut lasting almost four minutes, the camera (a steadicam), in close-up, pans along the faces of a chorus line of
Peter's friends singing something called "The Underground Song" to the
tune of Offenbach's "Gaiety Parisienne" from *Orpheus in the Under-
world*. The song was originally written for the 1977 Footlights show *Tag*
and is a typical example of Footlights humor. The camera, after scanning
the casts' garishly made-up faces and heads topped with bowler hats,
pulls back to reveal that they are dressed in frock coats, tutus, and net
stockings as they furiously belt out the names of London Tube stops while
frenetically attempting to do the Can-Can. The camera then pulls back
further to reveal the dinner guests supposedly being entertained but
largely ignoring the performers.

Slowly the camera begins to move around the back of the dinner table
to catch the climax of the song and the performers' mad dash off the stage
and into a narrow corridor leading to the kitchen. The camera, still without a cut, follows the troupe into the kitchen and then in rapid-fire

Andrew (Kenneth Branagh) gets sideways and spoils the party in *Peter's Friends*.
[Photographer: Clive Coote, Courtesy of Photofest]

succession captures individual explosions from each of the six as they shed costumes, make-up, and frustration over the leaden reception of their revue. This is tricky business because Branagh doesn't set the dialogue up in a neat order where the camera might pan naturally from left to right capturing individual bits of venting in sequence. In fact the explosions come randomly from actors scattered about the kitchen. The center is held by the housekeeper, Vera, and her young son, Paul, who offer consoling remarks about the performance. The short bursts of dialogue from each of the six performers also are meant to quickly establish their dominant personality trait: Andrew (splenetic), Peter (phlegmatic), Maggie (melancholic), Sarah (sanguine), Roger (wry), and Mary (volatile).[2] The scene and the shot climax as Mary insists they pose for one last group photo as they now all have graduated and this has been their last performance. The shot ends with the click of the still camera's shutter resulting in a black and white photo in freeze-frame as the film's credits roll.

Technically, this is perhaps the single most bravura shot in all of Branagh's films. One can only wonder how many takes it took to get it in the can and how sick his cast was of "The Underground Song" by the time they had a successful take. Interestingly, it is Branagh's character, Andrew, who is most emphatic that he is pleased to have school and "The Underground Song" behind him. In terms of the screenplay's conception, Andrew is one of the insiders, but in reality—though not ultimately banished along with the two genuine interlopers Carol and Brian—he's the ultimate outsider, having fled to America, Hollywood, commercial success, alcoholism, and a fragile marriage. In oddly prescient ways, the film becomes as much Branagh's story as Thompson's.

The film's premise is, of course, to bring this group and their additions back together again a decade later. As the credits roll, Branagh creates a montage of public figures (Thatcher, Bush, Ron and Nancy, Gorbachev, Sylvester Stallone, Boy George, Nelson Mandela, Queen Elizabeth, Mickey Mouse, Arrafat) and events (the Falklands, Tiananmen Square, the fall of the Berlin Wall) to span the decade, a device he would use again and modify in creating his summer of 1939 landscape for his film treatment of *Love's Labour's Lost*. Branagh likes to play with time less, I think, as a metaphysical issue than as a historical one. He generally prefers to ground his films in a specific historical or geographical milieu that can be immediately absorbed and read by the viewer.

In *Peter's Friends* the late 1980s are also heard as the film relies not on a Patrick Doyle original score, but on a series of popular songs from the decade. These songs range from Tears for Fears "Everybody Wants to Rule the World" to Queen's "You're My Best Friend" to Cindi Lauper's "Girls Just Want to Have Fun" to Tina Turner's brilliant "What's Love Got to Do With It?" According to Ian Shuttleworth, Branagh was the first filmmaker to receive permission from Bruce Springsteen to use one of his songs in a film—"Hungry Heart."[3] The use of pop songs to score a film had been a Hollywood standard at least since George Lucas's *American*

Graffiti (1973) but had been used most effectively, of course, by Kasdan in his *Big Chill*, adding another chorus to the complaints that Branagh was simply raiding Kasdan's film for his inspiration.

Country-weekend films are structured around arrivals, departures, and the big revelations (or murders in the mystery variety) in between. Branagh brings his guests in by plane (Andrew and Carol), train (Sarah, Brian, and Maggie), and car (Roger and Mary). He gives each couple and, most effectively, Maggie a moment to establish who and what they have become ten years on and what corrodes their lives and relationships. Carol and Andrew are seen at the airport just after their arrival from Los Angeles and are quickly defined by the limp one-liners they exchange ("You know what I hate the most about being a public figure?" "The public") and their American affectations (mountains of luggage for Carol and sunglasses for Andrew). Roger and Mary, the only members of the original six to have paired off, are more genuinely troubled. Several years ago, they had twin boys and one subsequently died of Sudden Infant Death Syndrome. This has made Mary manically possessive of Ben, the surviving son. She has also driven Roger into a guilty depression since the baby died under his watch. She is reluctant to leave Ben for the weekend, and Roger, patience extended to the breaking point, has to ease her away from the nanny, and then endure her repeated requests to stop on the car journey so that she can phone home to make sure all is well.

Maggie, along with Peter, the only one of the group without a mate, is given a leave-taking scene that gently mocks Roger and Mary's departure. Thompson does a wonderful turn with the moment. She, too, has hired a nanny—one to sit with her cat, Michael. Certain that the cat will be miserable in her absence, she has spread pictures of herself about the flat to console him while she's gone. She insists to the cat sitter that she will have to pull him away from her as she leaves because he is completely dependent upon her. Michael, cat that he is, will have none of it and scampers out of the room as soon as Maggie releases him from her embrace. In contrast to Roger and Mary's guilt and Maggie's melancholy, we discover Sarah and her latest lover, Brian, having a quick stand-up shag on the train that is also carrying Maggie to their country destination. Sarah is the beauty of the group, known for her sparkling eye and healthy libido, and Nina Simone is heard on the soundtrack singing "My Baby Just Cares for Me" as Sarah and Brian have at it. Tony Slattery's Brian is meant, I suppose, to be the English counterpart of Rudner's Carol. He is an underemployed actor, is married with a kid, sports Elvis Presley sideburns, and has a penchant for telling unfunny jokes in a loud and braying manner. His character is meant to irritate us as much as Carol's. She mistakes guests for servants, has her luggage moved into the master bedroom (Peter's, of course), refuses food (too fattening) and drink (revealing that she and Andrew are recovering alcoholics), and is a fitness freak.

In fairly efficient fashion Branagh gets all of these details of character and plot established by the time the guests have arrived and settled in. The natives, Peter, Vera, and Paul, are also established in several quick touches. Peter is not quite comfortable with his new role as lord of the manor. Vera plans to retire to the village (to "watch videos") and has agreed to stay on just for this last weekend; and Paul, now perhaps sixteen or seventeen, is looking to escape his menial life.

As discussed earlier, the structure of such films, once everyone has gathered, is to begin to break the group apart, generally in twos, to explore the ironies, bitterness, jealousies, longings, and missed opportunities that linger just beneath the surface of each character and their relationships with other members of the group. This might be called the Chekhov-effect for he was its master: repressed longings, misinterpreted gestures, conversations at cross-purposes, unintended slights, bittersweet comic bungling. All of these situations are at work in *Peter's Friends*, and not surprisingly, Branagh's Andrew, somewhat in the background in the arrival sequence, is at the center of many. Perhaps this is because his character has been farthest and longest away and there is more catching up to do; but perhaps too it's because Branagh himself is an outsider to this group of Emma's pals and their world, and part of the movement of the film is to bring him in from the outside.

The first extended sequences of characters pairing off in twos involve Andrew: first with Peter, then with Maggie. In the former Andrew helps Peter load up a basket with wood for the fireplace. The two engage in the jokey banter that always precedes a move into deeper matter. Peter: "Do you have wood in L.A.?" Andrew: "We have Hollywood." Andrew senses an unexpected sadness in Peter and gently probes for an answer but is brushed off. On Andrew's part the scene reveals his guilt in skipping off to America when offered a writing job in Hollywood. He and Peter were working on a play together when he left, so the guilt is deeper than just guilt over abandoning a friend; the departure had career and cultural consequences as well. Their exchange strikes a major chord among the six friends in the film: a failure to live up to bright expectations. This is not, of course, a natural Branagh theme. His own life, in 1992, had exceeded well beyond expectations, and his signature narrative, in concert with the heroic figure (Shakespeare's Henry V) he had ridden to fame, was one of triumphing against the odds. Andrew knows he has sold out, and not just in leaving England for America, but for leaving the dream of becoming a playwright to become a successful hack writer for an American television situation comedy starring his wife. Peter, though concealing a darker secret that will emerge at the film's climax, also thinks that he has failed to live up to his promise. The failed collaboration between the two is symptomatic of the sadness that prevails in the tone of the film: a sadness each feels over failing to achieve individually what they had once accomplished as a group in their undergraduate years. This nostalgia is typical of such works in fiction (think of Mary McCarthy's *The Group*) or film (*The Big Chill*), but here it seems all-pervasive, unleavened, with one or two exceptions, with any spontaneous rekindling of the old wit and energy that had marked their communal lives a decade before.

The sequence between Andrew and Maggie, which follows after a brief upstairs/downstairs exchange between Carol and Vera, is one of the film's most successful. As is his fashion when he has absolute trust in his actors, Branagh shoots their long exchange in a single extended take. The camera captures Andrew and Maggie, in long shot, as they stroll a gravel path through the estate's formal gardens. The path leads to a series of steps that the walkers slowly climb as they approach the camera. The scene becomes Maggie's monologue about a man who got away. This is Maggie's theme. We've seen it comically treated with Michael the cat, and now we get the absurdist version about her relationship with a colleague in publishing.

Thompson provides the film with a brave and subtle performance. She has a natural ear for the timing necessary to deliver the ironic understatement that characterizes English intellectual humor. Thompson's sensibility bleeds wry wit. As Maggie and Andrew move along the garden path, she tells him the story of her failed romance. With perfect timing each beat of her tale is understated yet underlined in the same instant.

> "I was seeing an author. [pause] He committed suicide."
> "Sorry."
> "I didn't like him very much. [pause] Especially after he committed suicide."
> "How did he do it?"
> "Threw himself off a building. Couldn't even do that properly. [pause] It was only a three-story building. [pause] He would have survived, only a car ran over him."
> "What kind of books did he write?"
> "Self-help books."

Branagh here plays the straight man to Thompson's exquisite deadpan delivery, who lets her pauses set up the string of punch lines. As the strollers approach the steps, Maggie switches the conversation to the topic of

Peter as a potential mate, and we realize, along with Andrew, the unlikelihood of such a relationship just as they pass the camera at the top of the stairs. This is a moment when Bergman and Rudner's script, Thompson's delivery, and Branagh's quiet camera work cooperate to make the scene realize its droll comic potential.

Maggie's lonely longing is repeatedly contrasted with Sarah's insatiable sexual appetite, and the film now cuts to post-coital Sarah admiring herself in a mirror as Springsteen's "Hungry Heart" pulses on the soundtrack. The song continues while the film cuts from bedroom to bedroom as the guests dress for dinner. As the film reassembles the group in common quarters, first at the dining room table and then in the sitting room for coffee and drinks, it allows for further revelations about the past to be inadvertently revealed. More importantly, these lead to individual meltdown moments for each member of the group. In this sense the film is darker and more emotionally embarrassing than any of the relationships in *The Big Chill*. Crib death, AIDS, alcoholism, bulimia, guilt (generic and specific), gay sexuality, dysfunctional marriages, adultery, and broken promises (to oneself and others) all come into play. At these moments the film more resembles a group version of *Who's Afraid of Virginia Woolf?* than the traditional country-weekend film.

The film gives us an overload of these scenes since its democratic community spirit insists that everyone be allowed one or two big scenes of emotional distress. Carol bolts the dinner table when Mary reveals that Andrew and Sarah were once lovers. Andrew dutifully follows, and he and Carol have a major row up in their bedroom, exposing the real bitterness that lies beneath the cynical one-liners that have distinguished their relationship. Carol, dressed in a strapless gold and black satin gown, does get off one of the film's most tart lines when complaining about the evening: "I'm stuck down there in a freezing drawing room with the cast of Masterpiece Theater." The scene is mainly interesting for being shot in one take with Carol seated on a bench at the foot of the bed while Andrew paces back and forth in an arc from one side of the frame to the other. The camera never moves, providing the only sense of stability in the volatile recriminations erupting between husband and wife.

Later Andrew rejoins the group in the sitting room, and we are treated to a momentary respite in the emotional upheaval. Peter persuades Roger and Mary to play and sing something from one of their undergraduate reviews. Roger moves to the piano, and the two begin a version of Jerome Kern's "The Way You Look Tonight." As Mary reaches the first chorus, Maggie joins in, followed by Peter and then Andrew and Sarah, and the group is reestablished around the piano in momentary harmony. Andrew and Sarah and Peter and Maggie begin to dance as the camera pans around the Christmas tree in the middle of the room and the six voices harmonize on Kern's haunting melody. The Kern song makes a wonderful counterpoint to the hard-driving contemporary rock and pop that has dominated the soundtrack and momentarily brings the past to the rescue of the present. The harmony is short lived, though this brief scene does point its way toward Branagh's *Love's Labour's Lost*, where the songs of Kern, Irving Berlin, and Cole Porter become an essential feature of the film. The ringing of the telephone interrupts the idyll with news that Mary and Roger's Ben is running a slight fever. A doctor has looked at him and said all should be well by morning, but this sends Mary off into a nervous collapse.

The film now gives us a series of night scenes—actually inaugurated by the row between Andrew and Carol earlier—in which we witness the emotional breakdowns of existing or imagined relationships. Some of this is formulaic (Roger and Mary finally confront their guilt over the lost child, Maggie makes a disastrous move on Peter, etc.), but it does give the film a deeper reach and allows the actors (particularly Hugh Laurie, known primarily—until his starring role in *House*— as Bertie Wooster to Fry's Jeeves in the television series based on P. G. Wodehouse's stories) a range of emotion to explore and express. So Roger and Mary finally have it out after nine months of repressed recriminations; and after Brian announces to Sarah that he has told his wife he is leaving her for Sarah, Sarah gives him the cold shoulder. "You might have told me first" is her limp reply to his confusion: "But I thought this is what you wanted." Sarah loves the chase, not the kill. And Maggie, sadly misreading Peter's earlier remarks about their being natural partners, makes a midnight visit to his bedroom, where she slips off her robe and announces, "Fill me with your little babies." Peter, stunned and embarrassed, graciously declines saying that he's a "bit of a whoopsie" and not "in the vagina business." Maggie shoots back, "But you slept with Sarah," to which Peter replies, "Maggie, dear, the Archbishop of Canterbury has slept with Sarah." This scene is typical of the thin line the screenplay tries to walk between comedy, farce, and genuine bittersweet Chekhovian miscommunication. Oddly, there is both more and less going on here than in *The Big Chill*, which never tries to be clever in its repartee but which more convincingly manages to suggest the fall from grace of the 1960s American college generation of civil rights activists and Vietnam war protestors. Admittedly, the two films emerge from distinct cultural milieus and moments in England and America, but the Falklands and Thatcherism never seep into *Peter's Friends* the way

Vietnam and Alex's suicide haunt the characters and the edgy bonhomie of *The Big Chill*.

The night scenes end with a meeting in the kitchen between Carol and Maggie—the film's female polar opposites: Carol the brash American star and Maggie the reticent English mouse. Carol has hit the kitchen to secretly gorge on the leftovers of roast beef and Yorkshire pudding she had shunned at dinner, and Maggie arrives looking for wine and solace after her embarrassing proposition of Peter. Branagh's camera cuts back and forth between the two as Carol is given her moment to shine by drawing Maggie out, listening to her dilemma, and proposing to give her a Hollywood makeover: "Maggie, you're a very pretty girl but you make Mother Theresa look like a hooker." In a comic reprise of Maggie's desperate tapping at Peter's door hours earlier, Carol now taps at Maggie's door loaded down with her make-up kit, hair dryer, and exercise equipment.

The next morning finds many of the night's conflicts resolved. Roger and Mary are reconciled and make squeaky-bed love heard by several of their pals having coffee in the kitchen. When their lovemaking continues through the ringing of the telephone, it provokes smiles all around. Sarah and Brian have split, and Brian—after a teary phone conversation with his son—is collected by his wife, the first of the outsiders to escape or be banished. The tarted-up Maggie appears in the kitchen to some rave and some skeptical reviews and the new day begins.

The film now provides Paul, Vera's teenage son, with his big moment. He and Sarah have a conversation in which he tells her of his ambition to be a fighter pilot. This bit of the screenplay strikes me as being the most Branagh-inspired moment in the film. Paul reveals that his ambition has been kindled by the film *Top Gun,* which he has seen sixty-two times.[4] When Sarah asks if it's the Tom Cruise character he admires, he quickly corrects her by saying, no, "It's Kelly McGilliss. I want to go to her flight school." Alex Lowe, the actor playing Paul, is one of Branagh's regulars. They first appeared on stage together in the West End production of *Another Country* that began the careers of its two stars: Branagh and Rupert Everett. The play is set in an English boarding school and is loosely based on the early life of Guy Burgess, later to achieve fame and notoriety as one of the Cambridge spies working for the Soviet Union. Everett played the Burgess character and Branagh his more serious and intense friend, Judd. Lowe played Judd's "fag" (a lower form boy assigned to run errands for a senior master) in the production. He's one of the few Branagh regulars involved in the film. The inspiration and humor in his admiration for *Top Gun* reminds one of Branagh's Belfast dreams fueled by watching Hollywood movies (Steve McQueen's *The Great Escape* being one of his favorites) rather than anything connected with Emma's friends at Cambridge. Paul is also the only member, except his mother, of the working class in the film. There may even be a subtle transatlantic Shakespearean resonance at work here since Kelly McGilliss is something of an American version of Emma Thompson. McGillis starred in several popular films, most prominently Peter Weir's *Witness* and Tony Scott's *Top Gun*, in which she played strong women willing to take chances in worlds dominated by men: the Amish farming community and the Air Force. She also left Hollywood at the peak of her career for Michael Kahn's Shakespeare theater in Washington, D.C., where she played several starring roles, including Helena and Beatrice, roles also associated with Emma Thompson. To crown this implied connection between Branagh's biography and Paul's character, the transformed Maggie and Paul end up in bed together. Branagh, cleverly, manages to get his young protégé to share both his Hollywood-inspired dreams and his wife!

The film now shuttles back and forth between twosomes and threesomes as it did the day before, building to the reuniting of the group for dinner on New Year's Eve. These scenes are quicker than their predecessors since they are either about making up or falling apart rather than catching up. Brian flees back to his wife, Peter and Vera make up their differences about Peter's being gay, Maggie and Paul have their fling, Sarah and Andrew reminisce about their university romance, and Carol decides to escape to Montana where a film role awaits. Carol's decision, at least partially spurred by discovering Andrew and Sarah sharing a sentimental kiss, sparks the film's final and most flamboyant meltdown: Andrew's drunk scene. When Carol bolts, Andrew hits the bottle. By dinner he's ripe, and, by coffee and drinks (champagne as midnight approaches), he's rotten.

Branagh's Andrew lets it rip and embarrasses himself, his friends, and many reviewers, but he did receive the *Evening Standard* award in 1992 for best comedy performance in a film. When Fry's Peter snaps Andrew out of his narcissistic wallowing with the midnight announcement that he is HIV positive, Branagh's performance of contrition strikes a more genuine chord than his profane self-loathing. As he keeps repeating, "O Peter, I'm sooo sorry," he's invited to snuggle back in among the group gathered on the sofa and into the bosom of friendship.

This, too, like the *Top Gun* business with Paul, has a faintly autobiographical ring to it. Andrew (and Branagh) is being welcomed back into the group and forgiven for America, money, success and the inevitable backlash in the form of envy, jealousy, and self-loathing. Branagh was

The cast (Rita Rudner, Kenneth Branagh, Alex Lowe, Emma Thompson, Alphonsia Emmanuel, Imelda Staunton, Stephen Fry, Tony Slattery, Hugh Laurie, and Phyllida Law) cut up for the camera after the final shot of *Peter's Friends*.   [Photographer: Clive Coote, Courtesy of Photofest]

being both remarkably prescient and optimistic here—prescient because even though he took a few hard knocks from the sharpened knives of the British press film reviewers for *Dead Again*, and he and Emma Thompson had become the new, hot, celebrity couple, he was still riding the upward curve of his young career. By the fall of 1992, he had released three movies and was editing a fourth, all of which made their money back and two of which became solid commercial successes. At this time he was about to play (at age thirty-two) his third stage Hamlet, this time in a highly lauded sold-out production for The Royal Shakespeare Company, and Emma Thompson was about to enter the film stratosphere by winning the Oscar (in March of 1993) for her performance of Margaret Schlegel in the Merchant-Ivory film of E. M. Forster's novel, *Howard's End*. Branagh's fall from grace and success seemed only a mote in his own eye at this moment. And Branagh was displaying optimism in his autobiographical rendering because, as I've mentioned earlier, the group he's nestling into are Emma's friends, his only by marriage and adoption. The Branagh behind the camera creating the film is an outsider to the world the film depicts. The sense of malaise among this group of thirty-somethings (some of whom are about to, or already have, hit it big) extends beyond Andrew. Vera, the mother figure who cannot be satisfied, emerges from the kitchen, champagne glass in hand, to join the group in consoling Peter but also to announce the film's final bleak judgment of Peter and, by extension, of his friends: "You had all that promise. I hated seeing what you did with your life."

This stern pronouncement delivered by Phyllida Law with something of a velvet glare (tears gathering in her eyes, a gentle smile on her face) propels the reconstituted group back into the past as Peter produces the photo snapped at the end of the film's opening shot ten years earlier. They instantaneously launch back into "The Underground Song," and a freeze-frame captures them in a reprise of the earlier photograph. Only a too inquiring eye, perhaps, will note that two figures have been transposed in the two shots. In the first it is Peter who is in the center and Andrew on the periphery; in the last Peter is on the edge and it is Andrew who is neatly nestled in between Sarah and Maggie. Branagh's attempt to synthesize elements of his own disparate experience—Belfast, RADA, Shakespeare, Hollywood, Emma Thompson—and take them toward the center of British performance culture in the 1990s is as much at work in *Peter's Friends* as it was in *Henry V* and *Dead Again*.

Peter's Friends turned out to be the first bump on the road of Branagh's commercial and popular success.[5] The film failed to find an audience and was generally panned on both sides of the Atlantic. Because it was shot on the minuscule budget of three million dollars, it managed to recoup its production costs, but unlike *Henry V* and *Dead Again*, it didn't return a profit. American film critics have tended to respond more generously to Branagh's films than have their English counterparts. Richard Corliss, writing in *Time*, and David Ansen, in *Newsweek*, set the tone: "In its bantering way, the movie is ambitious to a fault. When it isn't addressing the lapsing of marital love or the exhausting of extramarital lust, it's got dead babies on its mind, and Aids . . . sounds promising, but *Peter's Friends* is awful, with glimpses of wit" (Corliss). "The clever, facile *Peter's Friends* doesn't bear much scrutiny, and its attempts at pathos are more opportunistic than earned. Still, Branagh knows how to put on a lively show. Any movie that provides this many laughs can be forgiven a lot" (Ansen).[6] Both Corliss and Ansen are willing, at least partially, to give Branagh the benefit of the doubt, and neither critic sharpens his pen to take a personal shot at the film or its director. Stanley Kauffmann, the longtime film critic for *The New Republic* and an enthusiast for Branagh's Shakespeare films, has similar reservations:

The screenplay . . . scurries in pursuit of bright dialogue like a whippet after a rabbit and sometimes pounces. (Commenting on a friend's dire misfortune, one man [Andrew] says, 'If there is a God, he takes long lunches.') But when a screenplay snuggles into such a warm form as this one, it needs more than the occasional zinger: it needs justification in theme or sheer pleasure in the characters' company. *Peter's Friends* has neither.[7]

Kauffmann has put a wise finger on the film's major flaw, especially for American audiences: we aren't given enough reasons to care about any of these characters except, perhaps, Thompson's Maggie. The film, despite Branagh's growing mastery with the camera and his resolute determination to trust his actors, never takes off to provide the giddy high spirits of the best moments in *The Big Chill*. The screenplay, though coauthored by an American, remains decidedly British in its irony, understatement, and focus on loss and missed opportunity. The film never allows the group to rekindle and display the energy and affection that drove their university experience a decade before. The film needs more scenes like the brief gathering around the piano for "The Way You Look Tonight" or Paul's daft infatuation with *Top Gun* to lift it up out of its sentimental and melancholy doldrums.

The film, ultimately, is more interesting for what it tells us about Branagh and his development as a film director than it is as simply a work to be enjoyed on its own merits. This can be true in the work of any auteur; some of Woody Allen's or Martin Scorsese's films come immediately to mind as falling into a similar category. Branagh's first three films established the rhythm of his career as a director. He came to international prominence and attention as a young, unknown British Shakespearean who made the first successful Shakespeare film in twenty years. Surprisingly he didn't, like Olivier, follow *Henry V* with another Shakespeare film but instead went to Hollywood and made a contemporary version of a Hitchcock noir thriller. Rather than cashing in on *Dead Again*'s commercial success and remaining in America to take on an even bigger Hollywood project, he returned to England to make a little comedy on a largely self-financed budget even smaller than the one he had for *Henry V.* It is obvious that Branagh from the outset was determined to set his own course, declining to be seen either as Olivier's successor as a stage and film Shakespearean or as Hollywood's hot new director. Branagh's aim was to keep a foot firmly entrenched in both worlds, and in the process he ended up getting the worst of both. He sacrificed Hollywood's commercial rewards and exposed himself to the barbed taunts of the English press always alert to flay the latest son (or daughter) of Albion to achieve precocious notoriety. *Peter's Friends* might have been chosen to try to allay the later, but it failed to charm the English film critics either.

Nevertheless, Branagh's first three films reveal important aspects of his energy, style, working environment, and project choice. For a newcomer he had the charm and persuasiveness to work the theatrical and film cultures on both sides of the Atlantic. For *Henry V* he did not rely simply on the cast from Adrian Noble's RSC production of the play, but instead was able to gather to his cause some of the greatest living Shakespearean actors of the past fifty years, including Paul Scofield, Robert Stephens, Judi Dench, Ian Holm, and Derek Jacobi. When in Hollywood he was able to convince his producers at Paramount to cast the then equally unknown Emma Thompson as his co-star and to allow them to double the screenplay's leading roles. When Branagh ran into trouble dealing with Donald Sutherland, originally cast as Franklyn Madson, he again convinced the studio to allow him to replace Sutherland with Derek Jacobi, another unknown in the Hollywood world. When his charm, even after the commercial success of *Dead Again*, was unable to persuade Hollywood to finance *Peter's Friends*, he used some of his own money to leverage its meager budget from English film funding sources.

These first three films also reveal Branagh's developing film practice and style: rehearsal periods before shooting, actor-centered production decisions, bold camera moves, long takes, and rich, romantic, or pop film scores. Each features an unusual and stunning opening scene or shot meant to immediately grab and provoke the viewer's attention—what Orson Welles has called "the riderless horse shot."[8] The hook that Welles believed every film needs to pull the viewer into its universe. Finally, we see Branagh gradually building a company on both sides of the camera, something also true of auteur-directors like Welles, Bergman, Fellini, Truffaut, Kurosawa, Scorsese, and Woody Allen. Branagh is never a director for hire. He picks his projects and gathers his own creative team from those he has worked with in the past.

Peter's Friends was released in the fall of 1992 as Branagh was in the final stages of editing his next film, *Much Ado About Nothing*, shot on location in Tuscany that summer. In December he returned to the stage to play *Hamlet* for the RSC in a heralded production directed by Adrian Noble, who had launched Branagh's Shakespeare career with *Henry V* eight years before. For the first time in the RSC's history, one of their Shakespeare productions opened in London at the Barbican, where it played through early March before moving up to Stratford for April and May, reversing the normal flow of the company's work. There were several reasons for this innovation, one of which was to allow Branagh to be working in London during the days on the final cut of *Much Ado*. In retrospect we can see that Branagh was, in December of 1992, at the zenith of the first twenty years (roughly 1982–2002) of his professional career.

He had established himself, through his first season with the RSC, his subsequent stage work with his own company, Renaissance, and his film of *Henry V*, as the boldest Shakespearean of his generation. His first film had been nominated for three Academy Awards, his second had been equally surprising in its subject matter and had turned a handsome profit, and his third had brought him back from Hollywood and into the more intimate British film world.[9] He had formed a professional and personal partnership with Emma Thompson who was about to emerge, with her work in *Howard's End*, *Much Ado About Nothing*, and *Remains of the Day*, as the leading British film actress of her generation, successes that were crowned by her winning the Academy Award for Best Actress in 1993. Thompson received her award in Hollywood as her husband was playing Hamlet to sold-out audiences in England; he had just turned 32; she 33. It was a heady time in Branagh's career and, momentarily, things were about to get even better.

Chapter 5

MUCH ADO ABOUT NOTHING

Peter's Friends was for Branagh a low-budget trial run experience for making *Much Ado About Nothing*. The former film was Branagh's first extended experience with shooting on location and using a single essential space both as the landscape for the film and as the administrative center for the cast and production team. Wrotham Park, the setting for *Peter's Friends*, allowed the filmmaker to experiment with the more complicated logistics that later came into play when, for six weeks in the summer of 1992, Branagh transported cast and crew to the Villa Vignamaggio in Tuscany to shoot *Much Ado About Nothing*.

Much Ado is Branagh's sunniest film. Even more than *Henry V*, it spurred the revival of Shakespeare on film in the 1990s, primarily because of its surprising commercial success. *Much Ado About Nothing* was the first Shakespeare film since Franco Zeffirelli's *Romeo and Juliet* (1968) to capture the young, fifteen- to twenty-five-year-old, major movie-going audience and to make money in a manner to catch Hollywood's attention. Branagh clearly pitched his film—in tone, atmosphere, casting, and delivery—to the high school and college audience and succeeded beyond, if not his own, then Hollywood's wildest dreams. Here was a Shakespeare film that competed with conventional narrative films at the multiplex rather than at the art house in the summer of 1993. The major releases of that summer included *Sleepless in Seattle*, *Rising Sun*, *The Firm*, *The Fugitive*, and the Spielberg blockbuster *Jurassic Park*.

The film's popular reception was buoyed, of course, by Emma Thompson's remarkable journey into the public's imagination in the mere ten months between the release (in England) of *Peter's Friends* and the release (in America) of *Much Ado About Nothing*. If Branagh was riding a great wave of success, hers was even more stunning. In less than a year, she had gone from being a minor English television comedienne to an Oscar-winning film star. *Much Ado* might well have won her an Oscar nomination for her performance as Beatrice if she hadn't just won the Best Actress Award for *Howard's End*. In fact, she was nominated again the following year for her performance of Miss Kenton, the spinster housekeeper, in another Merchant-Ivory film, *The Remains of the Day*, based on Kazuo Ishiguro's novel. Thompson's Oscar triumph certainly helped to keep her (and by extension, Branagh) in the entertainment news, but the audience headed for *Much Ado* was not coming from having just seen *Howard's End*. Branagh's film found its own following.

Branagh's choice of *Much Ado* was a risky one. No film of a Shakespearean comedy had ever found a wide audience, not even Zeffirelli's *Taming of the Shrew* starring Elizabeth Taylor and Richard Burton and made at the height of the actors' notoriety. *Much Ado*, unlike *Romeo and Juliet*, *Macbeth*, *Hamlet*, *Julius Caesar*, and *A Midsummer Night's Dream*, is not a staple of the American or British high school literature curriculum. In retrospect Branagh's decision to cast the film with a mixture of British stage actors, Hollywood stars, and several young unknowns appears to have been commercially calculated, but it was also equally capable of backfiring—as it did for the Warner Brothers' *A Midsummer Night's Dream* in 1935. In fact one of Branagh's strengths as a director was to keep the film from being pulled apart by highly eccentric performances by two of its biggest Hollywood stars: Keanu Reeves and Michael Keaton.

What keeps the film alive and allows it to transcend the potential failures of individual actors is its driving energy, cinematic high spirits, and core performances from Branagh, Thompson, and Denzel Washington. In Branagh's conception and delivery *Much Ado* becomes a festive version of *Peter's Friends*. Whereas *Peter's Friends* is almost relentlessly melancholy and even bitter, with only a few flashes of heat and light, *Much Ado* is the previous film's reverse. Here the gentles are at their recreation, to borrow a phrase from *Love's Labour's Lost*, and we are invited to enjoy their sport. Although the film follows the text into dark territory in Claudio's shameless treatment of Hero, Branagh is quick to restore the play's conventional comic ending (and the film's Tuscan sun) as a festive antidote to Shakespeare's critique of love and courtship in a patriarchal society.

Though scholars place *Much Ado* before *As You Like It* in the chronology of Shakespeare's plays, temperamentally it belongs, I think, with those plays that follow the sublime festive comedies (*Love's Labour's Lost*, *A Midsummer Night's Dream*, and *As You Like It*), plays such as *Twelfth Night* and *All's Well That Ends Well*, where Shakespeare begins to test the limits of both the form and the content of romantic comedy. For several centuries *Much Ado* was seen essentially as a "merry war of words" between Beatrice and Benedick. The bittersweet subplot involving Hero and Claudio was downplayed in favor of the Beatrice and Benedick comedy and Dogberry's delicious anticipation of Mrs. Malaprop. Unsurprisingly, our age has sought to restore, even emphasize, the play's darker underside with its searing indictment of conventional courtship. Several productions by The Royal Shakespeare Company, Cheek by Jowl, and West End producers in the 1990s went so far in this direction that they even managed to drain the wit, spark, and humor out of the Benedick and Beatrice relationship.[1] Branagh seeks to restore the balance largely by treating the play as a festive comedy. But, as I will argue later in greater detail, the power of the film image, especially the close-up, will allow him to make the Claudio-Hero relationship more vivid than it usually is in stage productions, without allowing Claudio's callow cruelty to cast a cold eye over the entire film.

As the opening sequences in *Henry V, Dead Again*, and *Peter's Friends* have revealed, one of Branagh's great strengths as a director and a signature element in his work is his ability to get his films off to a vivid start. The opening of *Much Ado* confirms and extends this mastery, and it signals his firm control of his Shakespearean material. Branagh's screenplay plucks Balthazar's song "Sigh no more, Ladies, Sigh no more" from its pivotal spot in the center of Shakespeare's narrative and uses it to verbally frame the film. In three variations the song opens and closes the film, in addition to appearing at its center. With an instinctive understanding of the ways Shakespeare's comedies increasingly come to depend upon song as a crucial element of establishing character, action, and atmosphere, Branagh sees how Shakespeare anticipates both Mozart's comic operas and American musical comedies in plays like *Much Ado* and *Twelfth Night*.

Branagh begins his film with words rather than images. The words of Balthazar's song, being recited by the off-screen voice of Emma Thompson, pop up in white letters on a black screen. With a wry, knowing tone Thompson slowly recites the words as they spread out across the screen:

> Sigh no more, ladies, sigh no more,
>   Men were deceivers ever,
> One foot in sea and one on shore,
>   To one thing constant never:

Then sigh not so, but let them go,
And be you blithe and bonny,
Converting all your sounds of woe
Into hey, nonny, nonny.
Sing no more ditties, sing no more,
Of dumps so dull and heavy;
The fraud of men was ever so,
Since summer first was leavy:
Then sigh not so, but let them go,
And be you blithe and bonny,
Converting all your sounds of woe
Into hey nonny, nonny.

I first saw the film in London in May of 1993 (after it had been released in the States) at a special screening for film critics to which members of British Actors Equity had also been invited. This alert audience gave the film its first laugh just at the sight of those words and the sound of Thompson's voice. Balthazar's song does establish *Much Ado*'s wry and witty approach to romantic relationships, acknowledging that "men were deceivers ever," but also that women should "cry no more but let them go," converting their songs of woe into a "hey nonny, nonny."

Here Branagh associates the song with Beatrice's keen intelligence, and it comes as something of a warning for the audience (as well as for the women in the play) to be skeptical of the film's driving romantic energy. The song is spoken, not sung, to underline its message without the sugar-coating of a melody. The song then reappears in the film at the central position it occupies in the text. Shakespeare's placement of the song is curious. It is sung by Balthazar as Don Pedro, Claudio, Leonato, and Antonio gather in the garden to lay the trap for Benedick. The song, about the fickleness of man when it comes to romance, is sung by a man to an audience made up exclusively of men about to deceive another man! All too often, in performance, the resonance of the song's lyrics to the action of the entire play can get lost in the Benedick comedy. Here in Branagh's adaptation, the song is sung by Patrick Doyle, the composer of the film score, as the men gather around the garden's fountain. Our familiarity with the song should alert us to its potential application to other events in the play beyond the impending duping of Benedick and Beatrice. The song makes its final appearance at the film's end when the reunited lovers and their friends swirl from the chapel area in the rear of the estate, through its courtyard, and out into the front garden in festive celebration. Now the song is sung by the full chorus of revelers and signals the dismissal of all "sounds of woe" with a "hey, nonny, nonny."

In the song's first appearance in the film, as Thompson reaches its second verse, the words dissolve from the screen as the camera pans out over an idyllic Tuscan landscape. In another of Branagh's uninterrupted shots, the camera, mounted on a crane, captures the villa in the distance, the valley below, and a group of picnickers lolling on a hillside, revealing bare chests (the men) and ample cleavage (the women), and finally it closes in on Emma Thompson, sitting in a tree, eating an apple, and reading Balthazar's lyrics from a book. Birds chirp and bees buzz on the soundtrack. Branagh's camera lingers just long enough on this group to let us see that we are in an Englishman's fantasy of late nineteenth-century Italy: Club Med Tuscano with resonances of Chiantishire—a contemporary haunt of the English seeking the sun. Quickly the camera cuts to horse and rider as a messenger (Alex Lowe) dismounts, announcing the impending arrival of Don Pedro and his soldiers home from the wars. After a series of quick verbal exchanges and visual glances that establish the Beatrice–Benedick and Claudio–Hero relationships, the camera cuts to a long shot of the men pounding home in the valley below. We zoom in on them lifting up and down in their saddles in slow motion, spread out across the wide screen in a line of seven. They punch their fists in the air as Doyle's score trumpets their thunderous arrival. Branagh gets his second visual laugh as we indulge his comic evocation of John Sturges's *The Magnificent Seven*. In fact the moment gets a laugh even from my student audiences for whom *The Magnificent Seven* is as unfamiliar as *The Fairie Queene*. They just don't expect such a giddy moment and such a line of familiar Hollywood faces galloping toward them in a Shakespeare film.

As the credits begin to roll, the camera cuts to the equivalent scene for the women as they race down the hill to the villa to bathe and dress to welcome the return of males. The men follow a similar ritual by leaping from their horses into outdoor bathing tubs. Branagh makes sure his camera captures enough male and female flesh to reinforce for the teenage market that this is Shakespeare stripped to the bone; or, as Sarah Hatchuel observes, he does this as a symbolic gesture to demonstrate how the film means "to shake the dust out of Shakespeare."[2] When the two groups have bathed and dressed, the men march toward the villa as the women come down the stairs into the courtyard, where an overheard shot captures their meeting as they form a giant X on the screen, making literal the battle of the sexes which is to follow. Branagh, in this extended opening sequence, has taken the Shakespeare film into new territory. The structure and content of his images, the pace and flow of their delivery, the Hollywood flavor of his cast, and Doyle's rousing score all boldly announce the arrival of a fresh approach to translating Shakespeare into the language of popular film.[3]

Branagh clearly created this opening sequence as the hook to capture the cohort of fifteen- to twenty-five-year-olds who constitute the vast majority of the movie-going audience. That he succeeded does not reduce the danger of his gamble. He was likely to offend not only the Shakespearean purists who prefer "high" Shakespeare to "low," but also those more enlightened souls who, over the previous two decades, had come to embrace Shakespeare on film. For them the triumphs in the genre were the great modernist classics like Olivier's *Hamlet*, Welles's *Othello*, Kurosawa's *Throne of Blood*, and Brook's *King Lear*. Branagh's film was announcing Shakespeare-on-film's liberation from the high modernist aesthetic and its art house audience. His *Much Ado* was headed to the multiplex and determined to compete there. To succeed Branagh had to find a new film audience for Shakespeare and he did—the *Clueless* generation. *Much Ado*, especially in its opening sequence, spoke the young audience's language and allowed Branagh to draw them into listening to and understanding Shakespeare's.

As Geoffrey O'Brien had astutely detailed in writing about Branagh's film of *Henry V*, Branagh, in his company's work with Shakespeare on both stage and film, was working toward a way of communicating

Beatrice (Emma Thompson) and Benedick (Kenneth Branagh), framed against a romantic Tuscan landscape, take a momentary break from their bickering in Branagh's film of *Much Ado About Nothing.* [Photographer: Theo Westenberger, Courtesy of Photofest]

Shakespeare's language to the contemporary ear.[4] If visually Branagh was willing to risk incorporating elements of Hollywood's "popular" film style, so verbally he strove for the "plain" style in speaking Shakespeare. Gone were the plummy tones of Olivier and Gielgud and their supporting casts, who all spoke BBC-received standard English barren of regional or international accents.[5]

As Branagh comments in the Introduction to his screenplay for *Much Ado*, "We wanted to tell the story with the utmost clarity and simplicity. . . . we wanted audiences to react to the story as if it were here and now and important to them. We did not want them to feel they were in some cultural church."[6] To capture this "clarity and simplicity," he wanted to build on the naturalistic way of speaking Shakespeare's verse that he had pioneered in *Henry V* and that allowed him to turn toward Hollywood:

> The film [*Much Ado*] presented the rare opportunity to utilize the skills of marvelous film actors who would embrace this naturalistic challenge. . . In crude terms, the challenge was to find experienced Shakespearean actors who were unpracticed on screen and team them with experienced film actors who were much less familiar with Shakespeare. Different accents, different looks. . .[producing] a Shakespeare film which would belong to the world.[7]

The idea of "Different accents, different looks" has become one of the hallmarks of Branagh's Shakespeare films and was adopted by other directors in the Shakespeare film revival in the 1990s, directors as diverse as Baz Luhrmann, Michael Hoffman, and Julie Taymor. No other directors, however, have made the mixture work quite as successfully as Branagh does.[8] In order to create a Messina universe where "different accents" and "different looks" could seem to commingle naturally, Branagh had to create an approach to *Much Ado* that jettisoned some of its prominent features. In *Much Ado* Shakespeare is moving away from the "Green World" escapist settings of the major action in plays like *A Midsummer Night's Dream* and *As You Like It* and into a more recognizable middle-class social milieu. *Much Ado* has a city, rather than rural, setting; its language is littered with references to fashion, social conventions, and class consciousness; and in its flirtation with rape and death, it more resembles Shakespeare's problem comedies than his festive ones. Branagh intentionally obliterated the play's social hierarchy to create the more leveling, democratic atmosphere associated with the forest experience in Shakespeare's festive comedies where English weavers mate with Ovidian goddesses, lovers unite over class and family boundaries, and a natural social harmony prevails.

Branagh accomplished this move with the film's rural Tuscan setting, with determination to shoot as much as possible in the open air, and with the film's late nineteenth-century costuming. The costumes are significant. The women all wear similar sheer cotton camisoles under mock corsets and the men are dressed either in identical military uniforms or in white linen vests worn over white shirts with open collars. The only note of dress that distinguishes Don Pedro's social preeminence is that his leather pants are black whereas Benedick and Claudio's are blue. Anthony Lane archly responded to Phyliss Daulton's costumes by remarking, "*Much Ado* could become Ralph Lauren's favorite movie."[9] But Lane fails to see that Branagh's approach stresses the democratic tendencies in Shakespeare's comic art, where we see the youthful egalitarian yearnings of emotion and romance—the holiday spirit that tests social limits by flirting with transgression. It is part of the stripping away of fashion, military rank, and social standing down to bare flesh that begins the film, and this festive license provides one explanation for Claudio's eventual confusion of Hero and Margaret: both maiden and maid are dressed in almost identical white cotton dresses. Fashion, except as a metaphor for the socially conventional manner in which the Claudio and Hero subplot unfolds, is absent from Branagh's adaptation of the play.

In many ways, because of the power of visual images, Branagh's treatment of Hero and Claudio is more emphatic than in the dozens of stage productions of the play I have seen over the past forty years. We rarely forget Beatrice and Benedick; we rarely remember Claudio and Hero. My own experience of the play in performance stretches back to John Gielgud and Margaret Leighton in New York in 1959 and subsequent Benedicks and Beatrices have included Sam Waterston and Kathleen Widdoes, Judi Dench and Donald Sinden, Martha Henry and Alan Scarfe, Maggie Smith and Brian Bedford, Michael Gambon and Penelope Wilton, Derek Jacobi and Sinead Cusack, David Selby and Kelly McGillis, and Alex Jennings and Siobhan Redmond. I can't name—or summon the image of—a single Claudio and Hero, not even in Michael Boyd's bleak production (The Jennings–Redmond pairing) for The Royal Shakespeare Company in 1996 where the poor cast, following the director's conception, had to work hard to drain the play of all its natural humor (and complained about it in private). In production the play typically belongs to Beatrice and Benedick and Dogberry, though I have seen several where the actor playing Don John turned him into a marvelously funny melodramatic villain.[10]

We rightly think of Branagh's film as sunny and upbeat; he clearly imagines Shakespeare as leading the long line of English authors who send their characters to Italy to discover the joys of the flesh. But his film does not back away from the ways in which Shakespeare exposes the cruel complications of conventional romance played out under patriarchal rules and regulations. Largely through the impact of the close-up, Kate Beckinsale's Hero and Robert Sean Leonard's Claudio are firmly imprinted on our imaginations. Beckinsale's soft, doe-eyed Hero is often caught in a two-shot with her more exquisitely defined and outspoken cousin who both teases and defends Hero's clear but silent infatuation. Beatrice often speaks for her socially conventional younger friend who lacks the independence of mind to speak for herself. Robert Sean Leonard's Claudio is even more embarrassed and confused. The camera repeatedly captures him responding to both good news and bad with the flush of a cheek and a tear gathering in the eye. Leonard's Claudio is lost in a sea of inchoate emotions and uncertain conventions. When he turns to his friend, Branagh's Benedick, as immature males have done for centuries seeking confirmation of their taste in women, he is comically abused rather than stoutly supported. Branagh's screenplay retains all of Benedick's skepticism about romance and marriage. Benedick dismisses Claudio's romantic pieties and the language of commercial value in which he expresses them. Mocked by his friend and confused in his affections, it is little wonder that Claudio so readily accepts Don Pedro's offer to do his wooing for him.

The Masked Ball is the first scene to dramatize Claudio's romantic insecurity. The fast-paced editing of the scene, the emphasis on masks of animals of prey, the pulse of the film score, and the role reversals all suggest the release of social rules and sexual roles associated with holiday and carnival.[11] Branagh films the scene so that, alternatively, the scene circles around Claudio and Benedick. Claudio, of course, is confused by the conflicting reports he overhears (and too eagerly mis-notes) that Don Pedro has wooed Hero for himself. Once again the camera captures Leonard in close-up giving us his hurt little lost boy expression that only becomes more pronounced as his face swells with relief and embarrassment when he discovers the truth (and success) of Don Pedro's efforts on his behalf.

Branagh's Benedick, interestingly, seems genuinely stung by Beatrice's barbs about his being "the Prince's jester." His reaction is in keeping with his approach to the character. Most Benedicks assume the role of supreme self-confidence, of the aloof wit in full command of his emotions. Our pleasure comes in watching this facade crumble as Don Pedro's trick begins to do its work. In traditional productions Benedick would typically demonstrate the cool reserve exuded by, let's say, Denzel Washington instead of the more broadly comic features Branagh gives the character. Rather than firing off ripostes with a distanced superiority, Branagh's Benedick is clearly working hard to be witty. In the scene where Benedick is being "limed," he resorts to slapstick and pratfalls as he struggles to get a canvas garden chair to unfold properly so that he can eavesdrop on the Prince and the others in comfort. His unsuccessful efforts send him to the ground. Later he covers a barely stifled cry (in response to the barbs directed at him by his friends) by mimicking the "caw" of a raucous crow.[12]

When Branagh delivers Benedick's famous soliloquy about his rediscovered passion for Beatrice ("I will be horribly in love with her"), he scrunches up his face and twists his mouth in comic distortion to underline the humor of Benedick's conversion. Tellingly, he never addresses the camera directly here as one might expect in such a confidential revelation. Branagh's Benedick is still the class clown rather than the confident mocker of love sure of his mind and at ease in making the audience his ally. He remains slightly off-center to us until he has made his ultimate commitment to Beatrice. To further underscore the physical comedy of the scene, Branagh moves to the garden's fountain, around which the other men had gathered for the reprise of Balthazar's song and the baiting of Benedick, to prepare himself for Beatrice's arrival to call him into dinner. Again he relies on broad physical comedy by trying out several positions in which to make himself casually attractive. Branagh has noted that he used Tony Curtis's attempts to transform himself into a version of Cary Grant in preparation for wooing Marilyn Monroe in *Some Like It Hot* as a model here.[13] Shakespeareans aren't prepared for a goofy Benedick, but Branagh had his eye squarely on another audience for his performance, and it worked for them. Most—not all, but most—of my female undergraduates have found his clowning winning. Some of it is connected to Branagh's natural boyish charm (physically, he's not a conventional leading man) and his willingness to be vulnerable, and thus silly, in an unguarded moment; some of it is connected with the film's intent to bring Shakespeare down from his elite pedestal (that "cultural church" Branagh mentions) and into the conventions of the popular romantic film comedy (the *Some Like It Hot* resonance); and some of it is surely connected with Emma Thompson's Beatrice.

Branagh could infuse his own performance with such broad comedy and his film with such ripe, romantic energy without destroying the more subtle and wary elements in Shakespeare's tale because of Thompson's performance as Beatrice. It is as though the part was written with her strengths as an actress and comedienne in mind. Branagh made her the film's radiant, sentient center. Intelligence, generosity, and wit illuminate every aspect of her performance. Thompson's Beatrice can register emotion, underline irony, change mood, raise alarm, deflect attention, suppress sorrow, and enhance wit by the mere tilt of her head, the lift of an eyebrow, the flick of an eyelid, or the purse of a lip. She can also capture the right inflection of Shakespeare's muscular prose and deliver it in a tone and rhythm properly suited to the camera. The economy with which she allows us to understand her previous romantic relationship with Benedick, her embarrassment at unintentionally encouraging Don Pedro's marriage proposal, and her outrage at the patriarchy's treatment of Hero is film acting worthy of association with Katharine Hepburn, Claudette Colbert, and Irene Dunne, the self-confident, fast-talking, sassy heroines of the great screwball comedies. It's hard to imagine another actress in the history of the movies who has given three such varied and mature performances in successive films as Thompson's Margaret Schlegel (*Howard's End*), Beatrice (*Much Ado*), and Miss Kenton (*Remains of the Day*).[14]

Thompson's Beatrice anchors the film; she gives it weight and ballast and grounding. This allows Branagh's camera and Doyle's score to perform some cinematic high-flying without ignoring the wit and social critique at work in Shakespeare's play. Nowhere is this levitation more evident than in the overlapping images of Benedick and Beatrice that climax the first half of the film. Benedick, in response to the hidden message of affection he is certain was buried inside Beatrice's truculent invitation to come in to dinner, begins to dance about in the fountain as the film segues from *Some Like It Hot* to *Singin' in the Rain*. Beatrice, having overheard the report of Benedick's love (and her scornful pride) from Hero and Ursula, expresses the release of her emotions by taking to a swing. Director Branagh superimposes their splashing and high-flying images in slow motion as once again Patrick Doyle's score soars into a romantically triumphant crescendo. This is the film's festive climax. Its atmosphere now darkens as we turn from Don Pedro's plot to play cupid in the Benedick–Beatrice relationship to Don John's anti-cupid efforts to explode the romance between Claudio and Hero.

Denzel Washington and Robert Sean Leonard's performances make Branagh's American gamble pay off. But assigning the roles of villain and clown to Hollywood stars Keanu Reeves and Michael Keaton proved more problematic. Reeves, rumored (like Jack Lemmon in *Hamlet*) to have approached Branagh with the request to be included in his next Shakespeare film, is an actor without affect. His handsome face is a mask—a great plus in films like the *Matrix* series—but a liability in roles requiring a greater range of expression. One can see why Branagh cast him as Don John, for the role is conceived as a one-note ("If I had my mouth, I would bite") character. Reeves also fits in with Washington and Keaton as young actors who had recently starred in big Hollywood films: *Malcolm X*, *Batman*, and *Speed*.[15] Unfortunately, Reeves's performance doesn't work; it's the weakest link in the film. Reeves makes his Don John uniformly lugubrious and in the process makes him neither lethal nor comic. The performance is leaden and Branagh's attempts to help by repeatedly shooting him in the shadowy cellar of the villa or by showing him being given an oily massage by Borachio didn't help and only left the film open to the charge of homophobia by some of Branagh's critics.

If Reeves's Don John is relentlessly sullen, Keaton's Dogberry is all manic energy—a daring reprise, with variations, of his Beetlejuice character. It is in the nature of comedy that villains get trumped by clowns even when, like Dogberry, they are oblivious about what they have inadvertently uncovered. Branagh, with the experience of playing Touchstone in *As You Like It* fresh in his mind, is on record as finding Shakespeare's great clowns unfunny.[16] Perhaps this is why he has repeatedly cast American comedians, from Keaton to Billy Crystal (*Hamlet*) to Nathan Lane (*Love's Labours Lost*), to play them in his films. He certainly gives Keaton wide latitude to turn Dogberry into something almost pathological in his eye-popping, head-swiveling, word-eating performance. Dogberry and Verges, played by Ben Elton, ride about on Monty Python–inspired pretend horses, creating a malapropism of gesture to mirror Dogberry's famous fracturing of language. It almost works, especially as a contrast to Reeves's inert Don John. The two performances might have seriously unbalanced a film equally unhinged in its focus, but Branagh was firmly in control of Shakespeare's romantic intentions, including his handling of the Claudio–Hero subplot.

Shakespeare can discredit Hero simply by having others report that she "talked with a man out her window" on the eve of the wedding. Branagh understands that our age requires a greater presumptive sin and that film demands that we see the supposed transgression. Therefore, he takes Claudio (and us) to a vantage point where we see a man and a brunette in a white shift, not talking out of, but making love in, a window. We, as well as Claudio, are implicated in the voyeuristic pleasure of being allowed to peek in at what is going on in that frame. The moment is a complicated one because the camera catches on Leonard's face the familiar blush of embarrassment we have come to expect from his Claudio. He tries to cry out, but Don John claps a hand over his mouth and moves him out of the frame. The audience, particularly the young, are moved to sympathize with Leonard's Claudio. Leonard makes him seem so forlorn and innocent that Branagh's film is in danger of sentimentalizing Shakespeare's tougher tale. But when the film ultimately arrives at the wedding scene (and its immediate aftermath), it delivers.

By setting the wedding outside of the villa's small chapel, Branagh gave ample space to Claudio's immature, petulant tantrum.[17] Claudio savagely shoves his bride to the ground and makes a triumphant circuit of the scene, overturning benches and ripping down the wedding decorations that festoon the setting before nestling in next to Denzel Washington's elegant Don Pedro to reestablish what he smugly believes to be the primacy of the patriarchy. Leonard's Claudio rips into Beckansale's Hero with a preening verbal and physical violence. He deliberately chooses to attack her at her most vulnerable moment: the public ritual where we pledge our most private commitments to one another. Don Pedro lends the support of the male social order to Claudio's rude behavior, and all too quickly, Richard Briers's Leonato joins in on the attack on his daughter as well. He grabs her violently by the hair to pull her away from the scene of her shame. If the film invited us to sympathize with Claudio when he became the easy victim of Don John's deception the previous evening, we, now in the cold light of a hot day, are equally indicted in Hero's victimization. It's a powerful and crucial moment in text and film. As the men (and the power structure) stand united against Hero, only Benedick and the Friar go to their knees to join Beatrice in consoling Hero. Benedick, the man's man, refuses the knee-jerk reaction we might have expected from his impudent tongue. As the socially conventional romance between Claudio and Hero collapses, Beatrice and Benedick's unconventional wooing relationship rises from its ashes.

Beatrice and Benedick now move into the chapel. There, first through her tears and anger and then through his commitment to her aggrieved passion, they create a ceremony and construct a vow that issues not from social practice and religious tradition but from the pair's own emotional and imaginative response to Hero's crisis. Branagh shoots a kneeling Beatrice in profile over Benedick's left shoulder so that we react to her outrage from his perspective. It's an awkward shot but appropriate: they are not squared to the camera because they are not yet square with each other. Beatrice's roiling anger and her frustration with the social and gender limitations in taking appropriate retaliatory action in the male world of "honor" leads her to kick over, in an exasperated parody of Claudio's earlier behavior, the communion bench on which she has been kneeling. She cries out, "O that I were a man for his sake, or that I had any friend would be a man for my sake!"

Branagh's Benedick is transformed by her passion. Earlier we had seen his exaggerated cocky jester melt into the explosive comic romantic in the gulling scene. Now both of these excessive portraits are clipped, darkened, and matured as we watch his agile mind absorb and comprehend the issue that has spurred Beatrice's fury. For the first time in the film, Branagh allows Benedick to look directly into the camera's eye as he confronts his emotional and intellectual commitment to Beatrice. Anne Barton notes that Branagh does not fully mine the comic potential of Benedick's soliloquies because of "his insistence upon looking everywhere except into the camera."[18] I agree with Barton that had Branagh coolly confronted the camera directly, he would have given us a less edgy and contorted performance, a version of the more self-assured Benedick we have come to expect from performance tradition. But Branagh clearly wants to stress the insecurity of his Benedick's anti-romantic stance. This Benedick is not able to be fully at ease with himself or the camera until he has confronted and confessed his affection for Beatrice and broken with the bachelor world he has championed. Now he steadies and fixes his gaze, for to finally engage the camera is to engage Beatrice. Branagh plucks out the word "soul" to underscore his steadfast query, "Think you in your soul that Count Claudio has wronged Hero?" It is a word Claudio has flung about recklessly when turning on his bride. Thompson, in Beatrice's reply, chooses to emphasize "thought": "Yea, as sure as I have a thought or a soul," completing the marriage of mind and heart, thought and soul, between them. Their pact is then sealed by the vow that the entire scene has moved toward: "Enough. I am engaged. I will challenge him." Benedick's commitment to action completes Beatrice's outrage and creates a surprise: a constant man. The words that lead man to woo and wed will now be as consequential as those that lead him to war.

If Branagh flirts with pandering to his teenage audience's sentimentality in his generous treatment of Claudio, he redeems himself with his intelligent and clear-eyed handling of the climactic moment in the development of Benedick's relationship with Beatrice. The most stunning moment in Shakespeare's play comes as it reaches what convention insists will be its romantic climax. The wary lovers inch toward the expected mutual revelation of their love for one another. When Benedick finally expresses the typically grand and hyperbolic male wooing sentiment, "Come, bid me do anything for thee," Beatrice does not respond in conventional kind, but snaps back, "Kill Claudio." Thompson delivers the line with her eyes ablaze. Branagh's Benedick instinctively responds, "Ha. Not for the wide world." The film confronts this moment directly and holds it for a beat before Benedick makes the final stage in his journey from bachelor to bridegroom, from wise guy to wise man.

Vincent Canby's stunned reaction to this moment is revealing. He sees that its power is directly related to the film's sunny high spirits:

Everyone seems to smile too much and to laugh too quickly. Yet I also suspect that if it weren't for this helium-high manner, Mr. Branagh would not be able to discover the moments of pathos that, by contrast, unexpectedly illuminate the comedy and give it value. Benedick's suddenly abject, intensely felt admission of his love for Beatrice, in a chapel during one of their otherwise barbed arguments, takes the breath away. Because it is such a surprise amid the tumult, it has an emotional impact I've never before experienced in Shakespeare, on stage or screen.[19]

Michael Anderegg excellently describes Branagh's technical accomplishment in making the scene so powerful, noting that "the four minute scene involves six camera set-ups arranged in forty-one shots." For Anderegg the scene provides "an ideal welding of essentially 'theatrical' and essentially 'cinematic' elements—the theatrical is transformed into the cinematic."[20]

Branagh's handling of this intelligent and crucial move, like Thompson's performance throughout, is what allows us, as Canby realizes, to release our critical, skeptical selves to enjoy the film's exuberant excesses captured by Branagh's Gene Kelly–like splashing in the fountain, superimposed on Thompson's high-flying in a swing, that crowns the neatly compressed scenes of the unmasking of hidden affections. Branagh's film does foreground the serious gender issues at work in the play, brought into precise focus in the chapel scene, which makes possible the film's seemingly paradoxical indulgence in giddy romanticism. Branagh understands that even as Shakespeare's comedies critique the follies and cruelties of love's social conventions, they also provide evidence—however fleeting—for love's powers to cross class and gender divisions, as witnessed in the relationships between Titania and Bottom, Ganymede and Orlando, Cesario and Orsino, Toby and Maria, and even Hal and Falstaff. Here Benedick, by being willing to challenge Claudio, does become a man for Beatrice's sake and allows her anger the access to the world of masculine, physical retribution that is denied to her gender.

In working out, in film language, the remarkable relationship between Beatrice and Benedick, Branagh may have been inspired by the great Hollywood screwball comedies of the 1930s. As already indicated, his film, in cast and atmosphere, is loaded with Hollywood conventions and ideas. As he remarked just prior to the film's release in May of 1993, "If I can't make Shakespeare live for a broad audience with all the Hollywood that got packed into that film [*Much Ado About Nothing*], then I doubt I will

Dogbery (Michael Keaton), Claudio (Robert Sean Leonard), Don John (Keanu Reeves), Hero (Kate Beckinsale), Beatrice (Emma Thompson), Benedick (Kenneth Branagh), and Don Pedro (Denzel Washington) pose for a cast photo and reinforce the company ethos at the heart of Branagh's film of *Much Ado About Nothing*. [Photographer: Theo Westenberger, Courtesy of Photofest]

be able to raise the funding for [future Shakespeare films]."[21] Beyond the inclusion of Hollywood stars like Washington, Reeves, and Keaton and obvious visual quotations from films like *The Magnificent Seven*, *Singin' in the Rain*, and *Some Like It Hot*, the deep structure of the film owes much to the screwball tradition most commonly associated with a string of comedies Katharine Hepburn made first with Cary Grant and then Spencer Tracy. The finest treatment of those films remains Stanley Cavell's *Pursuits of Happiness: The Hollywood Comedy of Remarriage*.

Cavell's analysis of those films reaches back to the films' resonances with Shakespeare's romantic comedies. Curiously, though the play's structure most closely resembles the comedy of remarriage pattern he sees at work in screwball, Cavell never mentions *Much Ado About Nothing*. But clearly, Beatrice and Benedick—even in the history of their relationship, which features a broken past—are the great models for the bantering pairs about which Cavell writes. He sees that these Hollywood comedies "may be understood as parables of a phase of the development of consciousness in which the struggle is for the reciprocity or equality of consciousness between a woman and a man" and that they embrace the early feminist agenda for the "creation of a new woman."[22] Cavell understands that such ideas are particularly American and they express "the inner agenda of a nation that conceives Utopian longings and commitments for itself."[23] It is precisely Cavell's "equality of consciousness between a woman and a man" that is at the heart of the Branagh–Thompson conception of Beatrice and Benedick. Thompson articulates their mutual understanding of the two characters:

> [They have] an archetypically perfect blueprint for a relationship. Total equals. We made, I suppose, as feminist a reading of it as possible, without changing the meaning of it altogether. It's a remarkable part, for me anyway, because she's so angry, she's so fucking angry! They [the men] went off to learn to ride and joust and things and she wasn't allowed to go because she was a girl, and I think the anger and confusion and bewilderment started then, and I think it's still very much with us.[24]

It's wonderful how Beatrice's indignation gets channeled through something of Thompson's experience and spirit here. One senses her own passion and competitive drive and her longing for that "equality of consciousness between a woman and a man" that motivates Beatrice's cool explosion: "Kill Claudio." The film balances the sentimentality of its treatment of Claudio (compounded by Branagh's teenage audience's awareness that Robert Sean Leonard had literally died for Shakespeare in his previous film, *Dead Poet's Society*) by giving full vent to Beatrice's anger and, through Benedick's pledge to challenge Claudio, its consequences. Branagh is skillfully negotiating screwball territory reminiscent of Howard Hawks's films, in particular, *His Girl Friday* (1939), where Hildy Johnson (Rosalind Russell) not only competes with the boys in an all-male environment (the City Hall press room), but also scoops the story and reclaims her brazen boss and former husband (Cavell's remarriage pattern at work again), Walter Burns (Cary Grant).

As *Henry V* revealed, Branagh had an instinctive gift for film rhetoric long before he began to understand film grammar. Visualizing big moments and having the courage to pursue them in ways that ran counter to conventional film wisdom was a hallmark of his work as a director from the beginning, as was his lack of timidity in employing a powerful film score to underline those big rhetorical moments. The use of a film score is a tricky business when dealing with a Shakespearean script because there is already so much music built into his verse and prose, and Branagh is well aware of the debate, acknowledging that the role of film score in a Shakespeare film is "an enormously debatable issue. On the whole, we have continued to follow our instincts about where the music is helpful, but I know the issue remains contentious."[25] However, it took Branagh longer to develop the skill to effectively make the little scenes work with the right mixture of the establishing shot, two-shot, and close-up, all delivered at the right rhythm to accomplish the results he sought.

As we have seen in the long opening shot in *Peter's Friends*, the steadicam gave Branagh the liberty to put his camera in motion to a far greater extent than he could using the traditional dolly mounted on tracks, as he had done for the long tracking shot at the end of the Battle of Agincourt. A steadicam is a large device, mounted on the shoulders and strapped to the back of a cameraman, that supports a Panaflex 35 camera and allows the cameraman to follow shots on foot without having the image jiggle and jolt as it does with the handheld camera so favored by the French New Wave directors in the 1960s. Branagh uses the steadicam for several scenes in *Much Ado*, particularly for the first reprise of Balthazar's song as the men gather around the garden's fountain. The camera slowly circumnavigates the fountain as the men lay the snare to entrap Benedick, a reprise of Branagh's fondness for circle shots established in *Dead Again*. But Branagh saves his boldest use of the device for the extremely complicated final shot of the film.

After the two pairs of lovers have reconciled, Branagh wants to provide a spontaneous, festive conclusion to the love matches that crown the story. He has textual warrant in that Benedick, iconoclast to the end, insists on reversing the normal order of such events. Rather than scheduling the wedding ceremony first and celebration after, Benedick invites the pipers to "strike up" and leads Beatrice into a dance, picking up on her metaphor and spirit, expressed earlier in the play, about the relationship between dancing and marriage: "wooing, wedding, and repenting, is as a Scottish jig, a measure, and a cinque pace."

In fact, dancing—as Branagh will realize again and even more fully in his film of *Love's Labour's Lost*—is a metaphor for understanding the spirit and structure of a Shakespearean comedy. Dances are group experiences where several couples are set in motion, are allowed to spin dangerously out of control, and then are restored (reconciled and reinvigorated) to a more formal rhythm and pattern. Comedies celebrate the communal rather than the individual, which may explain why we tend to take them less seriously than tragedies. Sadly, their reconciliations don't seem as profound as the disintegration of the individual and the destruction of community at the heart of the tragic experience. Branagh wants to create an image of that restored community at the end of his film, and he wants a shot that both captures and mirrors that festive celebration.

In perhaps the most extravagant shot of his film career, Branagh has his steadicam operator follow the entire cast as the members dance out from the wedding chapel, through an arch leading into the villa's courtyard, and then out through the front arch into the formal garden. There the celebrants join hands and continue the dance as the steadicam operator sits on a crane and is lifted high in the air to catch the buoyant spirits spinning below in an overhead shot that finally pulls away to pan the surrounding countryside, as confetti pirouettes in the air and the final reprise, now choral, of "Sigh no more" swells on the soundtrack. All this in a single hyperbolic shot! This is Branagh at his dizzy, over-the-top best. Ian Shuttleworth describes the moment and the complexities of Branagh's cinematic invention:

> Choreographing the scene was another matter—a question of sending couples and lines of dancers off in the right direction at the right instant in perfect synchronisation with the travels of the camera (not to mention hoping that the cameraman actually found the crane platform as he backed towards it). Moreover, only a limited amount of time was available before the sun moved directly into the line of the final crane sequence, with the risk of "whiting-out" the filmed images.[26]

The three-minute shot took fifteen takes in 100 degree heat to accomplish. One early, otherwise perfect take was ruined only at the end when the camera panned the Tuscan hill side only to discover a dairy truck bouncing along in the distance on an otherwise deserted country road.[27] The shot is a signature of Branagh's aesthetic intentions and cinematic style: "I felt that the last part [of the film] should wrap up the 'fairy tale' and have a flourish; I also suspected that there might be an element as people watched it of 'Christ, he hasn't cut yet!', and that might be fun. . . . Those all-in-one things create a kind of theatricality on the set, which is very bonding."[28]

A number of key Branagh ideas are at work here: using film technology to achieve what he calls "theatricality" as well as a sense of communal bonding between cast and crew (who must all have been frustrated at the number of takes required); a self-consciousness not just about his art but also about its reception—he wants the shot to call attention to itself ("Christ, he hasn't cut yet") and to create an added pleasure for a savvy movie audience; and finally, his desire for certain moments in his films (true of darker films like *Henry V* and *Dead Again* as well as his comedies) to have a "flourish." This shot, others like it (particularly the giddy opening sequence), the naturalistic, unaffected, conversational style he pioneers for speaking Shakespeare's rich and muscular language, and his unembarrassed embrace of popular Hollywood film images and idioms all help to achieve his goal of liberating Shakespeare from being contained in "some cultural church." The sheer exuberance and energy of his *Much Ado* is unmatched in the long history of the Shakespeare film genre and was the first Shakespearean comedy on film to reach a wide audience and compete successfully with commercial Hollywood fare at the box office. In fact, *Much Ado About Nothing* outgrossed Jack McTiernan's *Last Action Hero*, starring Arnold Schwarzenegger, when the two films went head to head on the first weekend of their release in May of 1993.

In many ways, *Much Ado*, rather than Branagh's later film of *Hamlet*, is the apotheosis of Branagh's career with the Renaissance Company he founded in 1987. Here he comes closest to reaching his ideal of creating a company that becomes a community in the process of making its art. More than the group of Emma Thompson's Cambridge friends gathered together to make *Peter's Friends*, the *Much Ado* cast and crew, in its wide variety of backgrounds and experiences, was much more representative of the Branagh ethos and aesthetic. This was the last time he would have the fullest range of his Renaissance team gathered together and enhanced by the American addition of Washington, Reeves, Keaton, and Leonard. His production crew included old Renaissance hands such as producers David Parfitt and Stephen Evans, designers Tim Harvey and Phyliss Daulton, composer Patrick Doyle, and textual and performance consultants Russell Jackson and Hugh Cruttwell. The cast featured such Renaissance regulars as Richard Briers, Brian Blessed, Jimmy Yuill, Gerard Horan, Alex Lowe, and, of course, Emma Thompson.

The magic they made under the Tuscan sun in the summer of 1992 couldn't be sustained. The film they made together, though surpassed artistically in my judgment by Branagh's *Hamlet*, is the finest achievement of the Renaissance ideal. *Much Ado About Nothing* remains the production where Branagh made his most accomplished synthesis of Stratford and Hollywood to create a film that made Shakespeare available to a wide-screen audience without making him unrecognizable to profes-sional Shakespeareans.

The most interesting of the film's critics, Courtney Lehmann, builds her reservations about the film on the very ground where I have tried to stake a claim for its success: the creation of an ideal community where popular and elite forms of art genuinely mix and mingle to produce an original synthesis. Lehmann's argument is complex and conditioned, I think, by a particularly American political consciousness. It centers on Branagh's casting of a prominent African-American actor, Denzel Wash-ington, in the role of Don Pedro. She reads his exile from the final celebration—the camera catches him for an instant framed in the arch leading to the chapel as the revelers swirl on without him through the courtyard—as Branagh's failure to create the inclusive community the spirit of his film promises.[29] I would argue that Don Pedro, like Don John, is appropriately excluded and he has no place or role in the new dispensa-tion. The patriarchy has momentarily crumbled in favor of Beatrice and Benedick's festive imaginations, and Don Pedro has no partner with whom to join the world of "earthly things made even." Branagh doesn't overplay or underline the moment and many viewers miss it entirely. Sources close to the film have told me that it was Washington himself who suggested that Don Pedro not join the final dance. The film veteran realized the shot was likely to be arduous and require many takes, and so he enjoyed watching his colleagues at work while sitting comfortably in the shade of the garden.

Hollywood always has had difficulty in knowing how to honor one of its most enduring genres: romantic comedy. At the time of *Much Ado's* release, only four such films had been awarded the Oscar for Best Picture in sixty years. After the three nominations lavished on *Henry V*, it was sur-prising that the much more commercially successful *Much Ado* was ignored. Thompson, of course, had just won the best actress prize for *Howard's End* and would be nominated again the following year for *Remains of the Day.* Branagh may have swerved too close to popular appeal for Hollywood (as Zeffirelli did years before in *Romeo and Juliet*), which still regarded Shakespeare as the product of the British cultural elite (Olivier) or maverick American avant-garde (Welles). In any case, the film was ignored every place except where it counted: the box office. Branagh's success opened the Hollywood financial coffers for the series of Shakespeare films that came pouring into release in the 1990s, most significantly Baz Luhrmann's *William Shakespeare's Romeo + Juliet.* Luhrmann's film was even more audaciously Hollywood than Branagh's, putting two young American film stars, Leonardo DiCaprio and Claire

Danes, at its center and surrounding them with a dizzying array of technical dazzle.

Most importantly, Branagh's film opened the way for Marc Norman's long-hawked project, *Shakespeare in Love*, to come to fruition. Enhanced by Tom Stoppard's transformation of Norman's original script into something wonderfully witty about the archetypical battle between creators and producers in the worlds of theater and film and by John Madden's sure-handed directorial approach, the film became just the fifth romantic comedy to win the Academy Award for Best Picture. So Branagh not only brought Hollywood to Shakespeare; he also brought Shakespeare back to Hollywood and, at least for the decade of the 1990s, made him a commercially viable property for the first time.

Chapter 6

MARY SHELLEY'S FRANKENSTEIN

I first interviewed Branagh in April of 1993 at the Shakespeare Memorial Theatre in Stratford as his stage performance of Hamlet for The Royal Shakespeare Company was coming to an end. It was a beautiful spring afternoon. His window was open, and the sounds of ducks and swans taking off and landing and kids splashing the oars of their rowboats drifted up from the Avon flowing gently below. His dressing room was spartan. The first-night messages were long removed from the big make-up mirror where they are usually tucked in around the edges. The small bulletin board on the wall held but a single item. On it a jagged lightning bolt cut through a night sky with the legendary words "IT'S ALIVE" printed beneath. *Frankenstein* was on the way and with it enormous changes in Branagh's life. He was thirty-two, the director of four interesting films, married to an Academy Award–winning actress, and the most promising classical actor of his generation. He was being heralded not only as the new Olivier but as the new Welles as well in a flattering cover story in *New York* magazine.[1] Branagh had it all, but that lightning bolt was about to strike, and its consequences would unsettle his life and career.

Branagh's first four films all had modest budgets ranging from three to twenty million dollars. Only one of them, *Dead Again*, was made and released by a major studio, Paramount; the others were all made as independent films participating in the early success of that new category spurred by the release, in 1989, of Steven Soderbergh's *sex, lies and videotape* and Branagh's own *Henry V.* Though Branagh spurned the many big-budget scripts sent to him by Hollywood studio executives in the wake of *Henry V*'s multiple Oscar nominations, instead selecting Paramount's quirky *Dead Again*, this latter film's success made Francis Ford Coppola's offer to direct a new film of *Frankenstein* eventually irresistible.

In accepting this project, Branagh was venturing into unchartered waters. He was moving away from the triple anchors of his artistic base: Shakespeare, his colleagues in his Renaissance Company, and, perhaps most importantly, his most intimate collaborator, Emma Thompson. *Mary Shelley's Frankenstein* remains Branagh's only experience in prime Hollywood territory: the big-budget, studio-financed horror film played out in epic style against the landscape of a dynamic historical epoch. This was a huge leap, in style and scale, from anything he had previously attempted.

Through his career Branagh had already revealed that he was a risk-taker, from his audacious confidence in taking on Henry V at age twenty-three for the most distinguished Shakespeare theater in the world, to creating his own Renaissance Company of players, to boldly leading that company into the world of film with the stunning success of *Henry V*, to selecting the noir thriller *Dead Again* as his first Hollywood project. But the move out from that tiny, spartan dressing room and the comfort of playing Hamlet (for the third time in his young career) in familiar surroundings into the dangerous world of *Frankenstein* would prove to be the risk he could neither ignore nor transcend. Branagh had established himself as a filmmaker with a style that brought Hollywood convention and energies to the moribund genre of Shakespeare on film. Now the trick would become an attempt to bring a Shakespearean dynamic to translating Mary Shelley's classic romantic tale of Promethean urges, and their consequences, into a film radically at odds with the movie versions of the novel created by James Whale in his *Frankenstein* (1931) and *Bride of Frankenstein* (1933), which set the pattern for the long line of *Frankenstein* films that followed over the next six decades.[2] These earlier versions plucked Shelley's tale out of its historical milieu—the moment the Enlightenment gave way to Romanticism—and relocated it to something like the present. Whale, and his successors, jettisoned Victor Frankenstein as an example of the Romantic hero, replacing him with the twentieth century's notion of the mad scientist in his white lab coat working his experiments with the aid of a series of Rube Goldbergesque technological gadgets. Whale further understood, perhaps as Bill Condon's recent *Gods and Monsters* suggests, that not only was the Monster the most cinematically vivid character in Shelley's novel, but it was the most potentially sympathetic (the "other" as outcast) rather than horrific, as well.

Branagh and his screenwriters, Steph Lady and Frank Darabont, wanted to return to Mary Shelley's conception in form and content. They wanted to preserve her frame for the story that allows, through the device of the Arctic explorer Robert Walton, for a multiplicity of narrative devices in relating the stories of both Victor Frankenstein and his creation. Such an artifice helps to both release and contain the novel's radical romantic energies.

Branagh's relationship with the film is paradoxical on several levels. The film received the first bad reviews, both humorously dismissive and viciously cutting, of Branagh's career, but it is now regarded by many cultural critics of *Frankenstein* films as the most interesting adaptation of Mary Shelley's novel.[3] The common assumption is that the film, following its negative critical reception, was a box office bomb, but it more than recouped its production costs in worldwide sales and rentals, making it the largest grossing picture (over 100 million dollars) in Branagh's directorial career. The film's title, however honestly intended, turned out to be as cleverly misleading as Baz Luhrmann's *William Shakespeare's Romeo + Juliet*. In pace, pulse, and performance, the film is pure Branagh. Branagh's neo-romantic impulses as a film director are fully indulged and often matched by his frenzied performance of Victor Frankenstein. The film never stops coming right at the audience with an excessive intensity. The film was competing in the minds of film critics, as well as the general public, not with Mary Shelley's novel, but with James Whale's two *Frankenstein* films and Mel Brooks's brilliant parody, *Young Mr. Frankenstein*. Neither audience was prepared for Branagh's full-scale cinematic embrace of the novel's romantic energies.

As we have seen, Branagh likes to open his films in a stunning fashion: Jacobi striking that match in *Henry V*, the prison sequence in *Dead Again*, the long, complicated steadicam tracking shot in *Peter's Friends*, and the words of Balthazar's song popping up on the screen in *Much Ado About Nothing*. For *Mary Shelley's Frankenstein* Branagh returned to old devices even as he tried his hand at some new ones. As the credits begin to emerge as a thin white line traveling toward us from the center of a black screen, we hear a woman's voice reciting a line from Mary Shelley's introduction to the 1831 edition of her novel: "I busied myself to think of a story which would speak to the mysterious fears of our nature and awaken thrilling horror . . . one to make the reader afraid to look around, to curdle the blood and quicken the beating heart."[4] Branagh then follows Shelley's voice with a legend that unscrolls on the screen and begins, "The dawn of the nineteenth century. World on the brink of revolutionary change," and ends with the evocation of the explorer Robert Walton, who,

Victor Frankenstein (Kenneth Branagh) in the midst of his preparations to bring the Creature to life in Branagh's film of *Mary Shelley's Frankenstein*. [Photographer: David Appleby, Courtesy of Photofest]

in his obsessive quest to reach the North Pole, "would uncover a story to strike terror in the hearts of all who venture into the unknown."[5] Patrick Doyle's score provides a percussive throb on "terror" and the "unknown" and then the camera slams us into a ship caught in the chaos of a fierce ice-storm. The ship's crew is being hurled from port to starboard (and subsequently overboard) as the first mate screams above the gale, pleading with the Captain to strike the sails. Branagh is picking up on the novel's own layers of narrative even as he transforms them into long-established film conventions: the opening voice-over narration and the legend-scroll. Both devices are meant as a path to the past that Branagh then violently interrupts with the quick cuts and fragmented action of the sea storm, ending with the ship's collision with an iceberg.

The film then cuts to the next morning when the crew, trying to salvage useful elements from the wreckage, hears a mighty "Howl" and Walton asks, "What's out there?" The storm, the howl, and the mystery of something monstrous in the human psyche all echo *King Lear*, and Walton's question is but a slight variation of the opening line of *Hamlet*: ("Who's there?") The howl and the question are the two monumental explorations of man's tragic fate by Shakespeare that Branagh clearly wants to evoke as precursors to Shelley's preoccupations in *Frankenstein*. The howl—repeated by several characters at key moments in the film—is the Creature's perpetual expression of his tragic outrage at being abandoned by his creator, and the answer to "What's out there?" is the ravaged, exhausted figure of Victor Frankenstein.[6] Branagh gives himself a film entrance meant to rival and revise his very first appearance on the screen in *Henry V.* Out of the mist and fog a hooded figure pulling a ghostly sledge, with a great coat suspended like a sail and dog carcasses dangling from its superstructure, struggles toward the camera. When the figure reaches the camera, it lifts its head, revealing Branagh's frostbitten face and ice-encrusted beard, and we glimpse the exhausted ego relentlessly pursuing the howling id. "Who are you?" the exasperated Walton demands. "I am Victor [long pause] Frankenstein."[7]

Branagh clearly wants this opening to evoke the mystery and dynamism of his opening sequences in *Henry V* and *Dead Again*, where his character in each was presented similarly as a shadowy, edgy figure meant to spark our interest and curiosity. This sequence, the film's invention, is quite differently conceived and narrated in the novel. "What's out there?" literally refers to the howl of the Creature. That question then gets visually transformed in the film into the representation of Victor Frankenstein emerging from the mist, thus linking Creature and creator. As this opening indicates, Branagh's film repositions Victor Frankenstein, rather than the Creature, as the focus of the narrative. Branagh reaches back beyond Hollywood's transformation of Mary Shelley's powerful myth to the novel itself to reclaim Frankenstein as the romantic hero of his own tragic tale.

Branagh's typically bold choice undoubtedly contributed to the film's jagged reception. The film never stops assaulting the viewer, and Branagh's Frankenstein is a wildly romantic figure. Branagh endows the character with a passionate Shakespearean intensity that the dialogue of the novel and screenplay just cannot match. Branagh, as always, wants it all: fairy tale, historical romance, love story with just a hint of incest, rebellion against the power and finality of death, and the quest to push the limits of science and knowledge all mixed together with a tragic Promethean creation myth.

These stories and styles keep rubbing up against each other as the film unfolds and implodes. After our beginning trapped in the ice of the frozen north, the film flashes back to Geneva in 1773 and the beginning of Victor's tale. Here the film creates a fairy-tale reality at clashing odds with the adventure-story opening. We are in the living room of the Frankenstein estate; the characters are all dressed in period costumes, but the set is a stylized playing space rather than an attempt at historical reproduction. The big vaulted room is empty except for a harpsichord placed in its center and a huge staircase without a balustrade curving up the back wall. Young Victor, age seven, and his mother (Cheri Lunghie) are dancing and Branagh's camera swirls around them, establishing one of the film's repeated visual metaphors and camera movements. The film wants to sweep us up in its romantic urges and dancing is its method. The film includes three other dances: the formal waltz held to celebrate Victor's heading off to Ingolstadt and medical school fifteen years later; the remarkable dance Victor performs with the newly born Creature (Robert DeNiro) as they struggle to find their balance in the sea of amniotic fluid and other chemicals (actually gobs of K-Y jelly) that have spilled out in Victor's lab when the Creature emerges from his birthing contraption; and the reiteration of this image as Victor swings about the recreated body of Elizabeth (Helena Bonham Carter), Frankenstein's Bride, in a mad Dance of Death as the Frankenstein mansion goes up in flames near the film's end. As the screenplay comments, "here we are treated to the most sweepingly romantic and hair-raisingly demented image of the film: Victor dances with his dead bride, showing her the way, begging her to remember . . . and now the "Waltz/Love Theme" really comes back to haunt us as the music swells, incredibly lush and deranged, dissonant and echoing through Victor's head. . . . and the waltz goes on, madder and madder, sweeping in glorious circles."[8]

These four dances, leading from innocence to experience and birth to death, are emblematic of Branagh's bold and robust film style, but they also reveal the film's ultimate weakness—its failure to fully integrate the myriad elements of Shelley's tale and its subsequent film tradition (here most notably the incorporation of the *Bride of Frankenstein* material) into a coherent cinematic narrative. The film, despite its many virtues, is in constant danger of spinning out of control. The viewer is never fully drawn into the power of Shelley's conception because Branagh, bravely, keeps challenging our expectations and then embarrassing our response by piling one excess on top of another. His cinematic imagination, held in check in his Shakespeare films because of his devotion to communicating the language with an assured precision, is here given free reign to indulge in the visual and symphonic elements of film grammar and rhetoric with few restraints.

Another example of an area in the film in which Branagh's reach exceeds his grasp is in its treatment of women. Here the loss of collaboration with Emma Thompson is perhaps crucial. Branagh and Thompson made a winning pair because they linked fire and ice. Branagh was all passionate commitment, Thompson wry detachment. Branagh's impulses tend toward tragic or comic excess, Thompson's ironic deflation. Her performances in *Henry V, Dead Again, Peter's Friends*, and especially *Much Ado About Nothing* all provided elements of a restrained wit that made a smart contrast with Branagh's more bravura work—as actor and director. I do not know if their marriage was under strain before Branagh began to shoot *Mary Shelley's Frankenstein*, but it was certainly in trouble by the time the film was released.

When I spoke with Branagh in May of 1993, he revealed that the *Frankenstein* screenplay was still undergoing rewrites, primarily to strengthen the role of Elizabeth. He elaborates on his notion in an essay published in the film's screenplay: "It was important to me to have a very strong woman's role in a film of this size, and not just a token love interest. All too often women are just peripheral elements of the picture, and I wanted Elizabeth and Victor to be two equal partners, utterly entwined from the beginning."[9] Elizabeth is not the only female figure the film seeks to recuperate or enlarge. Justine (Trevyn McDowell), largely ignored by other *Frankenstein* films, is restored and made an envious rival of Elizabeth for Victor's affections. After she is falsely accused of murdering William and hung by the mob, Victor raids her corpse for body parts with which to recreate Elizabeth, after she has been killed by DeNiro's Creature. The film, following subliminal hints in the novel, toys with the incest theme. At Elizabeth's entrance in the film, the camera catches a look of envy on the young Justine's face: a dangerous rival has entered and disrupted her fantasy paradise as Victor's playfellow. If Elizabeth's adoption by the Frankensteins troubles Justine's world, a female is also central to Victor's loss of innocence. As the dancing sequence that introduces us to Victor indicates, he is deeply attached to his mother. The film cuts from that moment to a decade later when Victor's mother, now pregnant with William, has come to his attic room to entice him away from his infatuation with building mechanical devices and experimenting with seeing how they might be animated by the flames from a candle. This is the film's first visual expression linking Victor to the "playing with fire" theme that will resonate throughout in counterpoint to the Creature's repeated association with Alpine and Arctic ice. Caroline Frankenstein lures Victor down from his study to once again join the dancing below, now in partnership with his father and Elizabeth.

In one of the film's most radical departures from the novel, Branagh has Caroline die not from smallpox, but from the complications of a breech delivery. The family waltz idyll is broken by the beginnings of

Caroline's labor. The gruesome scene that follows is Victor's initiation into blood and death and his father's (here made into a medical doctor in another departure from the novel) inability to save his wife. Ian Holm appears on that dangerous, open staircase with his hands, arms, and upper torso covered with Caroline's blood to confess, "I've killed my wife."[10] Death, the failure of medicine and science to protect life, and the loss of the mother (and the projected loss of a wife) all contribute to Victor's determination to discover the secrets of life as a means of triumphing over death. All of this will play out in Frankenstein's eventual creation of the Creature, who becomes the ultimate symbol of the "other." In Sandra Gilbert and Susan Gubar's pioneering feminist study of the nineteenth-century novel, *The Madwoman in the Attic*, the monster becomes a version of Eve, herself an archetype of filthy femaleness: "In this fierce, Miltonic world, *Frankenstein* says, the angel woman and the monster woman must die, if they are not dead already."[11]

Branagh's film, following a more conventional narrative line in its treatment of Caroline, Elizabeth, and Justine, catches at none of this. The focus is thrown back upon Victor Frankenstein, as it is throughout the film. In Branagh's treatment Victor Frankenstein becomes the bad mother rejecting his creation. Frankenstein suffers from immediate post-partum depression. His intellectual and emotional energies have all been spent on the act of creation. Once he gets DeNiro's Creature on his feet and moving in a parody rhythm of the film's waltz motif, he loses interest. The Creature's only flaw is its ugly helplessness. When it accidentally becomes entangled in the heavy chains of Frankenstein's laboratory equipment and is suddenly conked on the head by a pulley and sent spinning up in the air to hang suspended from the rigging, Frankenstein washes his hands of the experiment. In a reversal of the famous cry "It's alive . . . it's alive" uttered at the Creature's birth, Branagh's Frankenstein utters, "It's dead, it's dead, I've killed it." He immediately moves to tidy up his work by recording in his journal, "Massive birth defects. Greatly enhanced physical strength but the resulting re-animate is malfunctional and pitiful, and dead."[12] He places the journal in the pocket of his greatcoat and collapses.

The arc that takes the film, in its first hour, to this moment is nevertheless its strongest. When the film shifts from the Frankenstein estate in Geneva to medical School in Ingolstadt, Branagh changes styles. Geneva was all fairy-tale family romance suddenly destroyed by the death of the mother. Ingolstadt is all gritty realism. Branagh shoots the exteriors through a blue filter and the interiors through an amber one. The city is full of high cold stone walls cut through by narrow streets packed with people who are as grey as the landscape—none more so than Professor Waldman, to whom Victor immediately attaches himself. John Cleese delivers a terrific turn as Waldman, another instance where director Branagh stretches an actor by casting against type. Cleese's Waldman is cadaverous: sunken cheeks, false teeth providing him with an overbite, stringy grey hair, and a stubble beard. Waldman is the subversive professor engaged in unauthorized experiments with reanimation. He's a visual image of the simple lesson of Mary Shelley's novel: don't go there. He looks like walking death, appropriate for the film's version of Ingolstadt, which is in the grip of a cholera epidemic. Waldman is on the front lines of doctors vaccinating against smallpox and for his troubles is murdered by a low-life type who refuses to participate in the program. The murderer is subsequently hung, and his body and Waldman's brain become the key ingredients in Frankenstein's reanimation project.

The film's creation scene is its finest. Branagh and his designer, Tim Harvey, concoct a giant high-vaulted attic laboratory for Frankenstein: part gymnasium and part factory. Making a monster is conceived as strenuous work rather than delicate science. Branagh's Frankenstein is conceived as the romantic rebel rather than the mad scientist. In fact, rather than putting on the white lab coat associated with the deranged doctors and scientists of *Frankenstein* film history, Branagh's Frankenstein first dons a flowing robe and then strips to the waist in preparation for his frenzied performance. The sequence has three beats corresponding to conception, birth, and rejection, each lasting about two minutes. The first beat has fifty-one cuts with no single image lasting for more than three seconds. Frankenstein races about his lab, to the pulsating rhythm of Patrick Doyle's score, reminiscent of Doyle's music for the Battle of Agincourt. Stanley Kauffmann comments about this scene (and others), "I've never seen a leading man run, simply run, so constantly as Branagh's Dr. Frankenstein does. Four out of five times we cut to him he's running somewhere, even if it's only around his large laboratory."[13] Branagh's Frankenstein has to set in motion a huge mechanical contraption that consists of pulleys, chains, spinning wheels, a suspended rack, a huge copper sarcophagus, and a billowing cloth scrotum out of which protrudes a long glass tube that, at the climax of his efforts, Frankenstein will insert into the sarcophagus. Scientific reanimation begins to look like something very similar to an industrialized version of human insemination.

The pace quickens as Victor slams acupuncture needles, through slits in the kettle's sides, into the lifeless body within, and then we see eels awash in amniotic fluid sweep down from the billowing scrotum and into the penile tube and on into the sarcophagus. Victor throws a series of electrical switches and, in the midst of this rapid cutting from one creation activity to another, the camera catches Frankenstein standing on top of the giant kettle, blue electrical charges dancing in the air, insisting, "Live, live, live."[14] Suddenly, the Creature opens its eyes and Victor scurries to shut off the electrical power. But when there is no further sign of life from within the kettle, Victor walks away in defeat as the scene's frantic first beat ends.

The knocking of the creature's hand against one of the kettle's portals evokes the tale's most famous line as Victor turns and whispers to himself, "It's alive, . . . it's alive," and races back to unlock the lid as the kettle's liquid contents explode over his body and the Creature spills out onto the floor.[15] The jagged, quick cuts that distinguished the conception sequence now give way to slower, more fluid cuts as Victor and his creation slosh about in the muck of the afterbirth and Doyle's score disappears from the soundtrack. In the film's tenderest image, Frankenstein and the Creature cling to one another as they struggle to stand. After several failures, they eventually manage to become upright and for an instant or two they engage in a haunting parody of the waltz motif Branagh established at the outset to capture the fairy-tale quality of the Frankenstein family. As that dance was crushed by Caroline's death in childbirth, so Victor's momentary harmony with his creation is dashed when the Creature gets accidentally entwined in the chains of the conception machinery. Victor slips to the floor, inadvertently releasing a pulley that hits the Creature on his head and jerks his body up into the rafters to hang suspended over the laboratory. The creation sequence now enters its final beat, almost devoid of cuts, as Victor is captured in a long shot lamenting his experiment ("What have I done?") and rejecting his creation in the earlier-quoted words posted in his journal.[16] The last shot we have of Victor before he collapses on his bed is of his ravaged face reflected in a mirror. It's the only literal mirror shot we get in the film, but it is meant, certainly, to underline that Frankenstein will now and forever be inextricably linked with his creation. Walking away from the scene and writing down his version of the experiment's conclusion are not acts of closure but only further examples of Frankenstein's folly.

The creation scene is the climax of the first half of the film dominated by Victor Frankenstein's story. The second half belongs to DeNiro's Creature, and once again the film changes landscapes and styles. When the Creature slips into the plague-ravaged streets of Ingolstadt, he finds himself in the City of Death. He is hounded by its citizens until he manages to escape on a cart hauling dead bodies to a mass grave. The film now introduces the Creature into yet another fairy-tale world, this time that of

Hansel and Gretel. Following the general outlines of the Creature's story as recounted in chapters eleven through sixteen of the novel, the film quickly establishes the Creature's relationship with the forest family he secretly adopts. Branagh follows Shelley rather than Whale in giving his creature language, which he learns through exposure to the family by listening and observing through the wall that divides the simple log cabin from its barn.

Though DeNiro's face is a surgical nightmare with suture marks across his skull, around his left eye, and down through his lips, the film strives to make him a sympathetic rather than frightening figure. This quality led critics like Janet Maslin in the *New York Times* and Anthony Lane in *The New Yorker* to complain that DeNiro's Creature "would make a dandy guest on any daytime television show" and that the film might better be called "Oprah Winfrey's *Frankenstein*."[17] Whale's film made Boris Karloff's monster a mute. This did not prevent him from being sentimentalized, as in the drowning scene with the little girl, but it saved him from the embarrassment of having to express his complicated feelings of rejection in language that would be difficult to save from parody. Shakespeare's Caliban gets it right when he taunts Prospero with "You taught me language, and my profit on't / Is, I know how to curse." (1.2.363–364) Branagh's Creature learns language and his "profit on't" is that he knows how to suffer. The wall that exists between the Creature's physical monstrosity and his psychological demands cannot be bridged.

The Creature's idyll in the winter woods comes to an end when he is invited into the cabin by the blind grandfather (Richard Briers) who treats him with sympathy and respect. When their interlude is broken by the arrival of the family's father (a Branagh addition), the father beats the Creature and immediately packs up the family. When the Creature realizes he has not only been rejected but also abandoned, he sets the cabin ablaze, establishing his inability to reconcile the extremes of his emotions symbolized in the film by fire and ice. The film, following the Creature, now heads for the ice but keeps getting pulled back to Geneva and Victor's unfinished narrative. The real story is the relationship between the creator and the created, but it keeps getting sidetracked by Branagh's hyperbolic insistence on having it all—*Frankenstein* and *The Bride of Frankenstein* all rolled into one.

The film finally gets to the Alps once it has depicted the Creature's murder of young William and his framing of Justine for the crime. In this frozen landscape and with the encounter between maker and monster, the film momentarily finds itself again. In the film's most bravura shot (and the source for Branagh's handling of the "How all occasions do inform against me" soliloquy in *Hamlet*), the camera closes in on Victor hacking his way up a wall of ice and then slowly pulls back, in what we come to realize is a helicopter shot, to gradually frame Frankenstein as just a tiny black dot in a vast frozen landscape. When Victor Frankenstein reaches the summit, DeNiro's Creature comes flying into the frame with his black greatcoat billowing out from his sides, creating the image of a giant bat sweeping down on its prey. The Creature latches on to Frankenstein and their linked bodies hurtle down an icy tunnel into a frozen cave. Here the film finds its quietest moments as its relentless pace slows to a pattern of stately cuts between medium close-ups of the two men as the Creature reveals his torments and demands that Frankenstein make him a mate. Frankenstein is moved by the Creature's plea and acquiesces in his request.

In the novel, Frankenstein, the romantic wanderer, heads off on a version of the Grand Tour, eventually working his way to Scotland's Orkney Islands where he reassembles his lab and begins work on fulfilling his promise to the Monster. In the novel Frankenstein only abandons his labors when he discovers the "demon at the casement" peering in on his work. That image so revolts Frankenstein that he destroys the mate he has been creating as the Monster howls with "devilish despair and revenge."[18] Shelley, perhaps subconsciously, understands the maternal/paternal relationship between Frankenstein and the demon. Branagh's Frankenstein even more cruelly repeats his rejection of his Creation. His Frankenstein can't tolerate the horror of another birth. Branagh's film domesticates this decision. His Frankenstein changes his mind about creating a mate because of the demands of his own: Elizabeth. Branagh pulls the tale of maker and monster back into the family romance. Frankenstein's decision seals the family's fate. William and Justine have already been destroyed. The Creature now snuffs out Victor's father and heads, as promised in novel as well as film, to share Victor's bride on Victor and Elizabeth's wedding night. In its final working out of the Victor-Elizabeth-Creature triangle, Branagh's film cuts from one visual excess to another and spins out of control. What Branagh clearly envisions as a heart-beating climax of gothic horror comes dangerously close to parody. It's as though Branagh is releasing his own personal and artistic demons as the film pounds from one moment of cinematic hyperbole to another.

First, Branagh insists, even as Henry Clerval (Tom Hulce) and others are searching for the Creature, on giving the full lush romantic treatment to Victor and Elizabeth's wedding night. Their bedroom is ablaze with candles, and Branagh, again buff and bare, and Helena Bonham Carter engage in a series of passionate embraces. Flesh is pressed against flesh,

The Creature (Robert DeNiro) and his creator Victor Frankenstein (Kenneth Branagh) confront each other in the climactic scene in *Mary Shelley's Frankenstein*.
[Photographer: Peter Appleby, Courtesy of Photofest]

the camera swirls around them, and Doyle's score pulsates on the soundtrack. The screenplay calls it "the sexiest seduction imaginable."[19] In the midst of all this high passion, Victor hears the mournful tones of the recorder and he knows the Creature is near.[20] He immediately abandons his bride to join Henry in the search, leaving Elizabeth, of course, to the Creature's mercies. By the time Victor wises up and returns, the Creature is ravishing Elizabeth, and when Victor arrives, the Creature smashes his hand through Elizabeth's chest and rips out her heart.

As if this image was not excessive enough, the film now segues into *The Bride of Frankenstein* as Victor rushes the dead Elizabeth back to his laboratory, determined, with the help of some of Justine's body parts, to make himself a new mate. Like the reprise of the hit number in a musical comedy, Branagh treats us to a replay of the creation scene including his mad dance with the reanimated Elizabeth. The Creature arrives to demand his bride, and for a moment Elizabeth is caught in a manic tug-of-war between the two adversaries. In one fleeting stroke of wit amidst all this gothic indulgence, Bonham Carter's shorn and sutured Elizabeth actually steps toward the Creature subliminally recognizing that they are now kindred spirits. But the film can't tolerate such an ironic gesture and ambiguous closure to the tale. Bonham Carter picks up a kerosene lamp (a domesticated version of Victor's Promethean fire) crushes it in her hands, and explodes in a ball of fire as she races like a fury through the halls of the Frankenstein mansion, sending it to its fiery end.

Branagh tries to regain some measure of control in the film's final frames by returning to the novel's framing device and Walton's ice-bound ship. He devises one last image of fire and ice that might have been a haunting ending of a less lush and fervid version of the tale. After Frankenstein's death, he is placed upon a funeral pyre and doused with kerosene, but before Walton's men can light the fire, the ice begins to break-up and Victor's body begins to drift away out to sea. DeNiro's Creature suddenly appears, grabs a torch, and swims after the floating pyre, hauling himself up on its ice floe with the torch held aloft, himself now the image of the new Prometheus. He lights the pyre and cradles Victor in his arms as they ignite in a huge explosion: creator and created bound together at last.

In retrospect, we can now see that much of Branagh's early promise and power as a film director went up in flames on that bier as well. *Mary Shelley's Frankenstein* was the first critical failure of his career. His two Shakespeare films had been met with rapturous reviews, particularly in America. *Dead Again* was regarded as a charming and offbeat choice for a young Brit, known primarily as a classical actor, to make as his first American film, and its modest financial success only enhanced his reputation with Hollywood producers. *Peter's Friends* was considered a harmless and inexpensive folly. The film world, with the exception of some British newspaper movie critics always looking for the latest golden boy or girl to stumble, were not, I think, eagerly waiting for *Mary Shelley's Frankenstein* to be a failure.

But a grand critical failure it was. Even American critics like Stanley Kauffmann (*The New Republic*), Richard Schickel (*Time*), and David Ansen (*Newsweek*), who had praised Branagh's earlier films, could find little to applaud about *Mary Shelley's Frankenstein*. Ansen gets at both Branagh's stylistic intentions and their shortcomings: "You can see what Branagh is after . . . he wants to restore the passionate emotional scale of the early 19th Century to a tale that most people remember as a 1930s horror flick. But with his other eye firmly on the marketplace, he also wants to wow the MTV generation. What we get is Romanticism for short attention spans; a lavishly decorated horror movie with excellent elocution."[21] Ansen, at least, is willing to see what Branagh is trying to revive in Mary Shelley's tale. Richard Schickel's comments were typical of those reviewers who used the James Whale films as a standard by which to judge Branagh's: "Whale had real style. He understood that if it was too late to take this tale completely seriously, it was too soon to camp it up or make it an exercise in empty disgust. Delicately poising irony, dark sentiment and terror, he drew you into his web. Branagh never weaves one. He's too busy serving his own expansive ego."[22]

Schickel's charge is one that has been leveled at other actor-filmmakers, from Orson Welles to Kevin Costner, who place themselves at the center of their films. Only those actor-filmmakers with carefully crafted film personas like Woody Allen or Clint Eastwood have managed to escape the damning "expansive ego" label. Branagh is a romantic director. His imagination is attracted to big, powerful screen moments. Perhaps, paradoxically, his temperament and style were wrong for Shelley's novel, drenched as it is in the spirit of Romanticism. John Keats famously contrasted Wordsworth with Shakespeare by arguing that the former's poetry was an example of the "egotistical sublime" while the latter's was distinguished by its "negative capability."[23] Perhaps Branagh's artistic sensibility is too close to Victor Frankenstein's egotistical sublime to provide his treatment of Shelley's novel with the necessary distance. There's too much passion and not enough irony in Branagh's film. The director and actor just keep coming right at us with such intensity that we are eventually overwhelmed. Part of the problem is that Branagh, like many British classical actors, is not a conventional movie leading man or romantic hero. The British actors before Branagh who managed to combine successful stage and film careers, from Alec Guinness to Anthony Hopkins, were all essentially character actors rather than conventional leading men. Those who broke the pattern, such as Richard Burton, Peter O'Toole, Albert Finney, and Daniel Day Lewis, generally abandoned their stage careers once having become film stars. Others, of course, like Michael Caine and Sean Connery, never aspired to careers as classical actors. It is intriguing to conjecture how the film would have been received had Branagh cast someone like Russell Crowe as Frankenstein rather than himself.

Branagh's great strengths as an actor are all tied up with his intelligence, charm, and distinctive voice. Only his most delirious and loyal fans could have been thrilled by the romantic ardor and physical abandon he brought to his conception of Victor Frankenstein. He clearly conceived of Frankenstein as an interesting synthesis of Byron, Shelley, and Hamlet, and the bouncing shoulder-length locks and repeated willingness to shed his shirt were the physical manifestations of that romantic spirit. Branagh put Victor Frankenstein at the center of his film and then failed to make him either riveting or sympathetic. The frantic pace of the film, matched by Victor's relentless quest to uncover the secret of what animates life, never allows us time or space to fully identify with Victor's ambition. We are always on the outside looking in, and as a result, the film fails to build a bond between hero and audience. Whale's *Frankenstein* films circumvent this problem by relocating Shelley's tale to the early twentieth century, thus completely jettisoning the historical and cultural context of the novel. Whale's Victor, curiously renamed Henry, is a version of David J. Skal's mad scientist and is never presented as a sympathetic figure. Our identification is entirely with Boris Karloff's mute Monster struggling to find the light in a dim and shadowy world.[24]

Another part of the problem results from what George Levine and V. C. Knoepflmacher identify as the novel's most interesting feature: "*Frankenstein* invites, even requires, alternative readings because its mythic core is so flexible, polymorphous, and dependent on antithetical possibilities."[25] Steph Lady and Frank Darabont's screenplay overreaches in a manner similar to Branagh's hothouse film style. The screenplay veers between alternative tensions and suggestions in Shelley's novel without ever settling on a consistent approach to her protean material. Perhaps, most fatally, in wanting to return to the Lake Geneva landscape that gave the novel its birth, they failed to make the film speak meaningfully to its own time and place. In his essay, "Frankenstein Reimagined," Branagh hints at a series of contemporary scientific parallels with Frankenstein's story:

> For me the lasting power of the story lay in its ability to dramatize a number of moral dilemmas. The most obvious is whether brilliant men of science should interfere in matters of life and death. Today newspapers are littered with such dilemmas. . . . for example, should parents choose the sex of their child. We can see all these developments taking place. It's now an imaginable step, to prevent people from dying. . . . [Victor] is a sane, cultured, civilized man, one whose ambition, as he sees it, is to be a benefactor of mankind. Predominantly we wanted to depict a man trying to do the right thing. We hope audiences today may find parallels with Victor today in some amazing scientist who might be an inch away from curing AIDS or cancer, and needs to make some difficult decisions.[26]

Branagh is fumbling rather than focused here and that quality is apparent throughout the screenplay. The film simply never makes a convincing visual connection between Victor's Promethean quest to single-handedly create life and the perils and potentials of modern science. Because Branagh himself is so wonderfully sane, he wants his Frankenstein to be so, too (notice his preference for referring to him by his first rather than his last name). "Frankenstein" is tainted by tradition, but "Victor" remains relatively fresh and undiscovered. But ultimately Branagh's treatment of Victor makes the scientist out to be every bit as mad, perhaps even more so, than his predecessors in the long history of *Frankenstein* films. Science, for Branagh's Frankenstein, becomes a way of redirecting emotional and psychological energies that he desperately needs to repress: his oedipal attachment to his mother and the incestuous subtext of his relationship with Elizabeth. Branagh, in rushing so purposively away from tradition, ends up running smack back into it. Branagh's Frankenstein creates his monster in the desperate need to be self-sustaining, to free himself from his dependency upon women and death. His tragedy is to discover that once having created, he cannot nurture. He becomes exactly what he has striven to overcome: the bad mother.

Branagh's film is never tame. Following the cinematic instincts we saw at work in *Henry V* and *Much Ado About Nothing*, he always goes for the bold defining visual moment. In his early Shakespeare films, that boldness brought a new energy and vitality to the moribund genre. When Branagh tried to achieve something similar in approaching the *Frankenstein* story, his talents and Shelley's novel proved to be incompatible. Branagh's cinematic romanticism, coupled with the screenplay's refusal to find a constant focus, doomed his efforts to breathe new life into Mary Shelley's tale. His huge energies piled on top of Frankenstein's ambition drove the film into visual and aural excesses that ultimately deadened rather than enlivened its material. The film ended up mirroring Frankenstein's relationship with his Creature and drifted out to sea in a blaze of fire moving away from the audience it sought to capture and illuminate.

Chapter 7

A Midwinter's Tale

Branagh's two most ambitious films, *Mary Shelley's Frankenstein* and *Hamlet*, are the bookends for what is, perhaps, the overlooked gem of his work as a film director: *A Midwinter's Tale*.[1] If *Frankenstein* and *Hamlet* draw upon the epic tradition in British films most exemplified by the work of David Lean, *A Midwinter's Tale* is Branagh's homage to the great Ealing Studio comedies of the 1950s that propelled Alec Guinness to film stardom.

Though Branagh wrote the screenplay and directed the film, *Midwinter* is Branagh's only film in which he does not appear. Michael Maloney plays the Branagh character (the film is clearly autobiographical in its origins and energies) and does so with an uncanny ability to suggest Branagh's mannerisms, much as Branagh, several years later in *Celebrity* (1998), would mimic and mock the even more famous mannerisms of that film's director, Woody Allen. The film is clearly Branagh's bridge between *Mary Shelley's Frankenstein* and *Hamlet*; in it he purges his Hollywood ambitions, the grand romantic film style that came to an apotheosis in *Frankenstein*, and the personal toll that film's critical failure took on his career and his marriage to Emma Thompson.

Midwinter includes all the ironic distance and wit missing from *Frankenstein* without sacrificing Branagh's essential attraction to romance and sentimentality. The filmmaker was in full control and command of his medium and material and it shows in every exchange and frame of the film. *Midwinter* is Branagh's only non-Shakespearean film for which he wrote the screenplay. It is also his most personal film in that the screenplay reflects a bittersweet blend of Branagh's own experience as an actor and director caught between film and theater, Hollywood and Stratford, with his sensitivity to the traditions and vulnerabilities of the actor's life. For a relatively young man (he was thirty-four when he made the film), Branagh was remarkably alert to actors' insecurities and the way in which these anxieties are nurtured and nourished by the theatrical experience. The screenplay is remarkably acute and witty and ultimately loving about actors' foibles while at the same time exploring Branagh's own suddenly precarious situation as the newly tarnished golden boy of British cinema.

For Branagh, Hollywood was to be the money machine that would provide him with the resources to underwrite, or leverage backing, for his work with Shakespeare on film or stage. In fact, he used much of his earnings from *Mary Shelley's Frankenstein* to fund the 1.6 million dollar budget for *Midwinter*. He actually refused studio backing so that he could have total independence on the project and shoot the film in black and white. George Lucas had dangled before Branagh the part of Luke Skywalker in the second *Star Wars* trilogy, but he eventually decided to cast Ewan McGregor instead. Playing Skywalker in three films destined to be guaranteed box-office bonanzas would have ensured Branagh's financial stability for the next decade. Instead, with *Frankenstein*'s reception cutting off his interest in directing big-budget Hollywood films and with the loss of a lucrative percentage of the new Lucas trilogy, Branagh's film career appeared to be blocked both as a director and as an actor.

Branagh's move then, similar to following *Dead Again* with *Peter's Friends*, was back to a more familiar British landscape and tradition. *Midwinter*, in fact, shares a number of qualities in content and style with *Peter's Friends*, though this time Branagh explores, in ensemble fashion, the theatrical world of his own past rather than the Cambridge milieu that spawned Emma Thompson and most of the cast of *Peter's Friends*. *Midwinter* is both more firmly controlled and more entertaining than *Peter's Friends* because Branagh is working confidently from the inside of the film's central concerns rather than trying to capture a world he knows only by adoption. Branagh's camera is remarkably fixed and stable. Gone are the dazzling dolly, steadicam, and crane shots that dominated his earlier films. Now he is quite content to place his camera in a fixed position and to let a scene unfold with a minimum of angle-changes or cuts. The two devices that come to characterize the camera work in *Midwinter* are Wellesian in origin (via his cinematographer Gregg Toland): the wide angle lens and the deep focus shot. The film score is similarly restrained. *Midwinter* uses a single Noel Coward song, "Why Must the Show Go On," to frame the action (and to reappear at crucial moments in the narrative) and

Joe Harper (Michael Maloney) stares out at the motley crew of actors he has assembled for a benefit performance of *Hamlet* in Kenneth Branagh's film *A Midwinter's Tale*.
[Photographer: David Appleby, Courtesy of Photofest]

otherwise banishes any music under the dialogue except for some very quiet and delicate guitar chords from Gustav Holst's setting of Christina Rossetti's "In the Bleak Midwinter," courtesy of Jimmy Yuill, which creep in under a few tender moments late in the film.

If *Peter's Friends* and *Mary Shelley's Frankenstein* were Branagh's furthest shift away from working with a core group of his Renaissance Company actors, *Midwinter* brought him back home. Richard Briers, Michael Maloney, Gerard Horan, John Sessions, Patrick Doyle, and Nick Farrell were Renaissance regulars. To this group of men Branagh added several women known for their work on British television: Celia Imrie, Julia Sawalha, Hetta Charnley, and Jennifer Saunders. The most surprising addition to the cast, something akin to an English version of Branagh's use of American film stars in his Shakespeare films, was Joan Collins. Collins had expressed an interest in working in a Branagh film, and Branagh felt she brought the right sense of show business glamour to the role of Joe Harper's agent, Margaretta D'Arville.

The film's premise is that thirty-three-year-old actor Joe Harper, down on his luck and waiting to hear if he has been cast in a series of

Hollywood science fiction films, decides to play in and direct a production of *Hamlet* in the rural English village of Hope where he grew up and where his sister Molly is currently teaching. The purpose of the Christmas week production is to raise funds to save a local church that has become Molly's pet cause. The film follows the production from Joe's casting sessions in London, out to the abandoned church in Hope once the cast has been assembled, through a chaotic week of rehearsals, and on through the against-all-odds triumph of opening night. The tiny cast of seven (all except Joe playing multiple roles) is augmented by a designer (Fadge), Joe's sister, and his agent. At the narrative's climax, the cast members are joined by a variety of family members who show up for opening night along with an American film producer.

The film begins with a device reminiscent of Branagh's opening of *Much Ado About Nothing* and *Peter's Friends*: a song. Noel Coward's crisp and dry, essence-of-Martini voice sings:

> The World for some years
> Has been sodden with tears
> On behalf of the acting profession
>
> Each star
> Playing a part
> Seems to expect
> A purple heart
>
> It's unorthodox
> To be born in a box
> But it needn't become an obsession
> Let's hope we have no more to plague us
> Than three shows a night in Las Vegas
>
> When I think of physicians
> And mathematicians
> Who don't earn a quart of the dough
> When I think of the miners
> And waiters in diners
> There's one thing I'm burning to know. . .

The film cuts to Joe Harper in direct address to the camera: "It was late November, er . . . I think . . . and I was thinking about the whole Christmas thing, the birth of Christ, Wizard of Oz, family murders, and quite frankly I was depressed."[2] Branagh's use of black and white photography, a wry song from the 1950s, direct address by the film's hero, and the wonderfully droll ironic linking of Christmas, *The Wizard of Oz*, and family murders all call to mind the films of Woody Allen. This may seem, at first, an odd pairing. Branagh, after all, has credited the backstage film genre of the 1930s and 1940s from the Mickey Rooney–Judy Garland films to *42nd Street* as his inspiration: "[*Midwinter*] found its form finally through a version of Mickey Rooney–Judy Garland films, that thing about let's put a show on right here! And like all Mickey and Judy films, we wonder will they get to do the show, will there be an audience? All that excitement and old-fashioned romance about theater and movies is in there."[3]

In linking Mickey and Judy with Woody, Branagh is making another of those unexpected yokings of disparate traditions that distinguishes his film style. Like Allen he works with a core group of actors, mixing them with prominent outsiders who vary from film to film. Allen's core group, changing from time to time over the long arc of his career, includes Diane Keaton, Tony Roberts, Dianne Wiest, Sam Waterston, Mia Farrow, Alan Alda, and, of course, Allen himself. Allen then adds stars like Michael Caine, Julia Roberts, Goldie Hawn, Mia Sorvino, Helena Bonham Carter, and even Branagh to give each new film a distinctive flavor.

Allen's great subject is Manhattan; Branagh's is Shakespeare. Each director has an intimate and autobiographical attachment to his chosen territory. Both are comfortable, if such a term can ever be applied to the jittery neurosis of Allen's comic art, in projecting themselves into the heart of that territory. In their approaches to the material that feeds their art, Branagh is the romantic, and Allen is the skeptic, but each is also proudly sentimental about that material's sustaining impact on their lives. Allen is as unimaginable without Manhattan as Branagh is without Shakespeare. Woody loses touch with something vital when his films stray to California or Paris or even the Hamptons. Branagh's cinematic imagination is most alive when confronted with the continuing problem of how to make Shakespeare live on the screen with the power he releases in the theater.

So although Branagh acknowledges that the form of *Midwinter* is clearly borrowed from the Rooney–Garland films, the film's style is sweetly indebted to Allen. As Allen's best films are all love songs to a mythical Manhattan, Branagh's *Midwinter* (following Noel Coward's lead) expresses his devotion not only to Shakespeare but also to the vagaries of the acting profession itself. The view of actors and acting that emerges from *Midwinter* is as sparkling and generous as Allen's vision of Manhattan.

The flow of Branagh's film follows a pattern he established in *Peter's Friends* where ensemble scenes were punctuated by exchanges between two or three characters. Because the film wants to recreate the communal, family experience that develops among actors working together on a theatrical production, Branagh's camera tries to position as many members of the cast within the frame as frequently as possible. The film cleverly incorporates this growing sense of community by building it into its form and style. The film begins with Coward's off-screen voice singing "Why Must the Show Go On" over the credits and then cuts to a medium close-up of Joe Harper delivering his opening monologue. The film next cuts to a scene between Joe and his agent Margaretta, then segueing into a series of Joe's casting audition sessions before finally cutting to the assembled cast arriving, all seven crammed into a single station wagon, at the village of Hope. Form follows function as we move from solo off-screen voice to actor to interaction to ensemble. Once the core group of seven actors has gathered at the church, Branagh repeatedly sets up his shots to position as many of them in the frame as he can. Shooting in black and white with a wide-angle lens allows Branagh's cinematographer, Roger Lanser, to employ a series of deep focus shots that creates a depth of field in which Branagh can arrange and frame his actors.

Branagh, cleverly, uses several simple props or pieces of furniture around which to gather his cast: the station wagon, several benches, a long table used for communal meals and the first rehearsal read-through of the play, and the interior church steps separating the chancel from the nave. Branagh then alternates group scenes and shots with more intimate moments as the cast breaks down into smaller exchanges between two or three characters. The screenplay comically echoes Branagh's arrangement of his actors as Fadge (Celia Imrie), the slightly spacey designer, enters the film and begins to mystically commune with the church's atmosphere: "You know this place is incredible. I feel something very powerful here. Very strange and powerful. . . . You see, we must make the design all about space. People in space, things in space, women in space, men in space."[4] Tom (Nicholas Farrell), in his thick but well-meaning way, responds, "So we'd be sort of spacemen?"[5] Branagh's camera cuts back and forth between solo shots of Fadge and group shots of the seven cast members scattered around the church. The major arc of the film will be the way in which the cast members claim the church as a potent space for their production of *Hamlet*, even as the production (and the theatrical experience it symbolically embodies) is constantly being threatened by the world of film, especially the science fiction trilogy for which Joe remains a possible candidate for a leading role. Spacemen and Shakespeareans-

Henry Wakefield (Richard Briers), Carnforth Granville (Gerard Horan), Tom Newman (Nicholas Farrell), Nina (Julia Sawahla), Joe Harper (Michael Maloney), Terry DeBois (John Sessions), Molly Harper (Hetta Charnley), Vernon Spatch (Mark Hadfield), and Fadge (Celia Imrie) gather for the first rehearsal of *Hamlet* in *A Midwinter's Tale*.
[Photographer: David Appleby, Courtesy of Photofest]

in-space comically jostle with one another to define the tensions in Branagh's life as they are incorporated into the unfolding of *A Midwinter's Tale*.

The first communal moment in the church is followed by a series of scenes in which the cast members, paired off, settle into shared sleeping quarters: Carnforth (Gerard Horan) and Vernon (Mark Hadfield) in the crypt; Nina (Julia Sawalha) and Fadge in an upstairs gallery with a wonderful view down into the church; and Henry (Richard Briers) complaining to Joe (Michael Maloney) about being assigned sleeping quarters with Terry (John Sessions): "I don't see why I have to share with the pouffe, love."[6] Then Branagh brings everyone back together for a meal around a long trestle table. Individual idiosyncrasies begin to emerge as the group rubs up against each other. Branagh's camera slides down the table, catching individual exchanges rather than capturing the group as a whole in a single long shot. We are witnessing the legendary making of the theatrical family, but as yet individual needs and complaints and insecurities work against the making of community. Branagh, self-consciously, divides his film into a prologue and three acts with the first act coming to a close in an extended exterior scene between Joe and Nina. Nina is the most emotionally passionate about the project, and she bucks up Joe's flagging spirits even as she reveals her own wound at the loss of her fighter pilot husband in a crash over the Lake District. Branagh here is not only creating a backstory for Nina's personal relationship with Ophelia, but is also incorporating stage tradition, where the actors playing Hamlet and Ophelia in most productions end up becoming lovers as well. As Laurence Olivier, when queried, "Are Hamlet and Ophelia lovers?" once joked in response, "In my company, always!"[7]

Act Two begins with the cast plus Molly (Hetta Charnley) and Fadge gathered around the rehearsal table for the first read-through of the play. Branagh captures the read-through by montage and he reintroduces Noel Coward on the soundtrack singing the second verse of "Why Must the Show Go On":

> Why must the show go on?
> The room is sure not immutable,
> It might be wiser
> And more suitable just to close
> If you are in the throes
> Of personal grief and private woes
>
> Why stifle a sob
> While doing your job
> When if you lose your head
> You go out and grab a comfortable cab
> And go right home to bed
>
> Because you're not giving us much fun
> This laugh-cry-laugh routine's been overdone
> Hats off to show folks
> For smiling when they are blue
> But more cameo po-folks
> Are sick of smiling through
> And if you are out cold
> Too old and most of your teeth have gone
> Why must the show go on?
> I sometimes wonder
> Why must the show go on?

Coward's lyrics bounce along on the soundtrack as we watch a montage of images of the actors nervously jiggling their feet, chewing gum, and lighting endless cigarettes as the pages of the *Hamlet* text whiz by. The sequence ends with the cast staggering out of the church engulfed in cigarette and cigar smoke. The punch line generated by this scene comes a moment later when Vernon asks Fadge, "So what's the design?" and she replies, "Smoke . . . people in space, in smoke."[8] Stage smoke, as audiences at Stratford have learned, has been a staple of Royal Shakespeare Company productions over the past forty years. Branagh is not only tweaking designer-talk here but is also having a bit of fun at the expense of institutional Shakespeare. Fadge's "smoke" may well also be a playful echo of the interchange Branagh had with the director Ron Daniels when Daniels first approached him about playing Henry V at Stratford. When Branagh asked Daniels what he saw in the play, Daniels replied, "Mud."[9]

This exchange follows Fadge's presentation of her design for the set, and the moment allows for another tightly framed group shot with the actors gathered around Fadge's model. The camera captures Carnforth's face peering out through the model's back. The model is, of course, simply the church's interior uniting the film's meta-theatrical, meta-cinematic, and meta-religious (the theater as temple or sacred space) impulses. Branagh continues to follow the pattern of alternating shots that frame the group as a whole with those that spin off and away into the private lives and woes of the individual actors. Gradually, thanks to Shakespeare and Branagh, the two realities begin to intermix and mingle.

Henry, after fulminating about having to work with an actor in drag playing Gertrude, comes to learn of the buried secret in Terry's life (he has a son from a one-night heterosexual fling twenty years before) and becomes genuinely protective of his partner. Nina begins to transfer the passion of her grief for her dead husband into a commitment to the play and to Joe. Carnforth, the shy alcoholic in the group, always burying his misery in disguises and drink, discovers solace in a series of exchanges with Fadge and Vernon. And Tom, the film's comic portrait of the hopelessly self-centered actor, eventually finds a soul mate in Fadge. Father-son tensions, struggles with identity and narcissism, dealing with tragic loss, and being haunted by the past are all powerful themes in *Hamlet*, and they are reinscribed and gently mocked in the personal preoccupations of the play's cast. Branagh's film, in these moments, finds itself minding true things by what their mockeries be.

The group scene at the model looks not only back to how far (and fast) the cast has come in a few days, but also forward to Branagh's four-hour film of *Hamlet*. The shot of Carnforth peering out at the camera from the back of Fadge's model is repeated by Branagh at a crucial instant in his film of the play itself. At the conclusion of the "O what a rogue and peasant slave" soliloquy, Branagh's Hamlet peers out at the camera from the back of a Victorian toy theater model as he utters, "The play's the thing / Wherein I'll catch the conscience of the king." Kathy Howlett reads this moment and others like it as revealing the ways in which "Branagh's film self-consciously compares the theater in Shakespeare's time to the cinema of the modern age, for it is the cinematic medium that permits experimentation from a wide range of available perspectives and ponders the historical moment of its own possibility. *A Midwinter's Tale* . . . is as notably self-reflexive as *Hamlet*."[10]

Hamlet is at the center of *A Midwinter's Tale* in much the same way that *The Murder of Gonzaga* is in *Hamlet*. But Branagh's film works at catching our conscience rather than the king's. He wants to implicate us, as potential audience, in the precarious position live theater holds in contemporary Anglo-American culture. As Hamlet uses the theatrical event to expose the political corruption of the Danish court, Branagh uses film to engage our guilt about having abandoned the classical theater for pop culture. As Molly says when she discovers that Joe plans to put on *Hamlet* as the Christmas show to save the church, "Great. Hello kids. Do stop watching Mighty Morphin Power Rangers and come watch a four-hundred-year-old play about a depressed aristocrat."[11] As Shakespeare's play repeatedly underlines the connection between performance and power, stage and state, so does Branagh's film enact a similar struggle over cultural, rather than political, power.

A Midwinter's Tale is not only saturated with *Hamlet* as a cultural artifact and literary generator of meaning but is also an experience deeply rooted in performance history. The cast's banter is loaded with backstage gossip and lore that reaches back to Burbage's Globe Theatre: Terry DuBois's Gertrude evokes the cross-dressing reality of the Elizabethan theater, Henry Wakefield does an imitation of Henry Irving's Othello, and Molly finds Joe, in despair, going over the account books and muttering, "How weary, stale, flat, and unprofitable / Seem to me all the uses of this world!"—to which she replies, "That's not bad, Sir Laurence."[12] Branagh's film also serves as a comic homage to Olivier's 1948 film of the play, the only film of a Shakespeare play ever to win the Oscar for Best Picture. Olivier's black and white masterpiece is famous for its gloomy interiors, its fog-shrouded exteriors, its use of deep focus shots to capture characters radically separated from one another spatially as well as emotionally, its deeply Freudian approach to the play, and a curious, roving camera that keeps poking its nose—like the film's tragic hero—

into dark places. Branagh appropriates Olivier's film in the same way he does Shakespeare's play, simultaneously combining nostalgia, admiration, and parody. Fadge's visual image for the production, "People in space, in smoke," also parodies Olivier's film as well as those Royal Shakespeare Company productions mentioned earlier.

What Howlett does not see is that Branagh includes himself in that parody as well. Not only does *A Midwinter's Tale*'s screenplay, setting, budget, and modesty gently mock, in advance, Branagh's own epic, extravagantly ambitious, Technicolor film of *Hamlet* soon to be shot; the film also, in the details of Joe Harper's performance of Hamlet, looks back to Branagh's own performance of the part for The Royal Shakespeare Company in 1992. One of the most vivid images of that production was of Branagh's Hamlet, wrapped in a black great coat pulled tightly across his shoulders, standing alone on the Barbican Theatre's vast stage, speaking Hamlet's soliloquies directly to the audience. In *A Midwinter's Tale*'s version of *Hamlet*, Michael Maloney is wrapped in a similar great coat as he delivers the snippets from the great soliloquies, particularly "How all occasions do inform against me," enveloped in Fadge's smoke.

Two other significant moments in the film look both backward and forward in Branagh's Shakespearean career. The film jump cuts from a scene between Joe, Molly, and Vernon brainstorming about the mundane issue of ticket sales to a highly charged rehearsal of the closet scene. The camera captures, in close-up, Joe's face pressed tightly on top of Terry's as Hamlet hammers away at his mother: "Mother, for love of grace, / Lay not that flattering unction to your soul, / That not your trespass but my madness speaks / It will but skin and film the ulcerous place, / Whiles rank corruption, mining all within, / Infects unseen."[13] The exchange is highly charged because of Terry's troubled relationship with his own son. The moment also has backstory meaning in Branagh's career as well, for the shot of Joe's face pressed horizontally on top of Terry's is a mirror image of Branagh's own face, as Henry V, pressed against Scroop's (Stephen Simms) in the traitors' scene in Branagh's film of *Henry V*. There the shot was loaded with an awkward sexual tension as Branagh's Henry castigated Scroop for his betrayal and the way it endangered the homosocial bonding of Henry's "band of brothers" so central to Branagh's conception of the character and the play. In *A Midwinter's Tale* Branagh revisits the power of the shot, again exploring the complexities of male relationships, now in a more nuanced manner. Here Joe's Hamlet is almost eagerly comfortable working in a sexually intimate manner with a male actor playing a female role. It's all connected to the liberating power of a production committed, in Joe's words, to being "free and experimental."[14] Branagh, however, does not allow Joe the audience's fuller perspective on Terry's backstory. When Terry breaks off the scene on "Thou hast cleft my heart in twain" and brushes off Joe's excited encouragement to fully explore the emotional intensity of Gertrude's guilt, only we know that Terry is overly invested in the textual moment because of his complicated parental relationship with his son. Director Branagh creates an interesting distance here between himself and his multiple alter-egos captured in Joe's roles as director, entrepreneur, star, and Hamlet.

The other moment comes at the film's climax. The company has bonded. The dress rehearsal has been smashing. Spirits are soaring as Christmas Eve and opening night arrive. Unfortunately, so does Margaretta with the news that Joe, in fact, has been offered the lead in the Hollywood science fiction epic. The kicker is he must leave for Los Angeles immediately since shooting starts on Boxing Day (December 26th). Hollywood reality has intruded on theatrical nostalgia and the party's over. No Joe, no show. This device allows Branagh's film to record a variety of responses from Joe's fellow cast members with all—except Nina—eventually agreeing that he has, in fact, no choice. Hollywood is where they all would be headed if provided the same opportunity. Molly volunteers to step in for Joe, for one performance only, so that the show can at least go on once. Nina bolts in anger at Joe's decision and the others drift off, leaving only Carnforth to console Joe: "Easy on yourself old chap. I'm afraid we can't all afford the luxury of nourishing our souls. That's the prerogative of the romantics among us, I fear. These things happen. What does he say, 'If it be now 'tis not to come, if it be not to come it will be now, if it be not now, yet it will come, the readiness is all.'"[15] As Carnforth reaches Hamlet's famous lines, a solo guitar begins quietly to pick out the tune of Gustav Holst's "In the Bleak Midwinter" on the soundtrack.[16] Branagh's film, before its rousing comic finale, comes to a point of rest in the same passage that Shakespeare's tragedy does: Hamlet's quiet, self-controlled meditation on the fall of a sparrow. In an interesting reversal of Shakespeare's moment, Branagh has the Horatio character (Carnforth) deliver the lines to the Hamlet figure (Joe) as solace for good news rather than bad. It is another generous moment in Branagh's film as Carnforth has been something of the mutt in the cast, but here he is given prime focus and invested with one of Hamlet's most profound and bittersweet realizations.

As Russell Jackson notes, Hamlet's "the readiness is all" exchange with Horatio was a crucial moment for Branagh in the shooting of his *Hamlet* film. The scene came to frame the film's three-month shooting schedule as it was one of the first scenes in the film to be shot in January and then

Branagh, unsatisfied with his performance, returned to it on the film's pen-ultimate day of shooting in April. Jackson reports that Branagh "wanted to come back to it with the experience of the play behind him."[17] In that sec-ond take, Branagh's performance was quieter and less busy. As he delivered the famous lines, he allowed his body to mirror the sparrow's fall by gently sliding down a wall in Hamlet's study as he resigned himself to life ("Let be") as an uninterrupted human experience that continues its meandering progress even when our deep plots do pall. Branagh, as actor and director, treats this moment in his massive, vigorous film of *Hamlet* with the same quiet resignation and dignity that Gerard Horan brings to it in *A Midwin-ter's Tale*. Even Patrick Doyle's film score is as hushed and reverential in *Hamlet* as the quiet guitar chords of Holst's hymn are in *A Midwinter's Tale*. In both films Branagh comes closest in these moments to investing Shakespeare with something of the sacred; it's all tied up with his desire to link the sacred and profane, high art and low, elite and popular forms of entertainment. As Howlett perceptively notes about this impulse in *A Mid-winter's Tale*, "The ritual of putting on a play at Christmas time reveals the frame of a culture's collective values at the intersection of the traditional and the improvised, the sacred and the secular."[18]

From the Carnforth–Joe exchange the film dashes to its wonderfully anticipated comic conclusion. The form is the ultimate struggle to actu-ally "put on a play," and the route takes us, finally, through the company's production of *Hamlet*. The cast, triumphing over the disappointment of losing Joe, hustles to prepare themselves (and Molly) for the first-night audience. As the fog-bound production begins, Joe, of course, emerges from the rear of the church to rescue his tongue-tied sister on Hamlet's opening line: "A little more than kin, and less than kind." He's back, reuniting kin and kind in his decision to spurn Hollywood in favor of his new theatrical family. In a feat of compression worthy of Tom Stoppard's *The Fifteen Minute Hamlet*, Branagh gives us a montage of the production that takes us from "Who's there" to "Go, bid the soldiers shoot" in a fast and furious four minutes and fifty cuts. Branagh's film gives us the essence of the play, including jokes ("Good Hamlet, cast off thy coloured nightie and look like a friend on Denmark")[19], a passionate (and loaded) confrontation between Ophelia and Hamlet in the return of the love-tokens and letters scene, a touch of *The Mousetrap*, the murder of Polo-nius, and a rousing duel between Hamlet and Laertes. The audience gets actively involved in the duel, gasping at the violent parries and cheering on the protagonists, creating Branagh's image of Shakespeare as a popular dramatist capable of moving and inciting an audience otherwise only engaged by the Mighty Morphin Power Rangers.

The production not only has brought Joe back into the fold to be reunited with Nina but also has led to the sentimental reunions of Terry with his son (engineered by Henry), Carnforth with his mother, and Nina with her father. Most improbably, Joe's spurning of the Hollywood offer has brought the American producer (Jennifer Saunders) to the production to see what the competition is all about. She is much taken with Tom's Laertes and Fortinbras and offers him the science fiction film deal turned down by Joe. So Tom and Fadge, having become another backstage romance, are off to Los Angeles. *Hamlet* is, among many things, about the shredding of the family romance, and, as Horatio reports, the piling up of "carnal, bloody, and unnatural acts" and "deaths put on by cunning and forced cause." *A Midwinter's Tale* turns *Hamlet* on its head by using it as a vehicle for comic reconciliation rather than tragic destruction. Not only is its cast made into a community, but the communal effort involved in "putting on a show" works to heal larger breaches in their private lives as well.

Branagh celebrates this triumph of community the way Shakespeare typically does in his festive comedies: with a dance. In the last of the film's deep-focus group shots, he manages to position five dancing couples in the frame: Joe and Nina, Tom and Fadge, Molly and Vernon, Henry and Terry, and Carnforth with Nina's Dad. No symphonic score swells on the soundtrack, no confetti swirls in the air, no dazzlingly clever steadicam shot materializes, but the quiet, simple, straightforward—almost geometric—style of the film prevails even as Branagh indulges in one last sentimental touch. Moments earlier, Nancy Crawford, the Hollywood producer, has summed up her response to the cast's performance of *Hamlet* by saying, "The whole thing was like a Judy Garland movie."[20] This is precisely where Branagh's film universe lives: at the intersection of Shakespeare and Garland. *A Midwinter's Tale* is the answer to Noel Coward's "Why Must the Show Go On?" The film's landscape and tradition are English but its spirit is decidedly American. Branagh's energy and boundless optimism are American qualities and run against the grain of English irony and understatement. It's one of the reasons his films have generally been better received in New York than in London. H. R. Coursen, alert to the film's landscape and premise, is right to see that "What begins as murder in the cathedral ends as a community of the spirit, so that the setting gradually exchanges its ironies for its sacramental qualities."[21]

A Midwinter's Tale served as a crucial pivot in Branagh's career as a film director. Biographically, it was his means of recuperating his Shakespearean and theatrical energies after the critical bashing of *Mary Shelley's Frankenstein* and of preparing for his epic four-hour film of *Hamlet*. *A Midwinter's Tale* is another example of Branagh's genius for synthesis.

Here he uses film as a means of celebrating his attachment to the world of the classical theater. He compounded his accomplishment by linking his group of rag-tag English actors putting on a production of *Hamlet* with the American backstage movie genre most innocently expressed in the Mickey Rooney–Judy Garland films. Branagh was bold enough to gather comic rewards by extending his range of American movie references from The Andy Hardy films to George Lucas's *Star Wars* epics. In his two earlier Shakespeare films, *Henry V* and *Much Ado About Nothing*, Branagh had created cinematic energy by linking them to familiar Hollywood genres: the war film and screwball comedy. In *A Midwinter's Tale*, even though Branagh was quite consciously evoking the style and manner of the very British Ealing Studio comedies of the 1950s, his heart (and film aesthetic) drew him irresistibly to Hollywood.

In many ways, while *A Midwinter's Tale* seems, on the surface, Branagh's most homegrown film, it cannot escape the power Hollywood holds for Branagh's cinematic imagination and his creative energies. As Kathy Howlett rightly observes about *A Midwinter's Tale*, "Branagh's film embraces Shakespeare with a sophisticated awareness of generic expectations and constructs, not with creative exhaustion, but exhilarated by imaginative possibilities."[22] Branagh keeps finding ways to make Shakespeare fresh on film and to find in that combination the central concern of his career as an actor and director. As Douglas Lanier understands, for Branagh "Shakespeare serves as a point of emotional identification between otherwise isolated individuals, a means of articulating their loss of communal feeling and their desire for its re-establishment."[23] *A Midwinter's Tale* is a touching comic restorative for the first significant stumble of Branagh's development as a filmmaker. It also served as a comic exorcism of the *Hamlet* demons as Branagh moved toward realizing the most ambitious film of his career. In *A Midwinter's Tale* Branagh employed a lesson from the master. Shakespeare, in *Henry IV, Part One*, realized the power and potential of giving us the mock scene before the real one when he has Falstaff and Hal rehearse, in the tavern, Hal's impending confrontation with his royal father at Court. Mock king and truant Prince hurl gross insults at one another with comic brio, helping to dissolve the psychological tensions of the real king–prince encounter yet to come. *A Midwinter's Tale* served something of the same purpose as Branagh cleared his own psychological and aesthetic path to his long-anticipated full-text film version of *Hamlet*. As all of the cast members in *Midwinter* brought their own private backstory, or subtext, to their performances in *Hamlet*, so the entire film served that purpose for Branagh himself. Branagh, of all the English actors of his generation, is the most Hamlet-obsessed. He had played the role three times on stage and completed a full-text radio recording all by the age of thirty-two. His entire young career as an actor and director pointed toward his film of the play. The gentle, loving mockery of *A Midwinter's Tale* became the necessary territory through which Branagh had to travel to take on *Hamlet*: "Good night sweet parody and may flights of Christmas angels sing thee to thy rest."

Chapter 8

HAMLET

Branagh's *Hamlet* is the most ambitious and audacious Shakespeare film ever made—ambitious because Branagh set out to overturn seventy-five years of tradition in the approach to filmed *Hamlets*; audacious because he determined to shoot the full text of Shakespeare's longest tragedy and challenge the well-tested convention that commercial films should only last approximately two hours.

Hamlet films, reaching back to Sven Gade's 1920 silent version starring Asta Nielsen, take their visual clues from the play's labyrinthine mysteries and the hero's famed Danish melancholy. As a result, most *Hamlet* films have been shot in black and white and create a gloomy, gothic world dominated by a fog-shrouded Elsinore castle. Even *Hamlet* films shot in Technicolor and made by directors such as Tony Richardson and Franco Zeffirelli—noted for their bright, bold styles in such films as *Tom Jones* and *Brother Sun, Sister Moon*—imagine the *Hamlet* universe as dark, cold, and constricted, bound in by brick and stone as well as by the pale cast of thought.

The alpha *Hamlet* film is, of course, Laurence Olivier's Academy Award–winning version of 1948. All subsequent *Hamlet* films, even Michael Almereyda's quirky, personal contemporary version (2000) shot on location in Manhattan, are indebted in some significant fashion either to Olivier's cinematic style or to his Freudian approach to the text. Olivier made famous the imposing castle exteriors surrounded by fog, the interiors dominated by a series of winding stone staircases, and a prying camera exploring (via those staircases) the vertical axis as often as the horizontal. By casting as Gertrude an actress (Eileen Herlie) thirteen years younger than himself (Herlie was twenty-seven at the time) and by playing their scenes together with a strong Oedipal undercurrent, Olivier claimed the text for Freud and the twentieth century. Olivier's *Hamlet* is debilitated and paralyzed by his relationship with his mother and father. The actor, known for the robust physical vitality he brought to his stage Shakespearean roles, gives us a curiously passive Hamlet who is repeatedly brought to his knees, or even flattened, in his encounters with the Ghost and Gertrude. Olivier's screenplay also includes radical excisions from the text. All Shakespeare films trim the text, as do most stage productions. Most *Hamlet*s, on stage and screen, eliminate Fortinbras, Voltemand and Cornelius, Reynaldo, the second Grave-digger, and the English Ambassador. Olivier went even further by cutting Rosencrantz and Guildenstern as well.

Branagh's film makes a complete break with this tradition. In setting, atmosphere, film script and approach, Branagh boldly revises the dominant twentieth-century ideas about *Hamlet* in performance. Much, but not all, of his production choices were guided by his decision to film a full text, in this case a conflation of the Second Quarto and First Folio versions of the play. For fifty years, stage and film *Hamlet* productions, based on their approach to the play and subsequent editing of the text, had down-played or eliminated the play's larger social and political implications to focus on Hamlet's psychological struggle and its domestic impact on his immediate family. Olivier's Hamlet set the tone: he was morose and passive. When energized, as in his athletic dash up the winding stairs after discovering the presence of Claudius and Polonius in the nunnery scene, he was quickly reduced to a passive sprawl by a case of vertigo created by the sea crashing against the rocks below. He was similarly sent to his knees by the appearance of the Ghost in the closet scene, after initially showing some spark of vitality in his confrontation with Gertrude over her remarriage. This Olivier- and Freudian-inspired pattern of focusing on the domestic family romance turned sour, and Hamlet's fated inability to bring his emotional life under control dominated approaches to the play in the second half of the twentieth century.

By the 1980s this pattern had developed to such extremes that highly praised productions had Hamlet (Jonathan Pryce) literally invaded by the Ghost's demonic spirit so that Pryce spoke the Ghost's lines in a paroxysm of possession, or they had Hamlet (Mark Rylance) so reduced by his circumstances that he cavorted in his pajamas for most of the play in a wild (if also wonderfully comic) infantilism. Branagh's own stage *Hamlet* in 1988 for his Renaissance Company (directed by Derek Jacobi) was a further extension of the path from Olivier to Pryce to Rylance. He was wild and whirling—very much the rebellious child radically alienated by the drastically changed circumstances of his life caused by his father's murder and his mother's remarriage.

Branagh's route to his film version, like his film of *Henry V,* ran through another Royal Shakespeare Company production of the play directed by Adrian Noble. This production, in 1992–1993, featured the full text and a much more mature Hamlet from Branagh. But even though Noble used the full text, his production still concentrated on the family tragedy rather than emphasizing its larger social and political contexts. Noble, and his designer Bob Crowley, took the Scandinavian inspiration of the production's visual atmosphere from Ingmar Bergman's family masterpiece, *Fanny and Alexander* (1982). When Branagh made his film of *Henry V,* he relied heavily on many of the visual ideas from Noble's stage production; when he came to make his *Hamlet* film, he was making a break not only with the Olivier film tradition but also with his indebtedness to Noble and Crowley as well.

Branagh's decision to use the entire text of *Hamlet* stirred his cinematic imagination to create a style and landscape huge enough to contain it. Stylistically, his model was not Olivier or Welles or Zeffirelli, but David Lean. Lean, who started small with *Brief Encounter* (1945) and two exquisite films of Dickens's *Great Expectations* (1946) and *Oliver Twist* (1948), went on to become the finest director of epic movies in British film history. In *Laurence of Arabia* (1962), *Doctor Zhivago* (1965) and *Ryan's Daughter* (1970), Lean became the master of shooting in the widescreen 70mm format. Branagh boldly followed Lean into 70mm territory, and his *Hamlet* became the first British film to be shot in that format since *Ryan's Daughter.* In our time, *Hamlet* has most often been visualized as a play about impasse; Branagh wanted to restore its capacity for expanse, sensing that impasse is most effectively realized only when set against expanse.

The 70mm format meant Branagh needed to set his film in a landscape appropriate for such a treatment, and he found that landscape at Blenheim Palace in Woodstock, just outside of Oxford. Blenheim had been built in the early eighteenth century as a gift from Queen Anne to John Churchill, the first Duke of Marlborough, for his victory over the French in 1704. Blenheim is magisterial but Branagh's film makes it seem even bigger. When I first saw the film at a preview screening for critics at the Sony Building on Madison Avenue, I overheard the following whispered exchange between the two men seated behind me as the opening scene of the film unfolded before the Palace's gates:

"Where's that?"

"Blenheim."

"That's not Blenheim. I've been there and it's not that big."

The film's exteriors were all shot in and around Blenheim while its interiors were shot at Shepperton Studios, where Branagh's designer, Tim Harvey, created a great room trimmed in white and gold meant to echo a subtle merger of Versaille's dazzling Mirror Gallery and Inigo Jones's Banqueting Hall. Harvey explained, "Ken wanted the sets to be . . . far removed from the rugged medieval gloom one usually associates with the play."[1]

Branagh set the film in the late nineteenth century, though its political tone is much more Edwardian. Several critics of the film objected to its design and setting, complaining that they smacked of Ernest Lubitsch's film of Sigmund Romberg's *The Student Prince* (1927). Branagh does take inspiration from a wide variety of popular films, but here the influences are much more Boris Pasternack and David Lean than Romberg and Lubitsch. As the political background for his examination of the internecine civil struggle that destroys the House of Hamlet and leads to Fortin-

Hamlet (Kenneth Branagh) surrounded by the confetti released in celebration of the wedding of Claudius and Gertrude in Branagh's film *Hamlet*.   [Photographer: Rolf Konow, Courtesy of Photofest]

bras's brutal military invasion of Denmark in the film's final frames, Branagh draws upon Queen Victoria's Ruritanian Dream to populate the thrones of late nineteenth- and early twentieth-century Europe with her progeny and their offspring. Blenheim anchors Branagh's *Hamlet* in a European aristocratic world about to implode. Branagh's film is far more politically radical than most critics, with the significant exceptions of Mark Thornton Burnett and Harry Keyishian, have understood.[2] Branagh does want to capture the veneer of the late Victorian world but only so that his Hamlet can expose the rank corruption that "mining all within, / Infects unseen." (3.4.149–150).

Blenheim allows Branagh a space in which to link his epic impulses with his desire to restore *Hamlet*'s political dimensions. In historical terms Blenheim comes to represent the great palace Kaiser Wilhelm built at Potsdam as Wilhelm began to flex his military muscles within his extended family of English, Russian, and European monarchs. In the narrative, Branagh accomplishes this not only by retaining the role of Fortinbras (Rufus Sewell) but also by enhancing his presence in the film with frequent visual cuts to his war preparations and his advance on Poland when those events are discussed by others (primarily Horatio and Claudius) in the text. Branagh is embedding his *Hamlet* in the collapse of Europe as it stumbled into World War I.

In keeping with this historical context, Branagh conceives of his Hamlet as a soldier. When we first meet Hamlet, he's in a military uniform; he takes a keen interest in fencing; his bearing and manners are formal; he's polite and solicitous with Horatio and Marcellus; he is at clear pains to control and contain his grief over his father's death and his anger at his mother's remarriage; and his verbal attack is swift and precise. Olivier's Hamlet seems dreamy, passive, and abstract by comparison. Blenheim is a palace built as a reward for military achievement, and Branagh positions a military prince against its golden stones.

Following the geometry of his military setting, Branagh shot his film, with two important exceptions, on the horizontal. The film begins on the ground in front of the palace's gates rather than on its ramparts above.[3] The Ghost, rather than being the mysterious, looming disembodied voice and shadow of film tradition, appears to materialize from the giant statue of the old king that towers over Bernardo and Francisco in the opening sequence. Branagh's *Hamlet* is his only film to open without a prologue to hook the viewer into the visual storytelling. He's got to move fast because he has four hours of screenplay to shoot and no excess film time (montage and action without dialogue) to exploit to establish landscape and atmosphere.[4] We see "HAMLET" chiseled on a stone plinth, and the camera pans to a shot of Blenheim at night (a "gorgeous Winter Palace," the screenplay tells us, reinforcing Branagh's debt to David Lean) and then back to a slow pan shot, up from its base, of the statue of the old king.[5] The bell tolls the midnight hour, the statue's right hand appears to move and to pull its sword from its scabbard, we hear the sound of steel on stone, and Francisco turns in fright and is tackled by Bernardo as the text's famous first words come tumbling out: "Who's there?" From this moment on, Branagh's camera is in constant motion: it tracks, pans, cranes, zooms in and back, flashes back, and circles. Then, abruptly, it will hold an immense close-up of a tiny detail like a mouth, ear, pair of eyes, or pool of blood. The 70mm format is as powerful in these moments as in more obvious scenes like the first court scene or Fortinbras's army storming the Winter Palace at the end of the film. Branagh wants us to see and hear everything.

The film's interior landscape is distinguished by the great hall trimmed in white and gold and lined with mirrored doors. Branagh and Tim Harvey cleverly adapt this central space so that it serves multiple purposes as Claudius's court, Hamlet's playhouse, and Fortinbras's prize. The mirrored doors open into smaller spaces that come to include Hamlet's book-lined study, Ophelia's padded prison, Polonius's retreat, the palace's chapel, and Gertrude's bedroom. The great hall is always sparkling and dazzling, but its dark secrets lie hidden behind those mirrored doors. Not only is Branagh dispelling the gothic gloom associated with previous *Hamlet* films, but he is also playfully giving us film noir with all the lights on or horror with a Kubrick twist. If the Blenheim exteriors provide the external military world of the play—from old Hamlet's statue, to the Ghost's demonic dash through a purgatorial wasteland of bubbling, tormented earth, to the Gravedigger's cooler and more ironic burial plot, to the steady advance of Fortinbras's army—then the interiors are dominated by the painful progress of the domestic tragedy set in motion by Claudius's crime.

By using the full text, Branagh's *Hamlet* provides for extended attention to the Polonius family, Rosencrantz and Guildenstern, and the Players. The film provides a particularly powerful take on Polonius (Richard Briers) and his children. The film conceives of Polonius as newly appointed to his position of power. He's not an old holdover from the previous king's administration, but a younger politician promoted to first minister by the new king. He's Claudius's man and he's no fool. Branagh includes Ophelia (Kate Winslet) in 1.2 and groups the Polonius family together at the head of the line of dignitaries present to celebrate the marriage of Gertrude and Claudius. Polonius's gold military uniform is littered with medals and his children are handsomely, perhaps too handsomely, dressed. Michael Maloney's Laertes is already seen to be a bit of the dandy (the Paris influence), and Kate Winslet's Ophelia seems a touch uncomfortable at suddenly being too much in the sun (and son) of the public eye. Maloney's Laertes keeps a sharp eye on his sister, and when Ophelia shyly moves to comfort Hamlet as Claudius and Gertrude parade out of the hall at the end of the scene, Laertes quickly pulls her back into the family triangle.

In this first interior scene, Branagh's camera takes in the large audience packed into the hall to welcome the new king and his queen. The camera follows Claudius and Gertrude as they enter down two rows of courtiers, and it then pans up into the upper gallery packed with Danish citizens. For an instant, the camera picks out a woman (Melanie Ramsay) dressed in brown furs and then hurries back to Claudius and Gertrude. The woman will reappear, in Polonius's bed, in 2.1 as Polonius sends Reynaldo off to France to spy on Laertes. This touch is as revealing as it is crass. Briers's Polonius speaks from experience when he talks about the larger tether a man is given to walk than a woman when the blood burns. Reynaldo, puffing his tiny cigar, is played by the great French actor Gerard Depardieu, making sense of the Paris connection, and Reynaldo's casual attitude about having a conversation with a politician getting dressed after a sexual encounter suggests that he serves as Polonius's pimp as well. To heighten the scene's atmosphere of carnality and politics, Branagh originally shot it with a Great Dane sitting at Reynaldo's side. Unfortunately, as Depardieu and the dog arose to exit during filming, the Great Dane's paws couldn't get traction on the slippery surface of the set's black and white checkered floor, so this further wicked touch was left on the cutting room floor.[6] But Branagh did not sacrifice the prostitute's exit: she slips out of the room through a hidden door just beats before Winslet's distraught Ophelia rushes in through another with news of *her* lover's visit to *her* room. These visual details dance along with Shakespeare's dialogue, deftly shading the complex relationship at work here between sexual and political corruption and the ways in which the screenplay deepens the connection between the destruction of the Polonius family and the fate of Hamlet's own struggle with Claudius, Gertrude, and The Ghost.

Briers's Polonius is not only venal in himself but is also the cause of venality in others. Later, his son, full of sound and fury about his father's death, will immediately take the coward's way out in being quickly co-opted into the poison business by Claudius. Perhaps even more significantly for Branagh's film, Polonius's daughter has consummated her sexual relationship with Hamlet. The film, in a series of flashback shots, wants us to empathize with the young lovers. Their lovemaking is tender and sweet and is wrapped up in soft-focus photography and Patrick Doyle's melancholy Mahlerian score. But Winslet's Ophelia is, finally, her father's daughter. Though Polonius does manage to badger her into confession and submission in the earlier exchange (shot effectively in the palace's chapel) about her relationship with Hamlet, he ultimately can't control her appetite or will. Winslet's Ophelia resists and she escapes to her watery grave by cunning (by hiding her cell key in her mouth while undergoing shock therapy by hose and water) rather than by chance.

Michael Maloney's Laertes is a prig. He is clearly puffed up by his family's social and political advancement. He's another version of his father with a keen eye to catch the main chance while uttering pieties and platitudes. His exchange with Ophelia about Hamlet's romantic intentions is played straight with none of the wink and tease one might expect of a brother and sister making common cause against a prying and overbearing parent. Laertes is doing his father's business here but without the bullying. All these qualities of unearned certitude and shallow convention come into play in Laertes's angry return to Elsinore to avenge his father's death. Laertes quickly becomes putty in the hands of Derek Jacobi's slick and smooth Claudius. The film, by allowing all the details of the Polonius family to be so fully fleshed out, reestablishes its centrality to the personal and political reach of Shakespeare's tragedy.

In a similar fashion, but in a minor key, the film provides space and opportunity for Rosencrantz (Timothy Spall) and Guildenstern (Reece Dinsdale) to move through the narrative in their puzzled and clueless fashion. They arrive hanging gaily off the sides of a small train as it puffs its way to Elsinore through a wintery landscape.[7] Timothy Spall's bearded Rosencrantz, in particular, is an apt portrait of an aging European undergraduate. He wears a sporty cap and he uses a handsome walking stick with effect as a prop. Branagh's Hamlet is initially delighted to see them both, but neither is capable of hiding his guilt when Hamlet begins to probe about their sudden appearance in the provincial backwater of Denmark. Neither Spall nor Dinsdale stoops to easy humor to underline Rosencrantz and Guildenstern's shallowness. They seem genuinely perplexed both about Hamlet's odd behavior and about their significance as spies for Claudius. They are trapped between "fell and mighty opposites" without the slightest clue of how and why they are being taunted by Hamlet and manipulated by Claudius. Spall's delivery of the "cess of majesty" speech catches at this perfectly. He isn't trying to toady or curry favor with the king, but genuinely, with lovely little hand movements to illustrate his points, is giving him a lecture about king and country directly out of Wittenberg University's equivalent of Political Science 101. Spall and Dinsdale remain baffled until they are shuttled off to their unhappy fates in England. Their genial thickness makes a stunning contrast with Hamlet's mercurial cunning and Polonius's arras diplomacy.

Shooting the full text challenged Branagh's inventiveness as a director. He wanted his film to be big and bold and to move even as it honors Shakespeare's language: a tough task, but central to Branagh's project. What is most remarkable about the epic visual ambitions of Branagh's *Hamlet* is that the film does not abandon the actor's fascination with Shakespeare's language and his mad, Frankensteinesque determination to animate the complete text ("It's alive . . . it's alive") in a medium not known for its embrace of "words, words, words." Branagh understood that using the full text was a challenge "that can make you very canny and sharp and imaginative and inventive about how to communicate, how to make Shakespeare understandable, to make it . . . naturalistic and entertaining."[8] For Branagh, Shakespeare's language is not the means to an end, but properly expressed and understood, is the end itself. The intelligent attack on that language, which respects both its rhythms and powers to convey multiple layers of meaning, starts with Branagh himself and extends throughout his cast. The Branagh style, stressing crisp clarity over sweet sonority, is perfectly suited for film, where the big rhetorical rumble is at odds with the medium's naturalism. This approach is immediately recognizable in those actors who have worked with him on previous Shakespeare films—Derek Jacobi, Richard Briers, Michael Maloney, and Brian Blessed—but it is also evident in the work of Shakespearean outsiders from both sides of the Atlantic: Julie Christie, Kate Winslet, Charlton Heston, Robin Williams, and Billy Crystal. Language is essential to Branagh's romance with Shakespeare; it is not simply the launching pad for filmic inspiration and invention.

To release all that language and allow its energy to propel rather than paralyze his film was the ultimate challenge for the filmmaker. Branagh met it by combining in the film five crucial ingredients: landscape, cast, camera, editing, and music. As discussed, shooting in 70mm and selecting Blenheim Palace as the location for the film's exteriors provided Branagh with an epic size and scope to match the full unfolding of the multiple personal, social, and political layers of Shakespeare's text. Also, his casting decisions followed the successful pattern he had established in his film of *Much Ado About Nothing*, where he had mixed and mingled experienced stage Shakespeareans from his Renaissance Company (Thompson, Briers, Blessed) with several established American film stars (Washington, Reeves, Keaton) and a few attractive newcomers (Leonard and Beckinsale). In *Hamlet* he again built his cast around a core group of Renaissance regulars (Jacobi, Briers, Blessed, Maloney, and Farrell) and Hollywood stars (Lemmon, Heston, Williams and Crystal), many of whom had lobbied to be included in a Branagh Shakespeare film. To this group he added three British film actors (Winslet, Spall, and Christie), each of whom came from different film traditions. Winslet was the newcomer working on her second film, Spall was most widely known for his work on television and his appearances in Mike Leigh's largely improvised movies about English middle-class life, and Christie was the star of David Lean's *Doctor Zhivago* and the leading English film actress of the 1960s and 1970s. Christie had not appeared in a major film for fifteen years and had never done Shakespeare before on stage or screen. If some were perhaps overeager to work on a Shakespeare project with Branagh, Christie was reluctant, and Branagh had to exercise much of his charm and passion to convince her to join the cast.

Not only was Christie a great film actress too long absent from a major starring role, but she also brought with her all the associations with David Lean's epics that Branagh was attempting to evoke in his cinematic approach to *Hamlet*. The inclusion of Charlton Heston gave Branagh access to the Hollywood epic tradition reaching back to *Ben-Hur* (1959) and, as an added bonus, memories of Heston's work in Orson Welles's noir thriller *Touch of Evil* (1958).[9] Christie and Heston provided the beauty and the ballast to Branagh's epic intentions. They also provided two of the film's most interesting performances. Christie brings a delicate glow to her queen, creating a version of the character unique among film Gertrudes. She and Jacobi's Claudius make a handsome pair, sharing fine features, polished manners, and star quality. Brian Blessed's old Hamlet—in a series of flashback scenes—seems vulgar and overbearing in contrast. One can imagine Christie's Gertrude feeling liberated from his powerful dominance in her relationship with Jacobi's more gentle and solicitous Claudius. They seem the perfect couple and thus contribute to the duplicitous visual splendor of the world Branagh builds to both contain and baffle Hamlet.

Heston provides a similar surprise by bringing a wonderful gravitas to his Player King. Heston's face and physique are ideally suited for the 70mm format, and his deep, whiskey voice rumbles with authority. Age has lined his face and given his shoulders a slight stoop to soften his chiseled countenance and image. When Heston launches into Aeneas's tale to Dido about Troy, Branagh provides a flashback to Troy's devastation and silent cameo appearances by John Gielgud as Priam and Judi Dench as Hecuba. The film is crammed with such rich moments—this one corresponding to something like the Anglo-American Shakespearean Acting Hall of Fame in action. The great American epic film actor finds himself playing a character in Shakespeare who is evoking a dramatized scene from Virgil's *Aeneid*, a scene that is being acted out in mime by the two most beloved English Shakespearean actors of the twentieth century. And it all passes by and disappears in a flash.

Branagh was typically clever in the way he orchestrated cast and camera. In order to keep the audience's eyes alive and alert as Shakespeare's dense verbal images came flooding forth, Branagh used a series of complicated tracking and dolly shots that allowed him to often shoot several pages of text in a single take. Most often he arranged these shots when working with Shakespeare veterans Farrell, Maloney, Briers, Jacobi, and himself. By contrast, he shot the major moments of the less experienced Shakespeareans such as Christie, Williams, and Crystal with a stationary camera and relied on cutting to flashbacks or reaction shots as a means of sustaining flow and momentum.

For instance, he gave Nick Farrell's Horatio a long tracking shot along the expanse of Blenheim's front facade for his lengthy (fifty-six lines) account of the history of Denmark's relationship with Norway, followed by Horatio's efforts to put the Ghost's appearance into a historical context. He employed a similar strategy for the substantial exchange between Laertes and Ophelia, in 1.3, about Ophelia's relationship with Hamlet. Maloney and Winslet move along the west side of Blenheim with the tracking shot ending up in a rear garden where Hamlet is observing a cadre of young men engaged in fencing practice.

Several indoor dolly shots also deserve comment. As noted, Branagh has become increasingly fond of the liberty of using the steadicam in his films. Unfortunately, a 65mm camera, necessary for 70mm film stock, is too heavy (over ninety pounds) to be mounted on a man's shoulders in the steadicam harness. Alex Thompson, Branagh's cinematographer who worked as a young man as a focus-puller on *Lawrence of Arabia*, had a special dolly built in Italy that would allow him to maneuver the heavy camera in close quarters. Thompson recalled that it was remarkable that they managed to get a good print in just two or three takes on many of the film's extended dolly shots since these shots are tough for both the actors and the technicians.[10] One of the most stunning examples of the use of this technique in the film is the treatment of Claudius's reaction to Hamlet's murder of Polonius. Branagh has such implicit trust in Jacobi as an actor that he builds the scene around his ability to speak and move in one continuous flow of the action. In a single shot, Claudius learns of the murder from Gertrude, leaves his room and crosses the hall to hers, kneels by the pool of blood where Polonius tumbled to the floor, and fingers the small portraits of himself and his brother lying on Gertrude's bed, rises, returns to the hall to send Rosencrantz and Guildenstern to seek Hamlet, and then returns to his room to comfort his distraught wife. All of this action and movement is achieved in the process of shooting two pages of dialogue (forty-six lines of the film script) without a single cut. The camera tracks, pauses, circles, and retraces its path, matching Jacobi's efficiency with its own.

More obviously, Branagh employs a similar film economy in his handling of Hamlet's soliloquies. He films each in one long, unbroken shot, requiring the utmost concentration on the part of the actor and the cinematographer. Film acting is usually an endless series of snippets, tiny bits of dialogue repeated in endless takes, with reaction and point-of-view shots then all being stitched together in the editing process with montage, action sequences, establishing shots, matte shots, and digitalized sequences. Branagh's Shakespeare films require the actor's ability to sustain lengthy stretches of Shakespeare's verse and prose in a single take. For example, in Hamlet's first soliloquy after the great hall has emptied following the king and queen's exit, the camera begins its journey on the right, backs up to the middle of the room as Hamlet steps down from the dias, and continues to pull back slowly, keeping Hamlet in medium-long shot as he releases his anguish at his mother's remarriage. The camera needs to be close enough to capture Hamlet's pain but also distant enough to allow Branagh to give full voice to his anger. The camera follows Branagh down one side of the hall and then pivots so that the speech ends with Hamlet framed by the huge double doors opening into the hall opposite from the throne. Though it might seem natural and logical to provide a cut here, Branagh continues the shot as the doors open for the entrance of Horatio, Marcellus, and Bernardo. The unbroken shot continues as the camera circles the quartet and Hamlet is pulled away from his private anguish and back into the larger political world with Horatio's revelation about the ghost.

The first cut since Branagh launched into "O that this too too solid flesh would melt" now comes when Horatio promises to reveal "this marvel [the ghost] to you" and cues Hamlet to usher the trio into the privacy of his study just off the great hall. The sustained pace of this sequence allows first for the private explosion of Hamlet's repressed bitterness, then for the mercurial shift of his emotions into a lighter mood when he recognizes Horatio, and finally for his amazed reaction to Horatio's report. The absence of cuts here combines with the fluid, circular movement of the camera to create a scene typical of Branagh's way of capturing Shakespeare on film: he risks letting the actors, rather than the director and editor, create the rhythm and intensity of the moment. It is also how Branagh managed to make a four-hour film on a fifteen-million-dollar budget and a three-month shooting schedule.

Branagh makes interesting variations on this pattern in his handling of the three other major soliloquies. Branagh's Shakespeare films are distinguished by bold signature shots, what he calls "anchor images," that help create the tone and atmosphere of his cinematic approach to a particular Shakespearean text.[11] For Branagh, the key anchor image in his *Hamlet* comes in his controversial treatment of the "How all occasions do inform against me" soliloquy, where, as the camera cranes back and up, Hamlet's figure is seen as a tiny black dot trapped against a vast landscape of ice and snow and Fortinbras's army on the march to Poland. But his handling of the other soliloquies also produces a signature image in each. In the first, the image comes in the opening moment in which the camera captures Hamlet alone in close-up on the dais as the confetti celebrating the marriage of Gertrude and Claudius drifts down around him and a few white petals come to rest on his head and shoulders. Branagh watchers will remember the confetti dancing in the air in the famous final festive shot in *Much Ado About Nothing* and realize that Branagh, like Shakespeare, is making a turn from celebrating romance and marriage to uncovering their tragic potential.

In the "O what a rogue and peasant slave" soliloquy, Hamlet delivers his self-dramatizing attack on his own inability to move decisively against Claudius as he struts and frets among a student's treasures: books, masks, a globe, a drum, and a Victorian model theater. Branagh's Hamlet is self-consciously "acting" here—indulging his emotions, rather than concentrating them. What rouses him from complaint to action is spying the model theater that sparks his imagination. The camera follows him as he rises from his defeated slump and moves to the rear of the model for the soliloquy's climax: Branagh bends down so that the camera can catch his face framed in the model (recalling Cranforth's face similarly framed in Madge's model of the church in *A Midwinter's Tale*) as Hamlet dispatches the king, through the trap, to the "other place," upon reaching the lines "The play's the thing / Wherein I'll catch the conscience of the king" (2.2.616–617). The shot of Branagh's face peering out through the rear wall of the model theater becomes a perfect image for Hamlet's absorption with actors and acting and his growing understanding of the relationship between stage and state, drama and power.

The last such anchor image comes from the play's most famous soliloquy and is potentially the most resonant of the quartet. Branagh sets "To be or not to be" in the palace's great room lined with those mirrored doors. The camera follows Hamlet as he enters and moves toward one of the doors, unaware that Claudius and Polonius have hidden themselves behind it and are spying back at him through a two-way mirror. In a deceptively tricky shot, the camera peers over Hamlet's right shoulder, catching his full-length reflection in the mirrored door. As the speech builds, the camera slowly closes in until Hamlet is present in the shot only in reflection, as if trying to discover in that narcissistic "other" some clue to his recent discovery of the disparity between appearance and reality, loyalty and betrayal, deception and integrity. He is interrogating his own complicity in that disparity as well as puzzling out the whips and scorns of time. The image of Hamlet trapped in reflection, literally and figuratively, is the film's most stunning merger of text and technique.[12] The mirrored doors pick up and extend the play's many mirror images, from Ophelia's "glass of fashion" to the "mirror [held] up to nature" that Hamlet places at the heart of the actor's craft and the "glass" into which he intends to transform himself in order to show Gertrude her "innermost part." Hamlet has been pushed from the center to the periphery; suddenly he's on the outside looking in, and from that liminal position he develops a radical skepticism about his world. Branagh's Hamlet is troubled by the way he not only opposes but also reflects Claudius. And though he repeatedly tries to hold the mirror up to Claudius's and Gertrude's natures, it keeps throwing back images more of his own turmoil than of their transgression.

Branagh's handling of Hamlet's last soliloquy reverses the camera pattern used for "To be or not to be." There Hamlet was embedded in the deceiving glitter of Claudius's court, where he was confined and trapped by a demanding father and slippery uncle. Now impasse has given way to expanse as he finds himself in Fortinbras's world, conceived as a cold, snow-covered, rocky terrain resembling that little patch of Poland that Fortinbras is on his way to conquer. In the "To be or not to be" soliloquy, the camera slowly closed in on Hamlet; now in the "How all occasions" speech, the camera starts in close and then gradually cranes back and up, ultimately capturing Hamlet just as a black speck against a vast wilderness as he cries out the soliloquy's last lines: "O, from this time forth / My thoughts be bloody, or be nothing worth!" (4.4.65–66).

This moment is a perfect emblem for one aspect of Branagh's film style: a willingness to risk all on a single flamboyant shot. Too often Branagh's critics respond to the flamboyance without considering the keen intelligence—what Mark Thornton Burnett calls Branagh's "cunning"—behind the hyperbolic excess.[13] Here Branagh gives his Ham-

Hamlet (Kenneth Branagh) confronts Gertrude (Julie Christie) and chastises her for her tainted relationship with Claudius in Branagh's *Hamlet*. [Photographer: Rolf Konow, Courtesy of Photofest]

let a huge screen moment, but the extravagance of the shot is not self-indulgent: it is a searing critique of the character. Hamlet, in the vast expanse of landscape, has been reduced to little more than a tiny black dot making grand but impotent gestures. Branagh's Hamlet comes to resemble Branagh himself in his dual role as actor and director. Branagh sees that in many instances Hamlet is both "in the moment and observing himself."[14] He translates that awareness into his acute analysis of the extravagance of the "My thoughts be bloody" moment: "Here's a man [Hamlet] of grand passions where, in small rooms and with great intensity, his situation and his reaction to it can fill this vast screen and yet in a moment . . . he can see himself as a very small part of a very large picture that is almost overwhelming."[15]

The constant invention of Branagh's camera work is a key element in allowing his film to express so much text without losing its quick pace. Another device that contributes to this momentum is his use of flashbacks and visual inserts of action only narrated in Shakespeare's play. Branagh packs in dozens of these moments, from the early cut to munition manufacturers at work deep into the night to illustrate Marcellus's puzzlement over Denmark's war preparations in the opening sequence, to the appearance, late in the film, of old Yorick himself entertaining the king, queen, and young Hamlet in a cutaway from Hamlet's memory in the graveyard that the jester "hath borne me on his back a thousand times." The two most prominent packages of such flashbacks and cutaways concern Fortinbras's military ambitions and Hamlet and Ophelia's sexual entanglement: one deepens the film's political subtext; the other heightens its romantic backstory.

Fortinbras doesn't appear in the text until 4.4, only speaks twenty-seven lines, and is the character most often cut in film and stage productions of the play. In Branagh's film he is present, through both flashbacks and cutaways, from his first mention by Horatio in the play's opening scene. Branagh never lets us forget that Fortinbras is out there on the move and ready to strike. He's the film's Kaiser Wilhelm looking for any opening to make a military move on Europe even if it means rupturing a family dynasty. Rufus Sewell's hooded, hawk-eyed Fortinbras is crucial to the film's epic scale and to Branagh's understanding that *Hamlet* is about political, as well as personal, destabilization and collapse. Even when the text is silent about Fortinbras, Branagh finds a way to bring him back into the viewer's consciousness. Midway through the film, he includes a shot of Horatio reading a newspaper whose headlines chronicle Fortinbras's advance on Poland, and in the film's final scene Branagh repeatedly cuts away from the Hamlet-Laertes duel to shots of Fortinbras's army charging through Blenheim's snow-covered grounds in an obvious echo of the storming of the Winter Palace in history and film. In the film's final frames those troops do come crashing through the great hall's mirrored doors, emphatically reminding us that the end of the play is a political as well as individual tragedy. As Branagh jokingly remarked about this scene, "I'm making six films at once. This is *Die Hard.*"[16]

The other sequence of important flashbacks centers on the relationship between Hamlet and Ophelia. Again Branagh makes a bold choice. Some productions have subtly suggested that Hamlet and Ophelia are lovers (the intimacy of Nicol Williamson and Marianne Faithful in Tony Richardson's film of the play is one obvious example), but Branagh's film is the only production I have seen, on stage or film, that includes actual moments of their lovemaking. The flashbacks to their nude bodies in bed are sentimental and emotionally innocent. Ophelia has consummated their relationship as a means of consoling Hamlet in his grief over his father's death. The flashbacks occur when she is under parental and political pressure to reveal the nature of her relationship with Hamlet. The film insists that it is Polonius who complicates and corrupts Ophelia's attitude about her involvement with Hamlet and the consequences of their lovemaking. At a crucial moment, when Polonius is embarrassing Ophelia about Hamlet's "tenders" of affection in front of Claudius and Gertrude, the film flashes back to the two of them in bed as though it were Polonius's memory instead of Ophelia's. This has struck some critics, like Bernice Kliman, as an instance of sloppy editing on Branagh's part, but I think the moment works because it reaffirms Polonius's suspicious and salty imagination.[17]

Finally, there is Patrick Doyle's film score. Doyle's work, from *Henry V* on, has been a crucial element of Branagh's films. His score for *Hamlet*, appropriately, is more subdued, somber, and even lyrical than the insistent, often-jagged pounding of the music in *Henry V* or the festive upbeat melodies Doyle provided for *Much Ado About Nothing*. Doyle's score doesn't enter the film until the first appearance of the Ghost, when the music is meant to reinforce the Ghost's size and terrifying impact on Horatio, Marcellus, and Bernardo. Elsewhere, Branagh's pattern is to introduce the score only after a scene or soliloquy is well begun so that the music insinuates itself under the verse after the Shakespearean rhythm has already been established. Not surprisingly, the most obvious use of this technique comes in the "How all occasions" soliloquy where, by its climax, Doyle's score comes close to intentionally overwhelming Hamlet's words. As mentioned in the opening chapter, music, particularly music under dialogue, is rarely employed in stage drama but is an intimate element of film rhetoric.

A standard element for film scores is to compose themes identified with individual characters. Doyle, as in his score for *Henry V*, identifies characters with melodic motifs, which then lend themselves to varied restatement as the tragedy unfolds. Ophelia's theme illustrates Doyle's talent for original uses of classical influences. Her theme is almost a direct quotation from Mahler in its pronounced and repeated resolution of the seventh scale degree downward. Mahlerian too is the theme's progression between the reading of Hamlet's letter scene (where Ophelia is present in the film) and the mad scene, from soulful yearning and naiveté to elegiac mourning, as is the prevalence of horn and woodwind orchestration in these scenes. The Hamlet theme by contrast is small in compass, virtually contained within a fifth; it is short and convoluted, the melodic equivalent to being bounded in a nutshell.

Ultimately, the most fascinating element in Branagh's *Hamlet* is the way in which the film recasts the Freudian family romance, where the relationship between Hamlet and Gertrude is central, into a more robust, but still Freudian, political struggle between father, son, and stepfather.

Branagh's Hamlet is a military prince who more resembles Ophelia's idealized portrait ("the glass of fashion, and the mold of form") than any other Hamlet in recent memory on stage or film. We see his vital self emerge in the warm welcomes he gives to Horatio, Rosencrantz and Guildenstern, and the players. In each instance Branagh's eyes light up and a smile dances about his lips, revealing his genuine delight in old friends come from the wider world to brighten Denmark's prison. The flashbacks to his lovemaking with Ophelia are meant to reinforce the sincerity of his intentions fatally complicated by the news of his father's murder and Ophelia's betrayal in the nunnery scene. Branagh's Hamlet struggles to maintain a stable identity even as his personal and political ambitions are shattered. He never completely surrenders to his internal, psychological chaos. His antic disposition, especially with Polonius, Rosencrantz and Guildenstern, and Claudius, is always "put on." He's rough with Gertrude in the closet scene, but there is no overt sexual tension sparking between them: Branagh's Hamlet is much more intent on lecturing her about her sins than on acting out his repressed Oedipal desires.[18] The full release of his fury comes with the murder of Polonius, the one moment where Branagh's Hamlet loses his self-control as he repeatedly stabs the figure behind the arras. He only regains some measure of composure with the reappearance of Brian Blessed's Ghost to complete the triangle of the ruined family.

In his previous Shakespeare films, Branagh used Blessed to portray aggressive, paternal roles. As Exeter, in *Henry V*, Blessed was the king's burly champion vigorously urging him to invade France. Similarly, Blessed's Antonio in *Much Ado About Nothing* loomed as a protective paternal figure, presiding over the women at the film's opening picnic scene and later eagerly challenging Claudio and Don Pedro after their shaming of Hero.

Branagh conceives of Hamlet's father as a huge, powerful military figure. His giant statue, outside Elsinore's gates, frames the film. In the opening sequence, the ghost seems to emanate from the statue, and in the closing shot the statue is being razed by Fortinbras's troops. Branagh's film makes visually clear and compelling the ways in which Hamlet has mistakenly idealized his father, for Blessed's Old Hamlet bears a much greater resemblance to Hamlet's description of Claudius than that of the dead king. Both as the Ghost and, in several flashbacks, as the former king, Blessed is boisterous and overbearing, wearing a wide lecherous grin, resembling more a braying satyr than the graceful Hyperion of Hamlet's memory. This is a man, after all, who likes to take naps in the snow. Jacobi's brilliant Claudius is by far the more attractive and subtle man.

Branagh is certainly aware that his blonde Hamlet bears an uncanny physical resemblance to Jacobi's Claudius, while it is Rufus Sewell's swarthy Fortinbras who seems more the son of old Hamlet.[19]

Not only does Jacobi's Claudius resemble Branagh's Hamlet in appearance, intelligence, and good manners, but the two also are repeatedly linked in the film through the use of the two-way mirrored door in the "To be or not to be" scene and in the treatment of Claudius's attempt at repentance provoked by *The Mousetrap*. Branagh shot the moment with Claudius seated in the chapel's confessional and with Branagh's Hamlet slipping in on the other side of the screen to play scourge and minister. These two scenes link Hamlet and Claudius at their most vulnerable and reflective moments. Branagh's film makes manifest Hamlet's Oedipal identification with Claudius. Hamlet is trapped between a demonic ghost and a super-subtle stepfather. The ghost is the terrifying father, Claudius the puzzling one. Branagh's film twins and mirrors Claudius and Hamlet. Jacobi's polite, proper Claudius repeatedly gives Hamlet reflection, not difference. Hamlet's hatred of Claudius is deflected back into himself and internalized. Branagh's Hamlet is distinguished not just by his good manners and racing mind but also by a biting anger at himself that never gets released at its true objects—the father who won't stay dead and the stepfather who refuses to carouse—but only at their substitutes: Ophelia and Gertrude.

Branagh, through his conceptions of Ghost and Claudius, reveals his own creative struggle with the anxiety of influence as he engages them not only as actor but also as artist. Blessed, as Branagh's autobiography reveals, is the brassy, imposing friend urging him to risk all by taking on the Shakespeare establishment and to do so by appropriating roles (actor, director, Henry V, Hamlet) historically defined by others, primarily Laurence Olivier. Jacobi, on the other hand, represents that establishment itself: a product of Olivier's legacy as a member of the first company Olivier created at the founding of the National Theatre in 1961 and as the most famous Hamlet of his generation—the one Branagh remembers being thrilled by when he was sixteen. Jacobi also directed Branagh as Hamlet in 1988, played Chorus in his film of *Henry V*, and then played Franklyn Madson, the villain in *Dead Again* who met his fate impaled upon a giant pair of scissors. Branagh's career embodies these cross-currents of cultural and autobiographical forces that are not formally released and resolved until Hamlet sends his rapier whizzing through Jacobi's chest and Fortinbras's army comes crashing into Elsinore, smashing its mirrors and toppling its icons.

Branagh, like all artists, destroys as he creates, and all the rush and energy of his film career comes to a shattering head in his film of *Hamlet*.

In a real sense this film was where he was headed from the moment he left
Reading for RADA, inspired by that teenage train trip to Oxford to see
Jacobi's *Hamlet*. The film is a stunning achievement requiring and revealing all of Branagh's invention, intelligence, and impudence as an actor
and director. There's nothing quite like it in the history of Shakespeare on
film, and yet it was a commercial flop. Audiences were not, it proved,
ready for a four-hour Shakespeare film, at the art house or at the cineplex.
Frankenstein was a critical failure that ultimately found its audience and
turned a handsome profit; *Hamlet* was more generously received by the
critics (more so in America than England) but never found a commercial
audience. I'm sure Branagh would have preferred that their fortunes had
been reversed.

Chapter 9

Love's Labour's Lost

Branagh likes to follow a major film with one less expansive and expensive. Thus *Peter's Friends* brought him back to England and independent financing after making *Dead Again* in Hollywood for Paramount. *A Midwinter's Tale* was similarly a more personal and modest film, largely self-financed, following the big-budget extravaganza of *Mary Shelley's Frankenstein*; and the ninety-five minute *Love's Labour's Lost* was conceived as a short, bittersweet comic Valentine to Shakespeare and Tin Pan Alley after the four-hour excess of Branagh's monumental *Hamlet*.

Hamlet, like Oliver Parker's film of *Othello* released the year before, was financed by Castle Rock, the film and television production unit for Ted Turner's media empire. Its most famous, and hugely profitable, product was *Seinfeld*—the long-running television situation comedy. One of the sweet ironies of the American media business is that *Seinfeld* could end up subsidizing Shakespeare. Castle Rock was one of a number of smaller production companies that sprang up in the 1990s following the success of independent films like Steven Soderbergh's *sex, lies, and videotape* and Branagh's *Henry V*, both released in 1989. By the mid-1990s, Miramax had emerged as the leader of these so-called "independent" distributors buoyed by the critical and commercial success of films like *The Piano* (1993), *Pulp Fiction* (1994), *The English Patient* (1996), *Good Will Hunting* (1997), *In the Bedroom* (2001), and the Academy Award—winners *Shakespeare in Love* (1998) and *Chicago* (2002). It was perhaps inevitable that a match would be made between Branagh and Miramax's founders, Harvey and Bob Weinstein.

In 1997 Branagh signed a three–Shakespeare-picture deal with Miramax that was to include a musical adaptation of *Love's Labour's Lost* set in the 1930s, a version of *As You Like It* set in Japan, and a reimagining of *Macbeth* in modern Manhattan. *Love's Labour's Lost* (2000) is the only picture to emerge from that deal.[1] When *Love's Labour's Lost* became Branagh's second Shakespeare film in a row not to recapture the critical enthusiasm for his *Henry V* or the commercial success of *Much Ado About Nothing*, the Weinsteins determined that the 1990s revival of the Shakespeare film genre had run its course and it was time to withdraw from the field and bury the dead before committing to new Shakespeare projects. Subsequently, Branagh secured funding for his film of *As You Like It* from HBO Films. The picture was shot in April and May of 2005 and will be released in 2006.

Though in cast, scale, and landscape, Branagh's *Love's Labour's Lost* more resembles *Peter's Friends* and *A Midwinter's Tale* than either *Mary Shelley's Frankenstein* or *Hamlet*, the film is, in fact, both daring and ambitious. As Branagh repeatedly has pointed out, he sought to combine one of Shakespeare's least-known comedies (*Love's Labour's Lost* went virtually unperformed on stage for almost two hundred years) with a film genre, the movie musical, that had been moribund for decades.[2] He also insisted on casting actors with little or no experience (with the exception of Nathan Lane) as either singers or dancers on stage or screen. This is another example of Branagh's "let's put on a show" theatrical ethos. His energy and optimism about such ventures seems impervious to their obvious pitfalls, and it is remarkable how often he gets away with it, driven by an unlikely combination of Irish charm, Protestant work ethic, and chutzpah. For *Love's Labour's Lost* he actually gathered his cast together several weeks before shooting began and put them through an intensive workshop in singing, dancing, and verse-speaking. Branagh's desire to be a song-and-dance man reaches back not only to his infatuation with Rooney and Garland and Astaire and Rogers, but to his admiration of Jimmy Cagney as well. Cagney is the film actor Branagh most closely identified with when he was young, and he used Cagney as an alter-ego for the young Irish hero of his first play, *Public Enemy*. Branagh had a small role in George and Ira Gershwin's *Lady, Be Good!* at RADA, where he discovered, "I felt very much the secret song-and-dance man. One *could* be spotted in the chorus, I'd seen *42nd Street*."[3]

The surprising choice of *Love's Labour's Lost* also continued Branagh's pattern of mining his own stage past for film projects. He had played the King of Navarre in a production of the play during his season with The Royal Shakespeare Company in 1984–1985. So *Love's Labour's*

Lost was one of the small group of Shakespeare plays in which Branagh had performed at RADA, The RSC, or with his own Renaissance Company. As with *Henry V, Much Ado About Nothing* and *Hamlet*, Branagh knew the play from the inside. He also knew that the great early twentieth-century English playwright and director Harley Granville-Barker had written one of his most interesting *Prefaces to Shakespeare* about the play, in which he emphasized its reliance on styles and conventions that were "never very far from the actual formalities of song and dance."⁴ Granville-Barker went on to observe that "the actor, in fine, must think of the dialogue in terms of music; of the time and rhythm of it as at one with the sense—in telling him what to do and how to do it, in telling him, indeed, what to be."⁵ Richard David, the editor of the Arden edition of the play, commented, "It is this musical quality, evident in both construction and language, that gives the play its buoyancy, its coherence, and its feeling of release . . . if it is to be likened to opera, it must be to one of Mozart's Italian comedies. . . ."⁶ Branagh's imagination seized on such remarks, and he saw their applicability to a genre much closer to his own experience than Mozart—the American movie musical.

Love's Labour's Lost, like all of Shakespeare's festive comedies, is highly patterned. Shakespeare loves to mingle high and low comic elements in these plays, most often placing the romantic complications of several pairs of aristocratic lovers in relationship to a group of clowns who intentionally or unintentionally parody the aristocrats' behavior. The group experience, rather than the individual, is paramount. Shakespeare's manipulation of the lovers through the confusions of love and romance is like an elegant dance that goes awry when emotional rhythms trump established patterns. The lovers generally collide at several crucial moments with the clowns who, however excessive their eccentricities, tend to prove the steadier traders in the world of romance. Most often, the women, rather than the men, express a knowing sensibility about their emotions that aligns them with the clowns more grounded perspective. *Love's Labour's Lost*, in particular, is a comedy bewitched, bothered. and bewildered by language. The play is full of a young poet's dazzling delight in his own verbal gymnastics. The men indulge their lyrical leaps of fancy; the women display a witty intelligence in testing the men's sincerity; and the clowns, as one young bright wit puts it, "have been at a great feast of languages and stolen the scraps" (5.1.36–37).

Love's Labour's Lost, then, provides Branagh with an appropriate Shakespearean vehicle for his own flights of musical and movie fancy. The play was virtually unknown to the wide potential movie-going audience and thus was ripe for major trimming without howls of protest. As

Granville-Barker and David point out, the play is musical in its structure and in its highly stylized poetic conceits. Branagh had the imagination to see that Shakespeare's lovers break into sonnet as naturally as the romantic leads in movie musicals break into song and that dancing works as an implied metaphor for courtship throughout *Love's Labour's Lost*—from Berowne's opening query to Rosaline, "Did I not dance with you in Brabant once?" to the ultimate refusal of the women to "take hands and dance" to satisfy the men's wooing desires in the play's final scenes. Branagh realized that the play "responds very well to music":

> There are many references to music and dancing in it and the elegance, style, and wit of the play seemed to me to sit well in a context not unlike the Hollywood musicals of the thirties and forties. . . . Writers like Cole Porter, or Irving Berlin or George Gershwin whose lyrics are arguably as witty, in their own way, as Shakespeare was in his time and just as full of conceits and verbal trickery.[7]

Shakespeare's play concerns the desire of the young King of Navarre and three of his companions (Berowne, Dumain, and Longaville) to retreat from the world for three years to devote themselves to the scholarly virtues of study and contemplation and to avoid contact with worldly pleasures, including women. As soon as their communal oath to this edict is taken, they suddenly realize that the Princess of France and her retinue (including her companions Rosaline, Katherine, and Maria) are due to arrive to negotiate a political agreement between her father and Navarre.

The play's comic energy derives from the myriad ways women, love, sport, and wooing games overwhelm the men's resolve to withdraw from the world. Navarre's court is peopled with one of Shakespeare's richest arrays of eccentrics, including a fantastic Spaniard (Don Armado), his pert page (Moth), a clever clown (Costard), a schoolmaster (Holofernes), a curate (Sir Nathaniel), a country wench (Jacquenetta), and the local constable (Dull). Branagh follows his by-now-familiar casting pattern for his Shakespeare films by mixing Renaissance Company regulars (Richard Briers, Jimmy Yuill, Geraldine McEwan, and Timothy Spall) with young American (Natascha McElhone, Alessandro Nivola, Matthew Lillard, and Alicia Silverstone) and British (Emily Mortimer, Adrian Lester, and Carmen Ejogo) stage and film actors. Nivolo was fresh from *Face/Off* (1997), Lillard from *Scream* (1996), McElhone from *The Truman Show* (1998), Lester from *Primary Colors* (1998), Mortimer from *Notting Hill* (1999), and, most famously, Alicia Silverstone from *Clueless* (1995). Branagh, as with his magic mixture in *Much Ado*, again had his eye on the large fifteen- to twenty-five-year-old American movie-going audience. He also continued his practice of using a multiracial as well as multinational cast. Here he includes two Anglo-Africans, Adrian Lester and Carmen Ejogo, as two of the eight young lovers and subtly, as Stanley Kauffmann noted, refuses to pair them off with each other.[8]

Branagh was as ruthless in cutting the text of *Love's Labour's Lost* as he was generous in not pruning a word from *Hamlet*, but the film remains a little miracle of concision. In a mere ninety-five minutes Branagh gives us something like twenty-five percent of the text, all of the play's seventeen speaking characters, and ten song-and-dance numbers. Those routines include Cole Porter's "I Get a Kick Out of You;" Irving Berlin's "No Strings (I'm Fancy Free)," "Cheek to Cheek," "Let's Face the Music and Dance," and "There's No Business Like Show Business;" George and Ira Gershwin's "I've Got a Crush on You" and "They Can't Take That Away From Me;" George Gershwin and Desmond Carter's "I'd Rather Charleston;" and Jerome Kern and Dorothy Fields's "I Won't Dance," and "The Way You Look Tonight." All the songs were written between the late 1920s and mid-1930s except Berlin's "There's No Business Like Show Business," which was included in *Annie Get Your Gun* (1946).

The majority of these songs were originally sung by Fred Astaire either in stage (*Lady, Be Good!*) or movie (*Swing Time*, *Roberta*, *Top Hat*, and *Follow the Fleet*) musicals. Branagh's movie models are the great Astaire–Rogers films of the 1930s and 1940s. Hermes Pan, Astaire's long-time collaborator and choreographer, is the inspiration for almost all of the film's major song-and-dance routines. The two exceptions are the Busby Berkeley treatment of the "No Strings (I'm Fancy Free)" number for the women, which segues from the tents where Navarre has lodged them outside of his Oxbridge Academy to the swimming pool, where we are treated to an Esther Williamsesque water ballet and the hot and sultry version of "Let's Face the Music and Dance" inspired by Gene Kelly's *American in Paris*. Those numbers, along with Timothy Spall's wildly eccentric take on Porter's "I Get a Kick Out of You," are the film's least successful musical routines because they break the Astaire–Rogers–Pan pattern that makes such witty song-and-dance conversation with the Shakespearean material it replaces.

Branagh and Patrick Doyle raid the great popular songs of the 1930s with a keen eye to the ways in which they capture the romantic joy and sentiment released and resisted in *Love's Labour's Lost* once the men abandon their monastic oaths and follow their emotions into the world of romance. For instance, the first time the film breaks out of Shakespeare and into Gershwin comes in the opening scene in the text where Berowne, wisely, resists signing up for Navarre's strict regimen. The song, Gershwin

The Princess of France (Alicia Silverstone), Longaville (Matthew Lillard), Maria (Carmen Ejogo), Dumain (Adrian Lester), Katherine (Emily Mortimer), Berowne (Kenneth Branagh), and Rosaline (Natascha McElhone) provide a fantasy version of Astaire and Rogers in Branagh's flim of *Love's Labour's Lost.*   [Photographer: Laurie Sparham, Courtesy of Photofest]

and Carter's lively "I'd Rather Charleston," captures the exuberant natural energy that Navarre's decree seeks to suppress. The song—originally a duet between Astaire and his sister Adele in *Lady, Be Good!*—is begun in the film by Berowne as a reminder that for healthy young men, the urge to dance surely defeats the vow to study. The song's lyrics make it clear: "In you I never can detect / The slightest sign of intellect / You're mad on dances / Think of the chances / You neglect. / You never seemed inclined / To use your mind. / In fact, it's plain to see / That I'm the brains of this family. / Take a lesson from me." And the king then responds, "I'd rather Charleston." Carter's lyrics and Gershwin's bouncy melody nicely capture Berowne's mocking spirit. He is the smartest of the quartet (an early version of Benedick), and he knows from the start that their project is doomed. They aren't serious scholars or potential priests—they're young gallants or, in the film's terms, "men about town" who all would "rather Charleston" than commit to "barren tasks, too hard to keep, / Not to see ladies, study, fast, not sleep" (1.1.47–48).

The second song likewise makes a perfect fit with the Shakespearean situation. The women have arrived, floating into Navarre by punt. Each woman is associated with a color: red for the Princess, blue for Rosaline, green for Maria, and orange for Katherine. These colors begin as soft pastels and darken into their primary hues as the film progresses. The men are similarly coded, first by the color of their ties and later by the color of the flowers in the lapels of their tuxedos. The men greet the women; the king explains the oath he and his friends have taken and apologizes for not being a better host; negotiations begin. Lines, limits, and boundaries are established, but the men can't resist making inquiries about the women because, of course, each has had at least a brief previous encounter best expressed in Berowne's query to Rosaline: "Did I not dance with you in Brabant once?" Her reply, establishing the wooing pattern, is the exact echo of his question, with Natascha McElhone providing just a slight teasing emphasis to "I" and "you" in her response.

The men can't woo, but they can't resist either. This predicament leads seamlessly into the film's version of Jerome Kern's "I Won't Dance." Again the lyrics, with their Gallic flavor ("You'd be the idol of France with me," "I won't dance, Madame, with you," and "I won't dance, merci beau coup"), clever internal rhymes ("For heaven rest us, I'm not asbestos"), and understanding of the dangers of dance ("I know that music leads the way to romance"), express the compromised desires of the men to uphold their integrity or to lose themselves in love.[9] Kern's wonderfully bold beat mirrors the masculine aggression wrapped up in the "I won't dance" insistence that begins to glide away in the lyric's longer, more yielding lines ("My heart won't let my feet do the things they should do!"). The dance, itself, nicely uses the several steps leading up to the gates of Navarre and features Branagh doing a few Groucho Marx moves as he clowns around the seated Rosaline. As with the "I'd Rather Charleston" number, both songs capture and gently mock the men's predicament: they have set their minds against their hearts and the comedy is generated by the way in which desire eventually sways reason.

The climax of this movement in the play comes in 4.3 when each of the men enters alone, starting with Berowne, to declare his love by reading a sonnet to his mistress. Each is overheard by the others, and all are thus, in turn, comically unmasked. Since they all are now found to be mutually guilty of breaking their initial oaths, they immediately comment to another, "Shall we resolve to woo these girls of France?" Branagh relocates this sequence to the center of his film; sets it in the circular Oxbridge library of Navarre's academy; and uses both George and Ira Gershwin's "I've Got a Crush On You" and Irving Berlin's

"Cheek to Cheek" to replace the sonnets that express the men's romantic fantasies.

"Cheek to Cheek," from *Top Hat* (1935), is the best of the film's dance numbers as it spins gracefully out from Shakespeare's verbal pirouettes on the relationship among love, learning, and the dazzle of a lady's eye. Branagh's Berowne begins his great lecture on love to his smitten pals by tapping out Shakespeare's iambs under its opening lines: "Have at you then, affection's men-at-arms." Berowne circumnavigates the library as Branagh gives full voice to the long speech's insistence that love "adds a precious seeing to the eye; / A lover's eye will stare an eagle blind." When he reaches "And when love speaks, the voice of all the gods / Make heaven drowsy with the harmony" (4.3.341–342), the film glides amusingly from Shakespeare to Irving Berlin as Branagh begins to croon, "Heaven, I'm in heaven / And my heart beats so that I can hardly speak," as he and his fellow lovers lift up and off, twirling into the library's great dome, carried aloft by their giddy wooing spirits. C. L. Barber has written that Berowne's peroration on love "leaps up to ring . . . big bells lightly"—a spirit captured nicely here by Stuart Hopps's choreography.[10]

When the men return to earth, now attired in Fred Astaire's customary white tie and tails, they spill out from the library into the courtyard to be met by their respective Gingers, each woman dressed in a flowing pastel gown, and we are treated to the fantasy heavenly harmony among the four couples we are denied in Shakespeare's play. Each girl is allowed a solo dancing entrance; each male appears at one of the library's doors as first Berowne sings "Dance with me," and then Dumain chimes in on "I want my arms around you," followed by Longaville with "Those charms about you" and finally Navarre with the verse "will carry me through"; and then the four couples are dancing together strung out in a twirling chorus line across the courtyard. Hopps's choreography gives each couple a turn together before reuniting the group of eight as they "seem to find the happiness we seek / When we're out together dancing cheek to cheek." As the sequence finishes, the film cuts back to the men in the library, and we realize that the entire number has been a fantasy as the men now formally resolve to launch a full-scale wooing assault on the women: "For revels, dances, masks, and merry hours, / Forerun fair love, strewing her way with flowers." (4.3.376–377).

The film's other great communal number is its final song: George and Ira Gershwin's "They Can't Take That Away From Me." The ending of *Love's Labour's Lost* presents a challenge to the musical comedy form because, as Berowne observes in lines retained in Branagh's screenplay, "Our wooing doth not end like an old play; / Jack hath not Jill" (5.2.864–

865). Even though *Love's Labour's Lost* is an early comedy, Shakespeare is already defying comic convention. Just as the wooing games are heating up, a messenger (Marcade) arrives with the news that the French king is dead. Death intrudes on romance and abruptly ends the comedy's certain progress to multiple marriages. The women silence the men's festive impulse and test their lovers' sincerity by enforcing a year's period of mourning and denial. The play concludes with a debate, in song, between Spring and Winter and Don Armado's final remark: "The words of Mercury are harsh after the songs of Apollo. You that way, we this way." (5.2.931–932). Not only does the wooing not end like an old play; it doesn't end like a 1930s movie musical either.

Branagh's solution to this structural problem is to raid another, non-musical film romance of the period famed for its wry, bittersweet ending where the exigencies of reality deny the form's conventional happy ending: *Casablanca*. Branagh sets his film in the late 1930s, beginning the opening sequence on September 1, 1939—the day Hitler's army rolled into Poland. This specific historical moment creates, for Branagh, both a motivation for and a critique of Navarre's decision to retreat into the academy. The king and his fellow gentleman songsters off on a library spree are trying to avoid the unavoidable: entanglement with the wider world. In Shakespeare's play that wider world is figured as female and the men come to discover that learning is no match for love. Branagh's film complicates this issue by adding war to women as part of the world's call, and thus it deepens the impact of Shakespeare's refusal to allow his play to end with the conventional happy ending. The arrival of Marcade and his deadly news suspends the wooing. In the film, this moment is transformed into the arrival of the war and the call of the men from one set of arms to another. Branagh appropriates the great final scene from *Casablanca* (1942) as the men bid farewell to their respective Ilsa counterparts at a foggy airport. As the women's airplane disappears into the night, it sky writes, "You that way, we this way."

This moment is the climax of the film's extended farewell sequence dominated by the lovers' rendition of "They Can't Take That Away From Me." The women are in hats and fur stoles, the men in topcoats and Fedoras. The song's stanzas are shared out among the four couples with the lines alternating between male and female voices. Branagh's light tenor sets the tone for the tune's melancholy nostalgia and all eight singers join together for the repeated last line of each refrain: "No, no, they can't take that away from me." Patrick Doyle's orchestration, dominated by violins, flutes, and oboes, creates the haunting atmosphere of lost love Branagh seeks to achieve. And, significantly, we have song without dance. The dancing is over. The elaborate verbal play and flights of wit that distinguish *Love's Labour's Lost*'s fascination with language are realized in the Hollywood musical in song and dance. Who remembers the dialogue (or even plot) from *Top Hat*? Astaire and Rogers communicate in song and make love in dance. Their wit is expressed by the ways their bodies fly together, then separate, then tap together side by side, and then dazzlingly swirl back together again. After the arrival of Marcade, the possibilities of song leading to dance have been foreclosed. "We may never, never meet again / On the bumpy road to love," Ira Gershwin's lyric suggests: memory is all that remains. As the women's plane lifts off and Gershwin's melody swells on the soundtrack, the men are left with a single reality courtesy of Bogart's Rick: we'll always have Navarre. It's an inventive move on Branagh's part and was originally intended, I'm sure, as the film's final image. But it did not remain so.

When the film was first previewed, to an English audience in Wimbledon, Bob and Harvey Weinstein joined Branagh and his production team for the screening. The evening was not a success. The audience was clearly puzzled about how they were intended to respond to Branagh's radical treatment of unfamiliar Shakespeare. Branagh agonized for days before having a "eureka" moment and hitting on the idea of using mock black and white *Movietone* (*Cinetone* in England) news-of-the-week footage to embed the film in the September 1939 moment, to establish a light, even jocular, tone, and to enumerate narrative connections for what remained of the drastically pruned Shakespearean text. There are five of these news-of-the-week sequences and they are employed to bind the film's mixture of Shakespeare and Gershwin et al. while the film remains true to yet another movie convention of the 1930s. Branagh himself narrates these moments in the arch, rapid-fire, rat-a-tat-tat manner of the voice on such newsreels. He is also making a witty glance at Laurence Olivier's narration of the great BBC television series on World War II, *The World at War*, and his own narration of CNN's production of a similar series of programs on the Cold War, both produced by the same man, Jeremy Isaacs.

The first and last of these sequences reinforce the cultural and historical moment that makes sense out of Branagh's reimagining *Love's Labour's Lost* as a 1930s movie musical. H. R. Coursen intelligently outlines the links between Shakespeare's text and Branagh's setting:

> Branagh's interwar instant does not depend on historical parallels bound to
> break down under the most superficial analysis. The thirties . . . were a time
> of fantasy, of Hollywood films flying us down to Rio, or simply opening

the doors in front of our dimes and quarters to art deco luxury in which William Powell and Myrna Loy traded witty comments or in which Fred and Ginger cavorted to captivating songs. . . . It is to this moment Branagh's film takes us. It is a zone that repells any history but its own, but it invites the kind of game-playing that goes on in Shakespeare's play and that was going on in the thirties, in spite of empty smokestacks and dust-filled midlands. As in Shakespeare's play, some of the "happy endings" were deferred, in 1939 because of another Great War. Some of the endings were not happy.[11]

As Coursen's analysis suggests, Branagh, in the film's final extended black and white montage, returns to World War II, where the men have gone to prove themselves worthy in a reality counter to that of love and romance. As Doyle's full orchestration of "They Can't Take That Away From Me" builds on the soundtrack, we are given a mini-version of the war with shots of Navarre, Dumain, and Longaville in combat and Berowne nursing the wounded for the Red Cross. The montage culminates in the reunion of the lovers as part of a wild V-E Day Celebration. One is tempted to assign the feel-good inspiration for this sequence to Harvey Weinstein who, after all, urged Tom Stoppard to have Shakespeare marry Viola de Lessups at the end of *Shakespeare in Love*.

Even though this World War II montage sentimentalizes Shakespeare's less conventional and more abrupt ending, the film's conclusion does pick up on an important strand in Shakespeare's development of the relationship between Berowne and Rosaline. Natascha McElhone is perfectly at home expressing Rosaline's intelligence, and in a few deft exchanges she manages to suggest the essence of the character's tart but generous wit. The screenplay, wisely, retains almost all of her important exchange with Berowne when she sends him off to amuse the speechless sick so that he might learn that a "jest's prosperity lies in the ear / Of him that hears it, never in the tongue / Of him that makes it" (5.2.861–863). Branagh's Berowne, a bit of a 1930s sport with a mustache and sandy lock of hair dangling down over his forehead, instinctively responds, "To move wild laughter in the throat of death / It cannot be, it is impossible: / Mirth cannot move a soul in agony" (5.2.855–857). The film then, in the montage of the war scenes, finds Berowne working in a field hospital, administering to souls in agony. It is an appropriate touch and an act of recuperation for Branagh's film Shakespeare roles, from the untested warrior-king Henry V, to the malignant NCO Iago with his eyes on the General, to a Hamlet condemned to fighting solitary battles against a smooth opponent and a troubled conscience, to the witty

Berowne sent out into the world by the moment and his mistress to test his tongue against rude experience.

The middle three newsreel montages briefly fill us in on the events of King and Court and are used by Branagh to establish the identities of the play's clowns and their relationship (tenuous in the film) to the activities of the aristocrats. Branagh, following his past practice, cast these roles with a mixture of American and English stage and film comics, ranging from Timothy Spall to Nathan Lane. Their characters suffer the greatest compression (and transformation as the schoolmaster-pedant Holofernes becomes the Lady Professor Holofernia and Don Armado's pert page, Moth, is translated from a quick-witted boy into an old dullard). The film creates a flirtation between Richard Brier's curate (Sir Nathaniel) and Geraldine McEwan's Holofernia and gives them a sweetly daft dance version of Jerome Kern's "The Way You Look Tonight" that takes a stab at gently mocking the romantic antics of Berowne and company. Nathan Lane as Costard (a country clown reimagined as a city slicker) is perhaps the most successful of all the American comedians, including Michael Keaton, Robin Williams, and Billy Crystal, to whom Branagh has turned to reinvigorate Shakespeare's clowns. Branagh's film draws its inspiration from vaudeville and Broadway as well as Hollywood. Lane's Costard is part Bert Lahr and part Zero Mostel, and the play's Pageant of the Nine Worthies disappears into a Lane-led version of Irving Berlin's "There's No Business Like Show Business." This routine, which features the entire cast tapping and singing its way into show business history and delight, reminds us that lurking as influences on Branagh are such Broadway musicals adapted from Shakespeare as *The Boys from Syracuse* (1938), *Kiss Me Kate* (1953), and the more recent *Play On!* (1997), which linked Duke Ellington's music with a Harlem version of *Twelfth Night*.

The one element in the film where invention and imagination sag is in the Don Armado subplot. The relationship between Armado and his nimble page (Moth) is transformed from trading "fire-new words" to a series of Curly and Moe slapstick routines. Branagh does give Armado Cole Porter's great "I Get a Kick Out of You" as his big musical number, but he then undercuts the wit of the lyrics by illustrating them in a way that takes the air out of Porter's subversive dare. Armado, played by Spall, pops a champagne cork on "I get no kick from champagne," Moth sneezes away a line of coke on "Some get a kick from cocaine," and both of them buzz through the sky in a bi-plane on "I get no kick in a plane, / Flying too high with some guy in the sky/Is my idea of nothing to do, / Yet I get a kick out of you." Branagh knows better, but, as in the case of Michael Keaton's Dogberry, he remains baffled about how to treat Shakespeare's clowns.

Berowne (Kenneth Branagh), Longaville (Matthew Lillard), the King (Alessandro Nivola), and Dumain (Adrian Lester) await what they mistakenly believe will be the successful conclusion of their wooing games in *Love's Labour's Lost*. [Photographer: Laurie Sparham, Courtesy of Photofest]

Spall is a wonderful actor but his genius is for getting at the gentle every-man in us all (true of his Rosencrantz as well as his Koko in Mike Leigh's *Topsy-Turvey*) rather than for the wild fantastic. He gives his Armado a Dali-esque mustache and an exaggerated Spanish accent, but it doesn't work; neither does singing off-key. Nathan Lane's Costard, pulling a string of colorful silk handkerchiefs (and Jacquenetta's knickers) out of his pocket and wielding a flabby rubber chicken, runs comic circles around him.

What does work is the genuine high spirits Branagh's cast brings to the enterprise, especially Adrian Lester. Lester is perhaps most widely known to American audiences for his role in Mike Nichols's *Primary Colors*, but he was a brilliant Rosalind in Cheek by Jowl's all-male *As You Like It* in 1991 and the definitive Bobby in Sam Mendes's 1995 revival of Stephen Sondheim's *Company*. After *Love's Labour's Lost* he went on to play a vigorous and heartbreaking Hamlet in Peter Brook's production that toured the world in 2001 and Henry V at The Royal National Theatre as the Nicholas Hytner regime began with its successful effort (aided by Branagh's own performance in David Mamet's *Edmund*) to lure a new and younger audience to the South Bank. Lester has a winning light tenor voice, a body that moves to music with ease and grace, and a boyish countenance that lights up the screen. He's the most comfortable member of the group of lovers with the multiple demands Branagh's project makes upon them. It should be noted that Alicia Silverstone, so delicious in *Clueless*, is the least comfortable, especially with the patches of Shakespeare's verse she is required to speak. She just can't get her lips around Shakespeare's language and its rhythms. You can see her literally worrying the lines out rather than enjoying them. In casting Silverstone, Branagh clearly had his eye on her *Clueless* audience but Branagh's film is playing with Shakespeare in a much more stylized manner than did Amy Heckerling's translation of *Emma* into the world of a Southern California valley-girl. And Silverstone didn't bring that teenage audience with her into a world that mixed Shakespeare, the 1930s, and the American movie musical. The film failed to find an audience among the young generation for whom Branagh had become the Shakespeare champion, and it didn't appeal to the segment of the over-fifty crowd who are drawn to more sophisticated independent films and Woody Allen's comic pleasures. What happened?

Branagh knew the film was likely to be a tough sell since it was combining elements largely unfamiliar to the conventional movie-going audience. But there was also initial excitement that the film was just offbeat and clever enough to generate the word-of-mouth buzz that sends some independent films (*In the Bedroom, House of Sand and Fog, Topsy-Turvey, Sideways*) from the art house to the cineplex.

For the young the great songs of the 1930s carried no special resonance. Those songs were alive for me, not only in the Astaire–Rogers films that gave many of them their first expression, but also in the voices of Frank Sinatra, Ella Fitzgerald, Sarah Vaughn, and Tony Bennett. They got Porter and Gershwin and Berlin as deep under my skin as the popular music of my own generation, from Chuck Berry and Ray Charles to the Beatles and the Stones. But Frank and Ella do not sing to my students.

The sophisticated adult audience may have been put off, as Wendy Wasserstein was, by a perception that "all the numbers in [Branagh's] musical *Love's Labour's Lost* are always performed with an arched eyebrow. And when the eyebrow becomes too arched, we can't help but suspend our suspension of disbelief and wonder why anyone's singing to begin with. . . . dancing tongue-in-cheek is hardly as difficult or inspiring as cheek-to-cheek."[12] I understand Wasserstein's response, though if Branagh's eyebrow is arched, it is directed more at his treatment of Shakespeare than Irving Berlin. Except in the song-and-dance routines for the clowns, where parody makes sense, Branagh treats his movie musical material with something bordering on adoration. The problem lies more in the very American nature of the movie musical. Unlike the Western, which has been successfully transplanted to cultures and landscapes as diverse as Italy and Japan, the movie musical is not a genre that travels well. Like the stage musical from which it springs, it is a form that thrives on innocence and energy rather than irony and entropy, which is why Baz Luhrmann's *Moulin Rouge* was so disappointing. The movie musical, far more than Shakespeare, inherently resists the postmodern aesthetic; as a form—except in the hands of Bob Fosse—it refuses cynicism.

Academic critics, such as Ramona Wray and Gayle Holste, while acknowledging that Branagh's film was, in Wray's words, "by far the most radical interpretive gesture of his career,"[13] nevertheless found the film, according to Holste, an "ungainly hybrid."[14] Wray, in particular, is intellectually and politically troubled with Branagh's melding of Shakespeare's aristocratic comedy, song-and-dance routines, and the advent of World War II. She finds the film's juxtaposition of the historical moment with escapist fantasy problematic: "The immediate problem with a movement between external and internal events is that it has the effect of making the protagonists' flight into romance seem self-indulgently irresponsible. As a result of *Love's Labor's Lost*'s uncertain fit between global conflict and romantic retrenchment, such a withdrawal is at least partially politicized."[15] To add physical insult to ideological injury, Branagh's film, for others, fails to deliver in performance as well as conception. Stanley Kauffmann, the dean of American movie critics and a champion of Branagh's Shakespeare films, complains, "Actors who are not singers and dancers are asked to do a great deal of singing and dancing. Some of the singing may have been dubbed, but it is still uncompelling. . . . The dancing is worse."[16] Wray takes Kauffmann's objections several steps further: "The self-consciousness that clusters around Branagh . . . extends into the self-consciousness of the film's singing and dancing technique. Branagh's decision to cast non-trained performers for roles that demanded classical performative skills rides roughshod over a basic musical convention: even if a plot constructs a character as an amateur, he or she is expected to demonstrate superlative qualities of movement and voice."[17] For these critics, the film is as unsteady on its feet as it is unexamined by its ideological assumptions.

Branagh's *Love's Labour's Lost* is his most ambitious attempt to make an ensemble film in the spirit of *Peter's Friends* and *A Midwinter's Tale*. His experiment was typical of his cinematic imagination, which has tried boldly to link Shakespearean material with resonant movie genres. The film is an example of one strain in Branagh's aesthetic: the desire to make a company movie that uses star actors but creates none. Branagh is stretching his powers of synthesis here to their limits and is taking his Shakespearean material as deep into one of Hollywood's past glories as possible. What he ultimately can't satisfactorily accomplish is a successful blend of Shakespeare and Gershwin, England and America, war and romance. Courtney Lehmann thinks his error is to have traded "Derek Jacobi for Fred Astaire, as his actorly body attempts to take on the ultimate illusion of transcendence: Americanization," when he should have settled for trading Jacobi for Jimmy Cagney—the working class Irish-American song and dance man.[18] But there's no room for Cagney among the lovers in *Love's Labour's Lost*. Impish, hard-driving song-and-dance energy works for the style of George M. Cohan but not for Cole Porter and Jerome Kern.

What Branagh's film ultimately runs up against is the particularly American nature, whether led by Cagney, Astaire, or Gene Kelly, of the movie musical. John Updike, noting the European resistance to Hollywood musicals, speculates,

> There [is] something specifically American about these films—a brassy opportunism and a galvanizing work ethic. From the muscularity of the performers to the dizzily wheeling multitudes of choral dancers and swimmers, the atmosphere is cheerfully industrial. The style of the images may be insouciant—*Look, Ma, I'm tap-dancing*—but the message is power, the power released from every man by the emancipation of democracy.[19]

That spirit ties the American movie musical to the period spanning the middle of the century from the 1930s to the 1950s. America lost its innocence in the 1960s, and with that innocence disappeared the movie-musical genre, swallowed by Elvis, rock 'n' roll, and *Hair*. Dennis Potter, in his curious way, with *Pennies from Heaven* (1978) and *The Singing Detective* (1986), Woody Allen with *Everybody Says I Love You* (1996), and Branagh all have attempted to resurrect the form's loony spirit, but the genre and the times resist.[20] Only Baz Luhrmann's *Moulin Rouge* (2001) and Rob Marshall's *Chicago* (2002) have found an audience, and each did so by a triumph of style over substance in vehicles so saturated with cynicism that they preclude successful imitators.

The relationship between Hollywood and Shakespeare that was echoed in certain visual moments in Branagh's films of *Henry V, Much Ado About Nothing*, and *Hamlet* becomes more than a hint or an echo in *Love's Labour's Lost*: it is the creative energy that drives the film, provides its comic pleasures, and dictates its evasions and elisions. I concluded my review of the film in *Shakespeare Bulletin* in 1999 by noting that Branagh "found a teenage audience for his *Much Ado* whose box office helped fuel the resurgence of the Shakespeare film in the last decade; if Branagh's current exercise in movie nostalgia doesn't bring in their parents (and grandparents) his *Love's Labour's Lost* may well sadly signal the end of the revival."[21] Writing now, six years later, my remarks are sadly prescient. After the decade from 1990–2000 that produced roughly twenty Shakespeare films, the first five years of the new century have seen the release of only two new Shakespeare films—Christine Edzard's *The Children's Midsummer Night's Dream* (2001) and Michael Radford's *The Merchant of Venice* (2004).

Love's Labour's Lost also brought a hiatus to Branagh's steady work as a film director. He has continued to appear in films by other directors, including a much-honored performance of Reinhard Heydrich in *Conspiracy* (2001), and he made a heralded return to the stage in performances of Shakespeare's Richard III at Sheffield's Crucible Theatre (2002) and David Mamet's Edmund at London's Royal National Theatre (2003). Opportunities to direct projects not of his own creation arose during the years immediately following *Love's Labour's Lost*, but he turned them down, preferring, as in the pattern of his films, to spend time in more solitary pursuits after a decade dominated by company work.

But in mid-2005, his film-directing career gained renewed momentum. As of 2005, Branagh was in the midst of making his long-planned film of *As You Like It* with a cast that includes Bryce Dallas Howard, Kevin Kline, Alfred Molina, Adrian Lester, Janet McTeer, and Brian Blessed. He has also agreed to direct a film of Mozart's *The Magic Flute* to be set against the background of World War I with a screenplay by Stephen Fry. After a period of less hectic activity in the first years of the new century, it appears that Branagh's career as an actor and filmmaker is poised to return to the productivity and dynamism of his work in the 1990s.

Branagh turned forty-five in December of 2005. If the next twenty years of his career approach the achievements of his first two decades as an actor and filmmaker, he will have created a theatrical and cinematic legacy to rival those of Orson Welles and Laurence Olivier. Branagh not only will have revived but also will have significantly reshaped the Shakespeare film genre at the turn of the twenty-first century and will have become the first British actor to join the Hollywood veterans Eastwood, Redford, Beatty, and Gibson as actor-filmmakers of artistic power and commercial appeal.

INTERVIEW WITH KENNETH BRANAGH

I interviewed Kenneth Branagh for the third time in June of 2005 (previous interviews were in 1993 and 2001). He had just completed the principal shooting for his new film of *As You Like It*, his first since *Love's Labour's Lost*, released in 2000. The film features such Branagh regulars as Richard Briers, Brian Blessed, Richard Clifford, Jimmy Yuill, Gerard Horan, and Adrian Lester along with Kevin Kline, Bryce Dallas Howard, Janet McTeer, and Alfred Molina. Branagh was obviously pleased to be behind the camera again, working with Shakespeare, so we began by getting his fresh response to the five intensive weeks of work that he had just concluded. We then moved on to consider some thematic and technical elements that have come to define his film style over the course of his development as a filmmaker. Because I did not want to cover ground we had already explored in talking about his Shakespeare films in 2001, I have taken the liberty of including several exchanges from that interview here. Those excerpts are indicated by an asterisk (*). That interview was published under the title "Communicating Shakespeare: An Interview with Kenneth Branagh" in the *Shakespeare Bulletin* (Summer 2002).

Crowl: Can you tell me a bit about the *As You Like It* you have just finished shooting?

Branagh: We had a very tight schedule and budget, but we had a great deal of creative freedom. I've been working on this project for a long, long time, and it came together in a very pleasing way. The performances were very rich. I see the first cut of it on Tuesday [June 14, 2005]. As you know, there are always three parts to making a picture: the film you plan, the film you shoot, and the film you edit. So there's a whole new film that starts on Tuesday.

Crowl: Can you talk a bit about your conception and the radical relocation of the play's landscape and setting?

Branagh: The play is often regarded as a bit superficial, without the depth and weight of some of Shakespeare's other comedies. We have tried to explore some of the play's darker elements, particularly the usurpation that sets the plot in motion and is mirrored in the Orlando and Oliver relationship as well. We wanted very much to bring the violence of that into play by beginning with the overthrow, the coup, so as to keep alive as a counterbalance or undercurrent to the play's delightful and charming aspects, the play's sense of danger, the sense of the necessity to get into Arden where Rosalind arrives under the penalty of death. We wanted to keep alive Duke Frederick's threat as well as creating Arden as a magical place, a miraculous place, and to get away from the tradition of presenting Arden as a sylvan glade defined by a giant oak tree.

Crowl: And you have done that by relocating the action to nineteenth-century Japan?

Branagh: Yes. As always it's sort of an impression of Japan. We were trying to get at two ideas within the play: the idea of romantic love and the idea of the simple life, the latter being a pretty current one in our lives. Perhaps it was ever thus but the modern variations of it are, as you know, the retreat from the rat race, the cabin in the woods, people downsizing, moving to the country, living simpler lives. In Japan I always found in my visits there, which began about fifteen years ago, a connection to the landscape that was particularly calming. It is paradoxical because that calm exists right next to the roar, which is the other part of modern urban Japan. There are many examples of these sorts of miraculous places; Kyoto is the obvious example, very much on the tourist trail for obvious reasons, but where there are literally thousands of temples; they might be tiny or massive, but often one finds them through a small door, in a hugely busy street filled with traffic, that opens into a magical space as small as twelve square yards. Three stones, some grass, a water feature, and you are in another world. That tension between the restorative and healing and meditative powers of that quiet contemplative landscape against the roar and traffic of city and court life is caught very well in that culture and works as a very strong dynamic in *As You Like It*. It makes the contrast very sharp and very satisfying.

Also, it gets us away from the traditional Warwickshire greenery and into a visual possibility that is in tune with the kind of symbols of peace and meditation a modern audience might associate with a tranquil landscape.

Crowl: You were exploring a similar tranquil green space and issues of relating to the quiet life in your recent short film, *Listening*.

Branagh: Yes. You're right. Maybe it's time of life [laughs] or whatever. Where does one find peace? In *As You Like It* the forest does offer that, but it's also a forest where there are lions and snakes, where it is sometimes described as a savage place, as a desert place. There are descriptions of Arden in the play that jar against the traditional merry world of "cakes and ale" that so many productions inhabit. So the Japan setting seemed to allow for an Arden that could be dangerous and strange and meditative and weird and we've tried to evoke that. It also allowed us to incorporate the martial arts side of Japanese culture, particularly in Brian Blessed's conception of Duke Frederick as a neo-colonial European interloper. Using the military prowess of Japanese culture also lent a kind of edge to what we were trying to achieve. We were trying to maximize what film can offer by looking at the play through a different kind of prism.

Crowl: Your emphasis on what film can offer in the realization of Shakespeare makes for a nice segue into looking at common elements, interests, and patterns in your career as a filmmaker. Laurence Olivier and Orson Welles between them created the modern Shakespeare film, yet Olivier never became fascinated with film as a medium the way he was with the stage, and once Welles found film, he rarely returned to the theater. You seem to have struck a better balance between film and stage work than either Olivier or Welles. You have found a way to devote your energies as an actor and director to substantial work in both theater and film. As an actor-filmmaker your career strikes me as being closer to the American model defined by Clint Eastwood, Warren Beatty, Woody Allen, and Mel Gibson. What sort of pleasure does film-directing give you that you can't achieve as an actor?

Branagh: Part of it is what I have just described, Sam: a chance to investigate a view of a play or text that is legitimate, that's not a stunt or trick but that you believe comes organically from the text and would be impossible to realize in the theater. It's the overall engagement with the ideas and the thematic strands and working with the actors and the text (however cut and rearranged in the screenplay). To put that together as a filmmaker is the challenge and the reward.

*Crowl: One of the elements that distinguishes your work, and this genera-
            tion of Shakespearean film directors, is that you (collectively) are
            not shy about taking popular—what we call, for lack of a better
            term, "Hollywood"—films as models. One could say your *Henry V*
            follows the war movie genre or your *Much Ado* gathers its energies
            from screwball comedy or that *Hamlet* borrows from the David
            Lean version of the epic film and so forth. Rather than shying away
            from Hollywood as a source, you and your contemporaries—Rich-
            ard Loncraine and Baz Luhrmann, for example—embrace and
            exploit and play with Hollywood genres. Are you self-conscious
            about that?

*Branagh: Um. No. I think it's an honest expression of what has become the
            sum of your influences and, you know, your upbringing. My
            upbringing was not filled with the experiences of live theater but
            was filled with watching films, watching films on television, watch-
            ing television.

*Crowl: But one senses that those films were not those of the great European
            modernist directors like Bergman and Truffaut and Fellini.

*Branagh: Right. The films I watched when growing up were much more con-
            ventional and mainstream.

*Crowl: Hitchcock and . . .

*Branagh: Yes. The films I remember watching early on are things like *The
            Great Escape*, *Chitty Chitty Bang Bang*, and *The Sound of Music*
            [laughs].

*Crowl: But rather than rejecting the popular film as a model when you
            came to maturity as a Shakespearean and film director, you remain
            unembarrassed about finding energy and even inspiration in those
            Hollywood films.

*Branagh: I'm absolutely unembarrassed about that; it's at least as interesting an
            option. I was obviously inspired by the fact that Shakespeare himself
            can legitimately be called a populist. The theater he worked for was
            subject to the rule of the box office, something that is interestingly
            and comically treated in *Shakespeare in Love*. But it's true. And, as
            far as we know, he seemed to be a man who had a commercial

instinct or at least had to listen to how the public voted with its feet: you see in the records of the performances which plays held on in the repertory, and you see him trying to find some way through that. He was aware of, though I think not controlled by, what the public wanted and what the public were interested in; when it comes to making films of his work, one has to be aware of the same thing.

And, I'm sure we have spoken about this before, you can give yourself freedom by knowing that you probably won't come up with anything truly original, but perhaps it will smack of originality in the context of the times, and you won't be destroying the plays. Shakespeare, the sacrosanct literary genius that strides the narrow world like a colossus, ain't going to be hurt or affected by the small irritating buzz-fly of a not fully successful film. My feeling has always been that even when there is a passionate debate, perhaps hostility, about the treatment in the films, it becomes a helpful and creative thing. People declare themselves; they argue about how a treatment of a character or scene is contrary to the way it should be presented or played. That indicates that the plays are alive and that they are doing what they are supposed to do: provoke thought and response.

Crowl: One of the key elements in your film work, both in theory and practice, is sustaining the idea and the reality of community. You like to work with a core group of actors and a core creative team. You create, in the film experience, something like the famous notion of the theatrical family you treat so lovingly and humorously in *A Midwinter's Tale*.

Branagh: Well that's certainly where some of the parallels you mentioned with Eastwood and Woody Allen come into play. Allen has made almost as many films as Shakespeare wrote plays, and across many of those films, you find him working again and again with a core group of actors. Eastwood does something similar with Morgan Freeman and Gene Hackman. It was interesting to me that on this last film there was a real atmosphere of creative harmony, a mixture of discipline and lunacy, embodied by this group, which is neither cozy nor conflicted but simply rolls up its collective sleeves and gets to work on the thing.

Crowl: I can imagine. After all, you had Blessed back working with you on this one.

Branagh: [laughs] Very, very much so and being very surprising and brilliant actually. He plays both Dukes and in both cases gives remarkable performances. I think that's an area of the play that will be revealed in this film in a very rewarding way. The creative spirit of the people working on this film was really wonderful and much remarked upon by those who were working with all of us for the first time. I think they have produced something special.

Crowl: I was pleased to see that you and Kevin Kline were finally working together (after two previous films together) on a Shakespeare project.

Branagh: He was a natural for us. He gives a spectacular performance as Jaques. He commented on the same thing. It was a sense of the unusual nature of the strange cinematic ensemble where the cast, across a range of roles, showed their development over the several Shakespeare films they have made with me. Richard Clifford is in the film; Richard Briers steals the film as old Adam. Small part, Shakespeare's old role, but Richard seems to want to walk away with the picture. Adrian Lester is a minor revelation as Oliver.

Crowl: Yes. He was one of the best things in your *Love's Labour's Lost*. And now he gets to play one of the heavies.

Branagh: Yes but in both cases, Frederick and Oliver, the film opens up possibilities in the text to chart their rocky road to the final reclamation of their better selves. These actors are now very practiced at the art of working with Shakespeare on film. Their abilities have developed and matured over several films, which is what allows us to work on such a tight budget and shooting schedule and still achieve what I hope are excellent results.

*Crowl: An element in your films that is universally remarked upon is their attention to language. You have an ability to communicate Shakespeare and his language to this generation. It's not just the language itself, but the language's relationship to the camera. What did you learn in making *Hamlet*, for instance, about what you had to do with the camera to allow all that language to live and breathe without the film becoming static and dull?

*Branagh: Well, there's an attempt to create some kind of marriage—given that you are retaining that amount of text—between language and image, and you have a number of choices. The people with the primary responsibility for making that marriage come alive for the audience are the actors. Harnessing the actors' energy in an exciting way is one of the first things to examine, so that the film is not just about photographing people talking. For example, having rehearsed a scene with several characters, you come to feel as though the playing energy, the electricity between them as provided by the scene and by the performance, is something special, and that a long uninterrupted shot is best. The camera can then feed off their energy and glide with it, or it may move jerkily or smoothly, to capture the unique ability of those actors to maintain a tension in a long scene in a way that the camera can feel and that the audience can vicariously enjoy.

Thus, for me as a director, rehearsal becomes very important because it tells me how to move the camera. It's as if in rehearsal you begin to feel and hear the music and the rhythm of the play as it is expressed by this group of actors. And that tells you a little bit about how to cut it or how you feel it should be cut, whether you stage long scenes or short scenes, and then, as you investigate that, you attempt to bring in some other elements in this strange sort of marriage. It may mean that the material acknowledges, as it moves from the theater to film, that the film audience expects other kinds of experiences. The director with the camera becomes some sort of interloper. For instance, in *Hamlet*, the flashback sequences explain, in a way that isn't entirely reliant on the actors but uses instead the visual medium to illustrate in a non-patronizing way, what you think Shakespeare is trying to do in a way that supports an ongoing moment-to-moment excitement.

*Crowl: It's obvious that you don't storyboard. You haven't shot the film in your mind before you get to rehearsals. You establish a landscape and setting for the film, but then you allow what you are doing as a director with the camera to emerge from the chemistry that develops in rehearsal between and among the actors, right?

*Branagh: Yes. The dynamics in the rehearsal have an enormous input. The actors' work on character is crucial. You may debate with them about things they have decided upon for the character, but on the whole I think it is an honest process. My policy is to communicate with the actors—full disclosure! I hope and believe that I carry that through. But, in addition to harnessing the actors' work, to using the cinema to express and illustrate in different ways your approach to the material, and to having settled, as you say, on some form of setting, landscape, and world in which the piece is set, there are key images, anchor images that I have in mind before the filming begins. These images . . . would be images like Henry's walk carrying the dead boy after the battle of Agincourt; Hamlet on the plain watching Fortinbras march against Poland . . .

*Crowl: [Laughing] Hey, you're stealing my ideas about your work here.

*Branagh: [With a chuckle] No. Well, yes. It's true. The opening overture, if you like, from *Much Ado*, the end sequence [the "They Can't Take That Away From Me" number] from *Love's Labour's Lost* as it moves through the war, and the staging earlier of Berowne's big speech in the library. There are a number of these key images I share with the actors in advance. I like to offer those up in order to see if (a) there's agreement, or (b) if there's a better idea. So in a way you come with a plan, some sort of route map, before rehearsals . . . All of that goes into the mix. You hope that in advance you have created a world in which you know there will be enough visual interest, visual excitement for the audience, but one in which the contribution of the actor has free play for as late in the process as possible.

Crowl: You have created a substantial group of British and American actors who have developed a style for delivering Shakespeare's language on film in a manner that doesn't seem to be at odds with the medium.

Branagh: I think what you say is true. In the course of shooting the new film, a number of people got to see bits of the "dailies," and the almost universal response was how natural the language seemed; the issue of language simply didn't exist. They felt that the cast spoke the language—of course much of the play is in prose—in an entirely effortless way. The actors, as they say in sport, had taken it to a different level.

Crowl: Speaking of taking something to a different level—in revisiting your eight feature films, I was struck again by the importance of the film score in each. They range from the neo-operatic scores Patrick Doyle composed for films like *Dead Again* and *Hamlet* to the 1930s Berlin and Porter classics for *Love's Labour's Lost* to the driving pop songs used in *Peter's Friends*. It is obvious that music is an absolutely important feature in your film style. Where does that interest in music and understanding of its importance in film come from?

Branagh: Well, one's Irish background is crucial. From an early age you are conscious of the importance of music in family gatherings. The atmospheric impact of music—even the unaccompanied voice or single instrument—evokes a mood.

Crowl: Music as integral to the Irish landscape.

Branagh: Yes. Music as drama was ever present in the landscape I grew up in. Whether it was the drama of a single voice at a funeral or at a family gathering or celebration, everyone seemed to have a skill with it—my mother singing her old favorite "Marguerite" or my Uncle Jim singing "Take Me Home Again, Cathleen." All sung at slightly tipsy family gatherings. But all sung with tremendous pace and mood. I think that's where it all started from. I have always enjoyed playing music when I could. When I was fifteen or sixteen, I started playing the guitar a bit, and I find playing it particularly engrossing in my life now. Playing the piano and singing has always been a part of my life and it seems such a natural element in my approach to something like Shakespeare where there's magic in the web of it anyway; there's a poetry in the weave of it that just calls out for a particular kind of rhythm, pace, orchestration, color, mood, atmosphere that is implicitly musical. I find that in directing a scene or doing a speech that you hear it in those terms and begin to look at the language itself musically, looking at the punctuation musically. One often describes it to actors in terms of rhythm, and when all else fails and you run out of adjectives, you find yourself literally tapping it out.

Crowl: As indeed you did yourself when launching into Berowne's big speech: "Have at you, then, affection's men-at-arms!" in *Love's Labour's Lost*.

Branagh: Yes. Now that was a fun thing to do. Someone once said to me, "Now what is iambic pentameter?" and I said, "Watch that little bit in *Love's Labour's Lost* and it will show you in a very simple way what it is."

Crowl: Following on with the musical theme, I understand that your next film will be one of Mozart's great operas, *The Magic Flute*.

Branagh: Yes it will. I had no plans to do so, but I was approached by a man named Sir Peter Moores, who is a patron of the Arts in this country. He has underwritten the making of compact discs of the great operas sung in English in a desire to make them more widely known. He decided that the next step in reaching a wider audience was to make films of operas. His foundation approached me, among others, to prepare a screen treatment of the opera. Needless to say, I had never seen *The Magic Flute* and had only heard some of the famous bits. I had only seen a couple of operas and had not felt that the form spoke to me. The music was often sublime, but I was not gripped by the storytelling. When the offer to prepare a treatment came along, I began to listen with some care to *The Magic Flute* and became, you know, something like the nine millionth person to be charmed by its spell, and it was a great joy. We have cast it and will record the music in September and start shooting the film in January of 2006.

Crowl: I want to turn now and talk about your camera style. One of your signatures as a film director is the use of active, aggressive, romantic camera movements. You like to use the steadicam and the crane and to devise complicated shots that involve the concentrated efforts of cast and crew. One of the most interesting, yet little noted, is the opening shot of *Peter's Friends*. Do you remember how many takes you had to do to get a version that worked?

Branagh: My guess is that we had to do it fifteen or sixteen times. My experience is that when you decide to do something extravagant like that, there is ever only one take that you can use. You only need one, of course, but you rarely have any choice about which one to use. Of course, you can always chop several of them up to get what you want.

Crowl: But that spoils the whole point of the shot.

Branagh: Exactly right. For your interest, the end shot on *Much Ado* we did about seventeen or eighteen takes, and I think take thirteen was the one we actually used. We had a couple of interesting ones on this last film, when you see it. One was in that challenging scene with Phebe and Silvius and Rosalind and Orlando that becomes, as they all repeatedly declare their affections for one another, as Rosalind quips, "Like the howling of Irish wolves against the moon." There's a complicated steadicam shot in there that took us seventeen takes.

Crowl: Another Branagh camera pattern is the swirling circle shot. This pattern is most pronounced in *Mary Shelly's Frankenstein*, where it first appears as a family waltz and is later recapitulated in Victor Frankenstein's slippery attempt to get Robert DeNiro's Creature on its feet and moving. What appeals to you about such shots?

Branagh: Dancing is in Shelley's novel and dancing seemed to go with the look of that historical period and those romantics. There seemed to be a chance within this gothic framework to see the attraction of dancing for the children morph into the romance of the dancing between Victor and . . . and . . . Christ, Sam, I can't remember her name.

Crowl: Elizabeth. It was a long time ago.

Branagh: Elizabeth. And then the touching contact for the Creature—that dancing might involve morphing again into the intense parody of all that by the time we reach the end. The swirl of the dancing was also meant to capture the turmoil of Victor's brain and the breathless nature of the story. And it was partly literally attempting to sweep the characters and the audience off their feet not only with the story but with the giddy and intoxicating ideas that are behind it. Dancing was at the heart of the period's charm and also its grotesque perversions and the sets, that huge ballroom and staircase, were designed to try and exploit that—a kind of gothic squiggle of curlicues and revolutions. It got picked up in the science as well as Victor's labs featured instruments and experiments that whirled about. Movement, energy, gyrations: the sense of the world as a kind of engine was a key image I was trying to capture.

Crowl: You also used several circle shots in your film of *Hamlet*, though with a less frenetic pace. Alex Thompson told me you had a special dolly built in Italy that could hold that heavy 65mm camera and also allow you to move it very fluidly. I also understand that you actually shot several moments of ballroom dancing for that film which ended up on the cutting room floor.

Branagh: That's right. As you probably know, the DVD of *Hamlet* is finally going to come out—the full-length version—next August. Warner Brothers have finally agreed to its release and it will come out in a two-disc edition. They are planning a whole series of special features—and we are certainly trying to help them—and I hope that cut footage of the dancing is included. I was very pleased with that sequence, as you can imagine the effect of the dancing inside that room with the mirrored walls. It was rather irresistible to someone like me [smiles and chuckles].

Crowl: Pure Branagh.

Branagh: We did use a special dolly. I didn't want to use a steadicam. I wanted all the fluid movement you refer to but with a sense of weight to it. And without the float, which is the giveaway in the world of the steadicam. I wanted to get a sense of that palace as vast—that it would go on and on with secret door after secret door and that the audience was being invited to track through it. The movement was meant to introduce the audience to a world of surprise, like the opening shot in *Peter's Friends*, and an ever-unfurling story. I was trying, in those fluid movements, to get away from the contrivance and artificiality of cut . . . cut . . . cut. There's a sense of magic and wonder, I think, that develops from those endless takes that I find very attractive.

Crowl: Those endless takes are a way to combine the power of the actor with that of the director and crew. Sequences are allowed to unfold driven as much by the actor's craft as by the film editor's.

Branagh: Sure. And we certainly have some examples of that on *As You Like It*. We do have several long steadicam shots that involve a dance between actors and equipment and crew and location and landscape. When you film such shots, they involve enormous planning; they are attended by nerves and a sense of high but helpful creative tension. They are communal in requiring the utmost concentration by everyone working on the film and everyone's thrilled when they work. When you are going to sweep the camera 360 degrees, where are you going to put the crew?

Crowl: Yes . . . like the great shadow shot in *Dead Again* when Margaret Strauss is being murdered. You had crew everywhere I understand, even under the bed.

Branagh: Oh yes. It seemed like the entire lot at Paramount was helping us with that one. Those shots do give me enormous satisfaction, but the bottom line is that you still have to feel, even if only by instinct, that such shots serve the story well or are inspired by some element in the story you are trying to capture on film.

Crowl: Ken, thanks again for being so generous with your time and your ideas. I look forward to both your *As You Like It* and *Magic Flute*. It's good to have you back behind the camera again.

Branagh: Thanks, mate. Good talking to you again.

Kenneth Branagh Filmography

FEATURE FILMS

Henry V: 1989. 138 minutes. Renaissance Film Company, Ltd. Color. 35 mm. Produced by Stephen Evans and Bruce Sharman. Directed by Kenneth Branagh. Screenplay by Kenneth Branagh. Cinematography by Kenneth Mac-Millan. Music by Patrick Doyle. Design by Tim Harvey. Costumes by Phyllis Dalton. Edited by Michael Bradsell. Cast: Kenneth Branagh (Henry V), Robbie Coltrane (Falstaff), Emma Thompson (Katherine), Judi Dench (Mistress Quickly), Brian Blessed (Exeter), Derek Jacobi (Chorus), Robert Stephens (Pistol), Ian Holm (Fluellen), Richard Briers (Bardolph), Simon Shepherd (Gloucester), James Larkin (Bedford), Paul Gregory (Westmoreland), Geoffrey Hutchings (Nym), Charles Kay (Canterbury), Alec McCowen (Ely), Michael Williams (Williams), John Sessions (MacMorris), Paul Scofield (Charles VI), Jimmy Yuill (Jamy), James Simmons (York), Pat Doyle (Court), Michael Maloney (Dauphin), Shaun Pendergast (Bates), Harold Innocent (Burgundy), Daniel Webb (Gower), Richard Clifford (Orleans), Richard Easton (Constable), Edward Jewesbury (Erpingham), Geraldine McEwan (Alice), Christopher Ravenscroft (Mountjoy), Christian Bale (Falstaff's Page).

Dead Again: 1991. 108 minutes. Paramount Pictures. Color and black and white. 35 mm. Produced by Lindsay Doran and Charles Maguire. Directed by Kenneth Branagh. Screenplay by Scott Frank. Cinematography by Matthew Leonetti. Music by Patrick Doyle. Design by Tim Harvey. Costumes by Phyllis Dalton. Edited by Peter Berger. Cast: Kenneth Branagh (Roman Strauss/Mike Church), Emma Thompson (Margaret Strauss/Grace/Amanda Sharp), Derek Jacobi (Franklyn Madson), Andy Garcia (Gray Baker), Hanna

Schygulla (Inga), Wayne Knight (Pete), Robin Williams (Cosy Carlisle), Campbell Scott (Doug), Richard Easton (Father Timothy), Patrick Doyle (Policeman), Erik Kilpatrick (Policeman), Jo Anderson (Sister Madeleine), Vasek E. Simek (Otto), Gregor Hesse (Frankie).

Peter's Friends: 1992. 97 minutes. Renaissance Films in association with the Samuel Goldwyn Company. Color. 35 mm. Produced by Kenneth Branagh, Stephen Evans, and David Parfitt. Directed by Kenneth Branagh. Screenplay by Rita Rudner and Martin Bergman. Cinematography by Roger Lanser. Music coordinated by Gavin Greenaway. Designed by Tim Harvey. Costumes by Susan Coates and Stephanie Collie. Edited by Andrew Marcus. Cast: Kenneth Branagh (Andrew), Emma Thompson (Maggie), Hugh Laurie (Roger), Imelda Staunton (Mary), Stephen Fry (Peter), Alphonsia Emmanuel (Sarah), Rita Rudner (Carol), Tony Slattery (Brian), Phyllida Law (Vera), Alex Lowe (Paul), Richard Briers (Peter's Father), Edward Jewesbury (Solicitor), Hetta Charnley (Woman at Airport), Annie Davies (Babysitter), Chris Pickles (Chauffer), Nicki Wright (Brian's Wife), Ben Parfitt (Ben).

Much Ado About Nothing: 1993. 111 minutes. Color. 35 mm. Renaissance Films in association with the Samuel Goldwyn Company. Produced by Kenneth Branagh, Stephen Evans, and David Parfitt. Directed by Kenneth Branagh. Screenplay by Kenneth Branagh. Cinematography by Roger Lanser. Music by Patrick Doyle. Design by Tim Harvey. Costumes by Phyllis Dalton. Art Direction by Martin Childs. Edited by Andrew Marcus. Cast: Kenneth Branagh (Benedick), Emma Thompson (Beatrice), Denzel Washington (Don Pedro), Keanu Reeves (Don John), Robert Sean Leonard (Claudio), Kate Beckinsale (Hero), Imelda Staunton (Margaret), Phyllida Law (Ursula), Gerard Horan (Borachio), Richard Clifford (Conrade), Richard Briers (Leonato), Brian Blessed (Antonio), Michael Keaton (Dogberry), Jimmy Yuill (Friar Francis), Ben Elton (Verges), Teddy Jewesbury (Sexton), Andy Hockley (George Seacole), Chris Barnes (Francis Seacole), Conrad Nelson (Hugh Oatcake), Alex Scott (Boy), Alex Lowe (Messenger).

Mary Shelley's Frankenstein: 1994. 128 minutes. Color. 35 mm. Zoetrope Productions. Produced by Francis Ford Coppola, James Hart, and John Veitch. Directed by Kenneth Branagh. Screenplay by Steph Lady and Frank Darabont. Cinematography by Roger Pratt. Music by Patrick Doyle. Design by Tim Harvey. Costumes by James Acheson. Edited by Andrew Marcus. Cast: Kenneth Branagh (Victor), Robert DeNiro (Creature), Tom Hulce (Henry), Helena Bonham Carter (Elizabeth), Aidan Quinn (Walton), Ian Holm (Victor's father), John Cleese (Professor Waldman), Cherie Lunghie (Victor's Mother), Richard Briers (Grandfather), Trevyn McDowell (Justine), Robert Hardy (Professor Krempe), Celia Imrie (Mrs. Moritz), Gerard Horan (Claude), Mark Hadfield (Felix), Richard Clifford (Farmer), Richard Bonneville (Schiller), Jimmy Yuill

(Second Mate), Joanna Roth (Marie), Sasha Hanau (Maggie), Joseph England (Thomas).

A Midwinter's Tale (*In The Bleak Midwinter*): 1995. 97 minutes. Sony Pictures Classics. Black and white. 35 mm. Produced by David Barron. Directed by Kenneth Branagh. Screenplay by Kenneth Branagh. Cinematography by Roger Lanser. Music by Jimmy Yuill. Design by Caroline Harris. Cast: Richard Briers (Henry Wakefield), Hetta Charnley (Molly), Joan Collins (Margaretta D'Arcy), Nicholas Farrell (Tom Newman), Mark Hadfield (Vernon Spatch), Gerard Horan (Carnforth), Celia Imrie (Fadge), Michael Maloney (Joe Harper), Jennifer Saunders (Nancy Crawford), Julia Sawalha (Nina Raymond), John Sessions (Terry Du Bois), Ann Davies (Mrs. Branch), James D. White (Tim), Robert Hines (Mortimer), Allie Byrne (Tap Dancer), Adrian Scarborough (Young Actor), Brian Petifer (Ventriloquist), Patrick Doyle (Scotsman), Shaun Pendergast (Mule Train Man), Carol Starks (Audience Member), Edward Jewesbury (Nina's Father), Katy Carmichael (Mad Puppet Woman).

Hamlet: 1996. 238 minutes. Castle Rock Entertainment Production. Color. 70 mm. Produced by David Barron. Directed by Kenneth Branagh. Screenplay by Kenneth Branagh. Cinematography by Alex Thompson. Music by Patrick Doyle. Design by Tim Harvey. Costumes by Alex Byrne. Edited by Neil Farrell. Cast: Richard Attenborough (English Ambassador), Brian Blessed (Ghost), Kenneth Branagh (Hamlet), Richard Briers (Polonius), Julie Christie (Gertrude), Billy Crystal (First Gravedigger), Judi Dench (Hecuba), Gerard Depardieu (Reynaldo), Reece Dinsdale (Guildenstern), Nicholas Farrell (Horatio), John Gielgud (Priam), Rosemary Harris (Player Queen), Charlton Heston (Player King), Derek Jacobi (Claudius), Jack Lemmon (Marcellus), Michael Maloney (Laertes), John Mills (Old Norway), Simon Russell Beale (Second Gravedigger), Rufus Sewell (Fortinbras), Timothy Spall (Rosencrantz), Robin Williams (Osric), Kate Winslet (Ophelia).

Love's Labour's Lost: 2000. 95 minutes. A Shakespeare Film Company Production. Color. 35 mm. Produced by David Barron and Kenneth Branagh. Directed by Kenneth Branagh. Screenplay by Kenneth Branagh. Cinematography by Alex Thompson. Music by Patrick Doyle. Design by Tim Harvey. Costumes by Anna Buruma. Edited by Neil Farrell and Dan Farrell. Cast: Kenneth Branagh (Berowne), Richard Briers (Sir Nathaniel), Richard Clifford (Boyet), Carmen Ejogo (Maria), Daniel Hill (Mercade), Nathan Lane (Costard), Adrian Lester (Dumain), Matthew Lillard (Longaville), Natascha McElhone (Rosaline), Geraldine McEwan (Holofernia), Emily Mortimer (Katherine), Alessandro Nivola (King), Anthony O'Donnell (Moth), Stefania Rocca (Jaquenetta), Alicia Silverstone (Princess), Timothy Spall (Don Armado), and Jimmy Yuill (Dull).

SHORT SUBJECTS

Swan Song: 1992. 23 minutes. Samuel Goldwyn Films. Color. 35 mm. Produced by David Barron. Directed by Kenneth Branagh. Screenplay (based on a short story by Anton Chekhov) by Hugh Cruttwell. Cinematography by Roger Lanser. Music by Jimmy Yuill. Design by Tim Harvey. Costumes by Susan Coates and Stephanie Collie. Edited by Andrew Marcus. Cast: John Gielgud (Svetlovidov), Richard Briers (Nikita).

Listening: 2003. 23 minutes. Blackfriars Production. Color. 35 mm. Produced by David Barron and Malory Moseley. Directed by Kenneth Branagh. Screenplay by Kenneth Branagh. Cinematography by Alex Thompson. Design by Tim Harvey. Costumes by Susan Coates. Edited by Neil Farrell. Cast: Frances Barber (Woman), Paul McGann (Man).

A Chronology of Kenneth Branagh's Work as an Actor, Writer, and Director on Film, Stage, and Television

1982   *Another Country* (stage: actor)
        A Play for Tomorrow: Easter 2016 (television: actor)
        Too Late to Talk to Billy (television: actor)

1983   *The Madness* (stage: actor)
        Francis (stage: actor)
        A Matter of Choice for Billy (television: actor)
        To the Lighthouse (television: actor)

1984   *Henry V* (stage: actor)
        Hamlet (stage: actor)
        Love's Labour's Lost (stage: actor)
        Golden Girls (stage: actor)
        The Boy in the Bush (television: actor)

1985   *Tell Me Honestly* (stage: writer and director)
        Coming Through (television: actor)

1986   *Romeo and Juliet* (stage: actor and director)
        Ghosts (television: actor)

1987   *A Month in the Country* (film: actor)
        High Season (film: actor)
        Public Enemy (stage: writer and actor)

John Sessions: The Life of Napoleon (stage: director)
Twelfth Night (stage: director)
Strange Interlude (television: actor)
The Lady's Not for Burning (television: actor)
Fortunes of War (television: actor)

1988   *Much Ado About Nothing* (stage: actor)
       As You Like It (stage: actor)
       Hamlet (stage: actor)
       Discovering Hamlet (television: actor)
       Thompson (television series: several appearances as actor)

1989   *Henry V* (film: actor, writer, and director)
       Look Back in Anger (stage and television: actor)

1990   *King Lear* (stage: actor and director)
       A Midsummer Night's Dream (stage: actor and director)

1991   *Dead Again* (film: actor and director)
       Uncle Vanya (stage: director)
       Symphony for the Spire (television: actor)

1992   *Swan Song* (film: director)
       Peter's Friends (film: actor and director)
       Coriolanus (stage: actor)
       Hamlet (stage: actor)
       Tales of Gold (television: narrator)

1993   *Much Ado About Nothing* (film: actor, writer, and director)
       Swing Kids (film: actor)

1994   *Mary Shelley's Frankenstein* (film: actor and director)

1995   *Othello* (film: actor)
       Anne Frank Remembered (television: narrator)
       Shadow of a Gunman (television: actor)

1996   *Looking for Richard* (film: actor)
       Hamlet (film: actor, writer, and director)
       Cinema Europe: The Other Hollywood (television: narrator)

1997

1998   *The Proposition* (film: actor)
       The Gingerbread Man (film: actor)
       The Theory of Flight (film: actor)
       Celebrity (film: actor)
       The Cold War (television: narrator)
       The Dance of Shiva (television: actor)
       Universal Horror (television: narrator)

1999   *Wild Wild West* (film: actor)
       Walking with Dinosaurs (television: narrator)

2000   *Love's Labour's Lost* (film: actor, writer, and director)
       El Dorado (animated film: voice)
       How to Kill Your Neighbor's Dog (film: actor)

2001   *The Play What I Wrote* (stage: director)
       Conspiracy (television: actor)

2002   *Harry Potter and the Chamber of Secrets* (film: actor)
       Rabbit Proof Fence (film: actor)
       Richard III (stage: actor)
       Shackleton (television: actor)

2003   *Listening* (film: writer and director)
       Edmund (stage: actor)

2004

2005   *Five Children and It* (film: actor)
       Warm Springs (television: actor)

2006   *As You Like It* (film: actor, writer, and director)

Notes

CHAPTER 1

1. Kenneth Branagh, *Beginning* (London: Chatto & Windus, 1989), p. 23.

2. *A Midwinter's Tale* was originally entitled *In the Bleak Midwinter*. The film's American distributor balked at the prospect of selling a film with the word "bleak" in its title, so Branagh was persuaded to change it for the film's North American release. I have retained the new title as it is the one familiar to American readers.

3. As Shakespeareans are aware, there are three principle texts of *Hamlet*: the First Quarto, the Second Quarto, and the First Folio. What we commonly regard as a full text *Hamlet* is a conflation of the Second Quarto and First Folio texts with the occasional addition of an element of word choice or structure from the First Quarto.

4. The period between 1944 (the release of Olivier's *Henry V*) and 1968 (the commercial success of Franco Zeffirelli's *Romeo and Juliet*) was one of the richest in Shakespeare on film history. The 1971 failure of the highly publicized film of *Macbeth* by Roman Polanski to recapture and build upon the audience for *Romeo and Juliet* doomed the genre in Hollywood for the next two decades.

5. I am indebted to Tamar Thomas, Branagh's personal assistant, for many favors, including this accounting of Branagh's activities in 1992–1993.

6. James Mottram, "Kenneth Branagh Unplugged," *The Glasgow Herald Magazine* (September 25, 2004).

7. See Douglas Lanier, *Shakespeare and Modern Popular Culture* (Oxford: Oxford University Press, 2002), pp. 157-160, and Courtney Lehmann, *Shakespeare Remains* (Ithaca: Cornell University Press, 2002), p. 177.

8. Welles also played Falstaff in a stage version of his *Chimes at Midnight* script in Dublin for several weeks in 1960 as preparation for shooting the film.

9. Pauline Kael, *Movie Love* (New York: Dutton/Plume, 1991), p. 216.

10. See Sarah Hatchuel, *A Companion to the Shakespeare Films of Kenneth Branagh* (Winnipeg: Blizzard Publishing, 2000), pp. 142-163, and Samuel Crowl, *Shakespeare at the Cineplex* (Athens: Ohio University Press, 2003), pp. 25-46.

11. Samuel Crowl, "Communicating Shakespeare: An Interview with Kenneth Branagh," *Shakespeare Bulletin* 20, no. 3 (Summer 2002), p. 25.

12. I am indebted to Susan Crowl's keen musician's ear for help in understanding the technical nature of Doyle's scores and the ways they appropriately mirror and underline Branagh's film narratives.

13. Pierre Berthomieu, *Kenneth Branagh: Traînes de Feu, Rosées de Sang* (Paris: Jean-Michel Place, 1998), p. 11. Translation by Susan Crowl.

14. I was able to examine Harvey's story boards and related materials at The Branagh Film Archive at Queen's University–Belfast thanks to the generous cooperation of its director, Professor Mark Thornton Burnett.

15. See Crowl, "Communicating Shakespeare," p. 25.

16. Sarah Hatchuel, *Shakespeare, From Stage to Screen* (Cambridge: Cambridge University Press, 2004), p. 25.

17. Trevor Nunn, *William Shakespeare's Twelfth Night: A Screenplay* (London: Methuen, 1996), p. ii.

18. Quoted in David Rosenthal, *Shakespeare on Screen* (London: Hamlyn, 2000), p. 215.

CHAPTER 2

1. A steady stream of Shakespeare films were released in the post–World War II period, but the well ran dry in the 1970s and 1980s after the commercial failure of Roman Polanski's *Macbeth* in 1971. The next eighteen years saw the release of only three Shakespeare films: Charlton Heston's *Antony and Cleopatra* (1972), Derek Jarman's *Tempest* (1980), and Akira Kurosawa's *Ran* (1985). By comparison twenty major Shakespeare films were released in the 1990s following the success of Branagh's *Henry V* (1989).

2. The last film made by a member of the British Shakespeare establishment was Peter Brook's *King Lear*, made in 1969 and released in 1971.

3. Peter S. Donaldson, *Shakespearean Films/Shakespearean Directors* (Boston: Unwin Hyman, Inc., 1990), pp. 2–3.

4. Branagh had appeared, in supporting roles, in two films: *A Month in The Country* (1987) and *High Season* (1987).

5. See Kael's review of Branagh's *Henry V*, "Second Takes," in *The New Yorker* (November 27, 1989), pp. 104–105.

6. Unless otherwise indicated, all Shakespeare quotations are from *The Riverside Shakespeare*, 2nd ed. (Boston: Houghton Mifflin, 1997).

7. *New York Review of Books* (February 6, 1997), p. 12.

8. For a brilliant analysis of the workings of intimacy in Branagh's film, see Peter S. Donaldson, "Taking on Shakespeare: Kenneth Branagh's *Henry V,*" *Shakespeare Quarterly* 42 (Spring 1991), pp. 60–71.

9. Ibid., p. 67.

10. Ibid., p. 67.

11. Branagh's first conversation about the possibility of playing Henry V for the RSC was with the director, Ron Daniels. When Branagh asked Daniels what he saw in the play, Daniels replied: "Mud." Kenneth Branagh, *Beginning* (London: Chatto & Windus, 1989), p. 133.

12. Ibid., p. 224.

13. Williams and Dench did, however, star in a television situation comedy, *A Fine Romance*, from 1981 to 1984 that made Williams a household name in England.

14. Branagh, *Beginning*, p. 235.

15. Donaldson, "Taking on Shakespeare," p. 68.

16. Dench had appeared as Titania in Peter Hall's film of *A Midsummer Night's Dream* (1968), and Scofield was Lear in Peter Brook's 1971 film of the play.

17. "Taking on Shakespeare," p. 65.

18. They met working together as the leads in *Fortunes of War*, shot as a film, but released as a television mini-series.

19. *Beginning*, p. 225.

20. See Sarah Hatchuel, *A Companion to the Shakespearean Films of Kenneth Branagh* (Winnipeg and Niagra Falls: Blizzard Publishing, 2000), pp. 142–162.

21. *The New Republic* (December 4, 1989), pp. 29–30.

22. *Time* (December 13, 1989), p. 119.

23. *The New Yorker* (November 27, 1989), p. 104.

24. Ibid., p. 104.

25. Samuel Crowl, "Communicating Shakespeare: An Interview with Kenneth Branagh," *Shakespeare Bulletin* 20, no. 3 (Summer 2002), p. 24.

CHAPTER 3

1. Bruce Weber, "From Shakespeare to Hollywood," *New York Times*, (August 18, 1991), p. H16.

2. Ibid., p. H16.

3. Ibid., p. H16.

4. Samuel Crowl, "Communicating Shakespeare: An Interview with Kenneth Branagh," *Shakespeare Bulletin* 20, no. 3 (Summer 2002), p. 27.

5. Donald Sutherland was originally cast as Madson; and when he withdrew from the picture for "creative reasons" (i.e., an unwillingness to work at Branagh's

pace), Branagh lobbied hard, and successfully, with the producers to hire Jacobi.

6. Johanna Schneller, "Stratford on Sunset," *GQ* (September 1991), p. 94.

7. Ibid., p. 94.

8. Ibid., p. 104.

9. Kent Black, "Married . . . With Chutzpah," *Los Angeles Times* (August 18, 1991), Calendar, p. 27.

10. F. X. Feeney, "Vaulting Ambition," *American Film* (September 1991), p. 48.

11. "Married . . . With Chutzpah," Calendar, p. 27.

12. See Marcia Landy and Lucy Fischer, "*Dead Again* or A-Live Again: Postmodern or Postmortem?" *Cinema Journal* 33, no. 4 (Summer 1994), pp. 3–22; Courtney Lehmann, *Shakespeare Remains: Theater to Film, Early Modern to Postmodern* (Ithaca and London: Cornell University Press, 2002); Kathy Howlett, *Framing Shakespeare on Film* (Athens: Ohio University Press, 2000).

13. See Fredric Jameson, "Postmodernism and Consumer Society," in *Movies and Mass Culture* (New Brunswick: Rutgers University Press, 1996), pp. 185–202.

14. "Vaulting Ambition," p. 24.

15. See boxofficeguru.com for details on film grosses.

CHAPTER 4

1. I don't mean to suggest that Branagh broke completely with one of the hallmarks of his career, loyalty to those he has worked with in the past. He cast Alex Lowe, who had been in the cast of *Another Country* on the West End stage a decade before, and employed Roger Lanser as his cinematographer. Lanser was the cameraman on *The Boy in the Bush* a four-part mini-series for television shot on location in Australia after Branagh finished his run as Judd in *Another Country*. Branagh played the lead in the series.

2. I was faced with six personalities but only four humors, so I created two more!

3. See *Ken and Em: A Biography of Kenneth Branagh and Emma Thompson* (Headline Book Publishing, London, 1994), p. 201. Even if the soundtrack is derivative, it is also memorable. In 2003, ten years after the film's release, I was chatting with an Australian woman who works in publishing in London. When she asked what I was working on, I said, "Branagh's *Peter's Friends*." "Never saw the film," she quickly replied, "but it had a great soundtrack. I have the CD."

4. In what is perhaps an insiders' joke, this very Hollywood product was directed by an Englishman, Tony Scott. Scott is the brother of Ridley Scott and one of a group of English directors, including Alan Parker, Adrian Lyne, Hugh Hudson, and Roland Joffe, who all made commercially successful Hollywood films in the 1980s and 1990s.

5. Actually, Branagh received his first poor stage notices in 1992. In that busy year he managed to make his last stage performance under the Renaissance banner.

He played Coriolanus at the Chichester Festival in a production directed by Tim Supple and co-starring Judi Dench and Richard Briers.

6. Richard Corliss, *Time* 141, no. 2 (January 11, 1993), p. 50; and David Ansen, *Newsweek* 121, no. 1 (January 4, 1993), p. 51.

7. Stanley Kauffmann, *The New Republic* 208, no. 5 (February 1 1993), p. 51.

8. Welles makes this remark in the program "Filming *Othello*," which he made for German television in 1978.

9. He had also made a short film, starring John Gielgud, based on Chekhov's short story "Swan Song"; the film *Swan Song* was nominated for an Academy Award in the Best Short Subjects Category in 1992.

CHAPTER 5

1. I am thinking particularly of Michael Boyd's 1996–1997 production for The Royal Shakespeare Company starring Alex Jennings and Siobhan Redmond and of Declan Donellan's 1998 production for Cheek by Jowl starring Matthew Mac-Fadyen and Saskia Reeves.

2. Sarah Hatchuel, *A Companion to the Shakespeare Films of Kenneth Branagh* (Winnepeg: Blizzard, 2000), p. 126.

3. Branagh's bold opening may owe something to Franco Zeffirelli's visual overture to his *Taming of the Shrew* (1965). Zeffirelli provides a wonderful introduction to Padua by having Lucentio and Tranio arrive during the carnival celebrations marking the beginning of a new term at the university.

4. Geoffrey O'Brien, *The New York Review of Books* (February 6, 1997), p. 12.

5. Welles, of course, in *Othello* and especially in *Chimes at Midnight*, pioneered the use of international casts, but his Shakespeare films were often faulted (and sometimes praised) for the poor quality of their soundtracks.

6. Kenneth Branagh, *Much Ado About Nothing*: Screenplay (New York: W. W. Norton, 1993), p. ix.

7. Ibid., p. x.

8. Hollywood had once before tried something similar when Joseph Mankiewicz and John Houseman cast Marlon Brando to play Mark Antony opposite James Mason's Brutus and John Gielgud's Cassius. Though mocked at the time, Brando's performance today is the film's most stunning achievement.

9. *New Yorker* (May 10, 1993), p. 97.

10. For an example see Glenn Walken's performance in A. J. Anton's production (1972) for the New York Shakespeare Festival now available on video. The Ohio University School of Theater's production (1997), set just after the end of World War I, conceived of Don John, Conrade, and Borachio as militaristic Huns who did everything in unison and stole the comic show from Dogberry and the watch.

11. I owe a debt of gratitude to my former students Nicholas Long and Ann Pedersen, who educated me on the significance of this scene, particularly the masks, to Branagh's film.

12. It is moments like this that frustrate some Shakespearean critics of the film. Michael Anderegg's comment is typical: "Too often slapstick substitutes for comic finesse. . . . very little is earned in this film—we are constantly being told how to respond, what to think and feel." *Cinematic Shakespeare* (Boulder and Oxford: Rowman and Littlefield, 2004), p. 124.

13. Branagh, *Much Ado About Nothing*: Screenplay, p. 47.

14. Remarkably, Thompson would, in 1995, win her second Academy Award, this time for Best Screenplay (for *Sense and Sensibility*). She became the only person in Academy history to win an Oscar for both acting and writing.

15. To his credit, Reeves is an actor with Shakespearean yearnings. He starred in Gus Van Sant's *My Private Idaho*, an homage both to Shakespeare's *1 & 2 Henry V* and to Orson Welles's *Chimes at Midnight*. Later, in 1995, he would play Hamlet on stage in Manitoba, Canada.

16. Branagh, *Much Ado About Nothing*: Screenplay, p. xiii.

17. The chapel was an addition to the villa constructed by the film crew. They also had to cover up its swimming pool!

18. Anne Barton, "Shakespeare in the Sun," *New York Review of Books* (May 27, 1993), p. 11.

19. Vincent Canby, *The New York Times*, (May 7, 1993), Section C, p. 16.

20. Anderegg, *Cinematic Shakespeare*, p. 125.

21. Samuel Crowl, "Interview with Kenneth Branagh," *Shakespeare Bulletin* 12, no. 4 (1994), p. 8.

22. Stanley Cavell, *Pursuits of Happiness: The Hollywood Comedy of Remarriage* (Cambridge: Harvard University Press, 1981), pp. 17–18.

23. Ibid., p. 18.

24. Thompson is quoted in Ian Shuttleworth, *Ken and Em: A Biography of Kenneth Branagh and Emma Thompson* (London: Headline Book Publishing, 1994), p. 222.

25. Samuel Crowl, "Communicating Shakespeare: An Interview with Kenneth Branagh," *Shakespeare Bulletin* 20, no. 3 (Summer 2002), p. 27.

26. Ian Shuttleworth, *Ken & Em*, p. 224.

27. I owe this story, and much more in my account of the film, to Russell Jackson, former director of the Shakespeare Institute in Stratford-upon-Avon and the textual advisor on all of Branagh's Shakespeare films. See his account of working with the actors in the film during the weeklong rehearsal period that preceded the start of filming: "Branagh and the Bard," *The Sunday Times* (London) (August 29, 1993), p. 6.

28. Ian Shuttleworth, *Ken & Em*, p. 223.

29. See Courtney Lehmann, "*Much Ado About Nothing*? Shakespeare, Branagh, and the National-Popular in the Age of Multinational Capitol," *Textual Practice* 12, no. 1 (1998), pp. 1–22.

CHAPTER 6

1. *New York* (May 24, 1993), pp. 37–45.

2. A sampling from this list includes *Son of Frankenstein* (1939), *Frankenstein Meets the Wolf Man* (1943), *The Curse of Frankenstein* (1957), *I Was a Teenage Frankenstein* (1957), *The Revenge of Frankenstein* (1958), *The Horror of Frankenstein* (1970), *Frankenstein: The True Story* (1973), *Young Frankenstein* (1974), *Gothic* (1987), and *Frankenstein Unbound* (1990).

3. Some of the more interesting include the following: Robert Craig, "Lost in a Lost World: Looking at Victor and the Creature as Aliens in Kenneth Branagh's *Mary Shelley's Frankenstein*," *Journal of Educational Psychology* 18 (March 1997), pp. 126–132; R. J. Frost, "'IT'S ALIVE!' *Frankenstein*: The Film, the Feminist Novel and Science Fiction," *Foundation: The Review of Science Fiction* 67 (Summer 1996), pp. 75–94; A. C. Goodson, "Frankenstein in the Age of Prozac," *Literature and Medicine* 15, no. 1, (1996), pp. 16–32; Michael Laplace-Sinatra, "Science, Gender and Otherness in Shelley's *Frankenstein* and Kenneth Branagh's Film Adaptation," *European Romantic Review* 9, no. 2, (Spring 1998), pp. 253–270; and Lori Leathers Single, "Reading Against the Grain: The U. S. Reception of Branagh's *Mary Shelley's Frankenstein*," *Studies in American Culture* 21, no. 2, (October 1998), pp. 1–18.

4. This and all subsequent quotations from the film are from the following source: Kenneth Branagh, *Mary Shelley's Frankenstein: The Classic Tale of Terror Reborn on Film* (New York: The New Market Press, 1994), p. 32.

5. Ibid., pp. 32–33.

6. Frankenstein's creation, in Shelley's novel, is referred to by many epithets: "horror," "demon," "monster." Branagh's film always refers to him as the Creature. I follow Shelley when dealing with the Frankenstein myth, Branagh when referring to DeNiro's character in his film.

7. Ibid., pp. 38–39.

8. Ibid., p. 131.

9. "The Filmmakers and Their Creations," in *Mary Shelley's Frankenstein: The Classic Tale of Terror Reborn on Film*, p. 146.

10. *Mary Shelley's Frankenstein*, p. 44.

11. *The Madwoman in the Attic* (New Haven and London: Yale University Press, 1979), p. 244.

12. *Mary Shelley's Frankenstein*, p. 81.

13. *The New Republic* 211, no. 22 (November 28, 1994), p. 57.

14. *Mary Shelley's Frankenstein*, p. 78.

15. Ibid., p. 79.

16. Ibid., p. 81.

17. Janet Maslin, "A Brain on Ice, A Dead Toad and Voila!" *The New York Times* (November 4, 1994), Section C, p. 1. Anthony Lane, "Used Parts," *The New Yorker* (November 14, 1994), p. 141.

18. Mary Shelley, *Frankenstein* (New York: New American Library), Signet Classic Edition (1965), p. 159.

19. *Mary Shelley's Frankenstein*, p. 122.

20. The recorder is associated with the blind Grandfather in the woods—the one character who treats DeNiro's Creature with compassion.

21. *Newsweek* 124, no. 19 (November 7, 1994), p. 73.

22. *Time* 144, no. 19 (Nov. 7, 1994), p. 73.

23. See Lionel Trilling (Ed.), *The Selected Letters of John Keats* (New York: Doubleday Anchor Books, 1956), pp. 165–167.

24. David J. Skal, *Screams of Reason: Mad Science and Modern Culture* (New York: W. W. Norton and Company, 1998).

25. *The Endurance of Frankenstein: Essays on Mary Shelley's Novel* (Berkeley: University of California Press, 1979), p. xiv.

26. *Mary Shelley's Frankenstein: The Classic Tale of Terror on Film*, pp. 18–19.

CHAPTER 7

1. The film's original title, and the one under which it was released in England, was *In the Bleak Midwinter*. That title alludes to Christina Rossetti's poem set to music by Gustav Holst. Holst's tune, gently plucked on a guitar, serves as the only music on the soundtrack except for Noel Coward singing his "Why Must the Show Go On?" The American distributor, Sony Picture Classics, made Branagh change the title arguing that "bleak" was box office poison. Branagh's American title has the virtue of evoking Shakespeare's *The Winter's Tale* and its powers of restoration and theatrical miracles.

2. Kenneth Branagh, *A Midwinter's Tale: The Shooting Script* (New York: Newmarket Press, 1996), p. 1.

3. David Gritten, "Kenneth Branagh, On the Rebound," *Los Angeles Times* (June 3, 1995), Section F, p. 12.

4. Ibid., p. 22.

5. Ibid., p. 22.

6. Ibid., p. 24.

7. Laurence Olivier, *On Acting* (New York: Simon and Schuster, 1986), p. 83.

8. *A Midwinter's Tale*, p. 33.

9. Kenneth Branagh, *Beginning* (London: Pan Books, 1989), p. 133.

10. Kathy Howlett, *Framing Shakespeare on Film* (Athens: Ohio University Press, 2000), p. 186.

11. *A Midwinter's Tale*, p. 28.

12. Ibid., p. 50.

13. Ibid., p. 67.

14. Ibid., p. 11.

15. Ibid., p. 74.

16. Holst's hymn is a setting of Christina Rossetti's poem and is, of course, the source for Branagh's original title for the film. The version played in the film was arranged by Jimmy Yuill, yet another member of Branagh's original Renaissance Company.

17. Russell Jackson, "The Film Diary," in Kenneth Branagh, *Hamlet: Screenplay, Introduction, and Film Diary* (London: W. W. Norton and Company, 1996), p. 207.

18. *Framing*, p. 194.

19. *A Midwinter's Tale*, p. 83.

20. Ibid., p. 98.

21. H. R. Coursen, *Shakespeare: The Two Traditions* (Madison and Teaneck: Fairleigh Dickinson University Press, 1999), p. 172.

22. *Framing*, p. 200.

23. Douglas Lanier, *Shakespeare and Modern Popular Culture* (Oxford: Oxford University Press, 2002), p. 159.

CHAPTER 8

1. Quoted in Sarah Hatchuel's *A Companion to the Shakespeare Films of Kenneth Branagh* (Winnipeg and Niagra Falls: Blizzard Publishing, 2000), p. 29.

2. See Mark Thornton Burnett, "The Very Cunning of the Scene: Kenneth Branagh's *Hamlet*," *Literature/Film Quarterly* 25, no. 2 (1997), pp. 78—82; and Harry Keyishian, "Shakespeare and Movie Genre," in Russell Jackson (Ed.), *The Cambridge Companion to Shakespeare on Film* (Cambridge: Cambridge University Press, 2000), pp. 72–81.

3. The Blenheim location prohibited Branagh from shooting scenes on the palace's roof.

4. Branagh was acutely aware of this problem in the compromises he had to make in shooting the scenes involving Hamlet's encounter with his father's ghost: "I wanted to scare people. . . . That's where I felt that lack of money and budget and, quite frankly, lack of imagination on my part didn't bring it off as well as I had hoped. I think it was always going to be difficult in the context of what we were doing because it required time—time without dialogue. It required the sort of

movie time we didn't have the luxury of creating when we knew there was another three and a half hours to come." Samuel Crowl, "Communicating Shakespeare: An Interview with Kenneth Branagh," *Shakespeare Bulletin* 20, no. 3 (2002), p. 27.

5. Kenneth Branagh, *Hamlet: Screenplay, Introduction, and Film Diary* (New York: W. W. Norton & Company, 1996), p. 1.

6. In a further irony, as reported by Russell Jackson in his diary about the making of the film, Disney was shooting its remake of *101 Dalmatians* on the next soundstage, so Shepperton was overrun with dogs. *Hamlet: Screenplay, Introduction, and Film Diary*, pp. 176–177.

7. See Hatchuel's *Companion to the Films of Kenneth Branagh*, pp. 87–88 for an interesting source for this scene.

8. Crowl, "Communicating Shakespeare," p. 25.

9. Heston's reputation as a serious actor has always been higher in England than in America. He has performed several leading roles in the West End over the past two decades while never venturing an appearance on Broadway in that period. His role as a spokesperson for the National Rifle Association doesn't trail him across the Atlantic with the same immediacy it does in the States.

10. Author interview, London, October 25, 2003.

11. Crowl, "Communicating Shakespeare," p. 25.

12. This moment clearly is indebted to similar mirror shots in Orson Welles's *Citizen Kane* (1941) and *The Lady from Shanghai* (1946).

13. Burnett, "The Very Cunning of the Scene," p. 78.

14. Crowl, "Communicating Shakespeare," p. 26.

15. Ibid., pp. 26–27.

16. Branagh, *Hamlet: Screenplay, Introduction, Film Diary*, p. 205.

17. See Bernice Kliman's "The Unkindest Cuts: Flashcut Excess in Kenneth Branagh's *Hamlet*," in Deborah Cartmell and Michael Scott (Eds.), *Talking Shakespeare: Shakespeare into the Millenium* (London, 2001), pp. 151–167.

18. For a contrary reading of the film's Oedipal pattern, see Lisa S. Starks, "The Displaced Body of Desire: Sexuality in Kenneth Branagh's *Hamlet*," in Christy Desmet and Robert Sawyer, eds., *Shakespeare and Appropriation* (London: Routledge, 2000), p. 160.

19. Interestingly, this physical similarity between Branagh's Hamlet and Jacobi's Claudius was the first thing that struck Gerard Depardieu when he arrived at Shepperton to shoot his short scene as Reynaldo. See Branagh, *Hamlet: Screenplay, Introduction, Film Diary*, p. 182.

CHAPTER 9

1. *As You Like It* was shot at Shepperton Studios and features a typically Branagh mix of English and American actors.

2. In an interview with Mark Caro, Branagh commented, "Well here's one [a comedy] that Shakespeare wrote [*Love's Labour's Lost*] that wasn't performed for 200 years after his death and I'd like to do it in a genre that really hasn't worked for the last forty years. You know, tough sell." "Top Hat—and Tales," *Chicago Tribune*, Sec. 5 (June 22, 2000), p. 6.

3. Kenneth Branagh, *Beginning* (London: Pan Books, 1989), p. 72.

4. Harley Granville-Barker, *Prefaces to Shakespeare*, Vol. II (Princeton, NJ: Princeton University Press, 1947), p. 442.

5. Ibid., p. 432.

6. *Love's Labour's Lost*, The Arden Shakespeare (London: Methuen and Co., 1956), pp. xv–xvi.

7. "About the Production," Miramax Press Packet for *Love's Labour's Lost*, p. 2.

8. Stanley Kauffmann, "Well, Not Completely Lost," *New Republic* (July 10 and 17, 2000), p. 32.

9. The song has multiple lyricists: Jimmy McHugh, Dorothy Field, Oscar Hammerstein II, and Otto Harbach.

10. C. L. Barber, *Shakespeare's Festive Comedy*, (Princeton, NJ: Princeton University Press, 1959), p. 92.

11. H. R. Coursen, *Shakespeare in Space* (New York: Peter Lang, 2002), pp. 159–160.

12. Wendy Wasserstein, "Where I Seem to Find the Happiness I Seek," *New York Times*, "Arts and Leisure," (Sunday, June 4, 2000), pp. 15–20.

13. Ramona Wray, "Nostalgia for Navarre: The Melancholic Metacinema of Kenneth Branagh's *Love's Labour's Lost*," *Literature/Film Quarterly* 30, no. 3 (2002), p. 171.

14. Gayle Holste, "Branagh's *Love's Labour's Lost*: Too Much, Too Little, Too Late," *Literature/Film Quarterly* 30, no. 3 (2002), p. 228.

15. Wray, "Nostalgia for Navarre," p. 173.

16. Kauffmann, "Well, Not Completely Lost," p. 32.

17. Wray, "Nostalgia for Navarre," p. 175.

18. Courtney Lehmann, *Shakespeare Remains* (Ithaca, NY: Cornell University Press, 2002), pp. 185–186.

19. John Updike, *More Matter* (New York: Knopf, 1999), p. 666.

20. For a more optimistic and positive account of Branagh's film and the tradition of the American movie musical, see Michael D. Friedman's "I Won't Dance, Don't Ask Me: Branagh's *Love's Labour's Lost* and the American Film Musical," *Literature/Film Quarterly* 30, no. 3 (2002), pp. 134–143.

21. Samuel Crowl, "*Love's Labour's Lost*," *Shakespeare Bulletin* 18, no. 3 (2000), p. 38.

INDEX

Allen, Woody, 6, 10, 11, 69, 70, 109, 113, 117, 164
Almereyda, Michael, 129
Altman, Robert, 6
Anderegg, Michael, 87, 192
Anderson, Lindsay, 10
Annie Get Your Gun, 153
Ansen, David, 68, 108
Asherson, Renee, 33
Astaire, Fred, 10, 153, 156, 158
Attenborough, Richard, 15

Bale, Christian, 32
Banks, Leslie, 25
Barber, C.L., 156, 197
Barron, David, 18
Barton, Anne, 192
Beale, Simon Russell, 21
Beatty, Warren, 10, 165
Beckinsale, Kate, 81
Bennett, Alan, 56
Bergman, Ingmar, 46, 70, 131
Bergman, Martin, 56
Berlin, Irving, 8, 153
Berthomieu, Pierre, 16, 188
Beyond the Fringe, 56
Big Chill,The, 55, 62, 63, 64, 69
Black, Kent, 190

Blenheim Palace, 131, 132, 134
Blessed, Brian, 23, 28, 146, 147, 171
Bogart, Humphrey, 10
Branagh, Kenneth
    Academy Award nominations, 5, 35, 38
    actors as filmmakers, 10, 11, 18, 109, 117, 139–142, 165
    Beginning, 3, 187
    camera movement, 16, 23, 45, 57, 90, 91, 114, 118, 176
    casting, 28, 43, 44, 79, 83, 103, 115, 137–138, 160
    company ideal, 7, 8, 11, 12, 13, 16, 56, 92, 114, 127, 150–151, 163, 171
    creative team, 18, 46, 92, 171
    early life, 1–3
    editing, 45, 53, 65, 87, 103
    film style, 10, 11, 15, 17, 24, 34, 43, 52, 70, 91, 99, 105, 117, 123, 125, 126, 130, 140, 150, 158, 173, 174
    flashbacks, 31, 53, 143–145
    Hollywood, 38, 88–89, 94, 95–96, 114, 127
    music, 15, 24, 25, 49, 59, 63, 90, 100, 124, 145, 152–154, 157, 162, 174–175

Branagh, Kenneth (*Continued*)
  Olivier, Laurence, comparisons with,
    8, 9, 20, 22, 40, 95, 165
  opening sequences, 19, 40, 41, 57,
    75–77, 97–99, 134
  Renaissance Theater Company, 3, 35,
    92, 115
  Royal Academy of Dramatic Arts, 3
  Royal Shakespeare Company, 3, 21,
    46, 67, 95
  Thompson, Emma, relationship with,
    7, 47, 55–56, 67, 73–74, 83, 96,
    100–101
  Welles, Orson, comparisons with, 8, 9,
    40, 95, 165
Branagh, Kenneth, films directed
  As You Like It, 8, 165, 167–169, 172
  Dead Again, 13, 39, 41, 43, 45, 51
  Hamlet, 13, 16, 130, 133, 137,
    139–142
  Henry V, 19, 23, 26, 28, 32, 34
  Love's Labour's Lost, 155–156, 157,
    158
  Magic Flute, The, 8, 165, 175
  Mary Shelley's Frankenstein, 13, 16,
    97, 99, 100, 103–104
  Midwinter's Tale, A, 117–118, 121,
    123, 125
  Much Ado About Nothing, 13, 16,
    75–77, 81, 85–86, 87, 91–92
  Peter's Friends, 57, 62, 63, 69
Branagh, Kenneth, films acted in
  Celebrity, 113
  Dead Again, 13, 47, 49
  Gingerbread Man, The, 6
  Hamlet, 133, 137, 140, 146, 147
  Henry V, 5, 18, 23, 30, 35
  How to Kill Your Neighbor's Dog, 6
  Love's Labour's Lost, 151, 155, 159
  Mary Shelley's Frankenstein, 103, 107,
    109
  Much Ado About Nothing, 82, 83, 85,
    86
  Peter's Friends, 66
  Wild Wild West, 6
Branagh, Kenneth, plays directed
  King Lear, 38
  Midsummer Night's Dream, A, 38

Romeo and Juliet, 36
Twelfth Night, 36
Branagh, Kenneth, plays acted in
  Another Country, 3
  As You Like It, 4
  Edmund, 165
  Hamlet (Renaissance Theater
    Company), 130
  Hamlet (Royal Shakespeare
    Company), 6, 71, 131
  Henry V, 3, 21
  Much Ado About Nothing, 4
  Public Enemy, 4
  Richard III, 165
  Romeo and Juliet, 4
Branagh, Kenneth, television shows
  acted in
  Conspiracy, 165
  Fortunes of War, 21
Branagh, William (Pop), 1
Branagh, William Jr., 1
Bride of Frankenstein, The (film, Whale),
  96, 100, 107
Briers, Richard, 11, 28, 55, 85, 105, 115,
  135, 172
Brook, Peter, 4
Brooks, Mel, 97
Burbage, Richard, 20, 35
Burnett, Mark Thornton, 133, 142, 195,
  196
Burton, Richard, 30, 74

Cagney, James, 10, 47, 150
Cambridge Footlights Drama Club, 55
Canby, Vincent, 87, 192
Carter, Helena Bonham, 100, 107
Casablanca, 157
Castle Rock Entertainment, 149
Cavell, Stanley, 88–89, 192
Charles, HRH The Prince of Wales, 21
Charnley, Hetta, 115, 120
Cheek by Jowl, 75
"Cheek to Cheek," 153, 156
Chicago (film, Marshall), 164
Chimes at Midnight, 29
Christie, Julie, 15, 137, 138, 143
Citizen Kane, 9, 12, 13, 35, 42
Cleese, John, 56, 103

Clueless, 78, 152, 162
Collins, Joan, 115
Coltrane, Robbie, 27, 28, 31
Condon, Bill, 96
Cook, Peter, 56
Coppola, Francis Ford, 10, 13, 96
Corliss, Richard, 34, 68, 191
Costner, Kevin, 10, 55
Coursen, H.R., 22, 126, 158, 195, 197
Coward, Noel, 114, 116, 120
Crowe, Russell, 109
Cruttwell, Hugh, 18, 46
Crystal, Billy, 44, 84
Curtis, Tony, 82

Daniels, Ron, 121
Darabont, Frank, 97
Daulton, Phyllis, 46
David, Richard, 151, 152
Dead Poet's Society, 89
Dench, Judi, 3, 4, 5, 11, 27, 29, 32, 36, 80,
    138
DeNiro, Robert, 100, 105, 106, 108
Depardieu, Gerard, 135
Dial M for Murder, 39, 49, 50
Die Hard, 144
Dinsdale, Reece, 136
Doctor Zhivago (film, Lean), 15, 131, 138
Donaldson, Peter, 20, 27, 31, 33, 180, 189
Doran, Lindsay, 47
Doyle, Patrick, 13, 15, 18, 24, 25, 33, 41,
    46, 49, 76, 98, 103, 125, 145, 157

Easton, Richard, 11
Eastwood, Clint, 10, 11, 18, 109, 165
Elton, Ben, 84
Emmanuel, Alphonsia, 56
Evans, Stephen, 18, 36, 46
Everett, Rupert, 21

Falklands War, 32
Fanny and Alexander, 131
Farrell, Nicholas, 11, 115, 118, 139
Fassbinder, Warner, 42
Fiennes, Ralph, 21
Finney, Albert, 10, 47, 109
Fischer, Lucy, 51, 190
Follow the Fleet, 153

Fosse, Bob, 163
Frank, Scott, 39, 47, 52
Frankenstein (film, Whale), 96
Frankenstein (novel, Shelley), 96, 97, 101,
    102, 106
Friedman, Michael, 197
Fry, Stephen, 56, 165

Gable, Clark, 10
Gade, Sven, 129
Garcia, Andy, 13, 42
Garland, Judy, 117, 126
Gershwin, George, 8, 153
Gershwin, Ira, 153
Gibson, Mel, 10
Gielgud, John, 10, 80, 138, 191
Gilbert, Sandra, 102
Gods and Monsters, 96
Grant, Cary, 10, 82
Granville-Barker, Harley, 151, 152,
    197
Great Escape, The, 66
Gritten, David, 194
Gubar, Susan, 102
Guinness, Alec, 10, 109

Hadfield, Mark, 119
Hall, Edward, 52
Hall, Peter, 4
Hamlet (film, Almereyda), 129
Hamlet (film, Olivier), 9, 122, 129, 130
Hamlet (film, Richardson), 144
Hamlet (stage, Noble), 131
Hands, Terry, 4
Harper, Frances, 1
Harper, Speedy, 1
Harvey, Tim, 18, 103, 132
Hatchuel, Sarah, 10, 77, 188, 189, 191,
    196
Hawks, Howard, 89
HBO Films, 150
Henry V (film, Olivier), 19, 20, 22, 25,
    32
Henry V (stage, Noble), 27
Hepburn, Katharine, 47
Herlie, Eileen, 130
Herrmann, Bernard, 41, 49
Heston, Charlton, 138

Hitchcock, Alfred, 39, 40, 42
Hoffman, Michael, 79
Holm, Ian, 5, 11, 22, 29, 30
Holst, Gustav, 115
Holste, Gayle, 163, 197
Hopkins, Anthony, 109
Hopps, Stuart, 156
Horan, Gerard, 115, 119, 125
Howard, Alan, 4
Howard's End (film, Merchant-Ivory), 7, 47, 67, 74
Hulce, Tom, 106
Hussey, Olivia, 15
Hytner, Nicholas, 161

I, Claudius (television series), 44
"I'd Rather Charleston," 153
"I Get a Kick Out of You," 153, 160
Imrie, Celia, 115, 118
In the Bleak Midwinter (film, Branagh), 194, 195
"In the Bleak Midwinter" (song, Rossetti and Holst), 115, 124
"I've Got a Crush on You," 153, 155

Jackson, Russell, 18, 46, 124, 125, 192, 195, 196
Jacobi, Derek, 4, 11, 19, 26, 34, 36, 42, 43, 44, 130, 147
Jameson, Fredrick, 52, 190

Kael, Pauline, 23, 35, 188
Karloff, Boris, 105, 110
Kauffmann, Stanley, 34, 68, 69, 103, 108, 163, 191, 197
Kay, Charles, 23
Keaton, Michael, 13, 74, 83, 84
Keats, John, 109
Kelly, Gene, 11, 164
Kern, Jerome, 153, 155
Keyishian, Harry, 133
King Lear (film, Brook), 78
Kingsley, Ben, 4
Kliman, Bernice, 145, 196
Kline, Kevin, 165, 172
Knoepflmacher, U.C., 110
Kozintsev, Grigori, 15, 19
Kurosawa, Akira, 17, 19

Lady, Be Good!, 153, 154
Lady, Steph, 97
Landy, Marcia, 51, 190
Lane, Anthony, 80, 105
Lane, Nathan, 84, 160
Lanier, Douglas, 8, 127, 187, 195
Last Action Hero, 92
Laurie, Hugh, 56, 64
Law, Phyllida, 56, 68
Lawrence of Arabia, 131, 139
Lean, David, 15, 113, 131
Lehmann, Courtney, 8, 51, 93, 164, 187, 193
Leigh, Mike, 161
Leigh, Vivian, 7, 44
Leighton, Margaret, 80
Lemmon, Jack, 44, 83
Leonard, Robert Sean, 13, 81, 83
Lester, Adrian, 152, 153, 161
"Let's Face the Music and Dance," 153
Levine, George, 110
Lewis, Daniel Day, 21
Lowe, Alex, 56, 77
Lucas, George, 114
Luhrmann, Baz, 79, 93
Lunghi, Cheri, 100

MacMillan, Kenneth, 22, 31
Mad Woman in the Attic, The, 102, 193
Magic Flute, The, 8, 165
Magnificent Seven, The, 77
Mahler, Gustav, 15, 145
Maloney, Michael, 11, 13, 119, 123, 135, 136
Mark Taber Forum, 38
Maslin, Janet, 105, 194
McElhone, Natascha, 44, 155, 159
McEwan, Geraldine, 4, 11, 36, 160
McGilliss, Kelly, 65, 80
McGowen, Alec, 23
McGregor, Ewan, 114
Merchant of Venice, The (film, Radford), 165
Million Dollar Baby, 10
Miramax, 8, 149, 150
Monroe, Marilyn, 9, 82
Monty Python, 56
Moore, Dudley, 56

Morecambe and Wise, 2
Mottram, James, 188

Newman, Alfred, 49
Noble, Adrian, 4, 21, 46, 70, 131
North, Alex, 49
Nunn, Trevor, 3, 4, 17, 188

O'Brien, Geoffrey, 24, 78, 191
Olivier, Laurence, 2, 5, 7, 9, 15, 17, 40, 43, 44, 129, 130, 147
Othello (film, Welles), 15

Pacino, Al, 17
Palin, Michael, 56
Pan, Hermes, 153
Parfitt, David, 18, 46
Play Misty for Me, 10
Polanski, Roman, 5
Porter, Cole, 8, 152
Prince and the Showgirl, The, 9
Pryce, Jonathan, 130
Pursuits of Happiness, 88
Putnam, David, 36, 46

Ramsey, Melanie, 135
Rebecca (film, Hitchcock), 42, 49, 51
Redford, Robert, 10
Redgrave, Michael, 10
Reeves, Keanu, 13, 74, 83, 84
Reisz, Karl, 10
Remains of the Day (film, Merchant-Ivory), 47, 74
Richardson, Ian, 3
Richardson, Ralph, 10
Richardson, Tony, 10
Rising Sun, 73
Roberta, 153
Rogers, Ginger, 156, 157
Romeo and Juliet (film, Zeffirelli), 15, 73
Rooney, Mickey, 117
Rossetti, Christina, 115, 194
Rota, Nino, 15
Royal National Theatre, 161, 165
Royal Shakespeare Company, 95
Rudner, Rita, 56
Ryan's Daughter, 131
Rylance, Mark, 21, 130

Sanders, George, 44
Saunders, Jennifer, 115
Sawalha, Julia, 115, 119
Schickel, Richard, 108
Schlegel, Margaret, 67
Schneller, Johanna, 190
Schygulla, Hannah, 42
Scofield, Paul, 5, 32
Scorsese, Martin, 69
Scott, Campbell, 44
Scott, Tony, 66
Seinfeld, 149
Sessions, John, 115, 119
Sewell, Rufus, 133, 144
sex, lies, and videotape, 95
Shakespeare in Love, 11, 17, 94, 159
Shaw, Fiona, 21
Shelley, Mary, 96, 97, 98, 194
Sher, Anthony, 4
Shostakovich, Dmitri, 15
Shuttleworth, Ian, 59, 91, 192
Silverstone, Alicia, 44, 162
Singin' in the Rain, 83
Skal, David, 110, 194
Slattery, Tony, 65, 60
Sleepless in Seattle, 73
Soderbergh, Steven, 95
Some Like It Hot, 82
Sonnenfeld, Barry, 6
Spall, Timothy, 136, 160
Spellbound, 51
Springsteen, Bruce, 59
Starks, Lisa, 196
Staunton, Imelda, 56
Stephens, Robert, 28, 31
Stevenson, Juliet, 21
Stewart, Jimmy, 10
Stoppard, Tom, 94, 125, 159
Strayhorn, Billy, 41
Streep, Meryl, 47
Student Prince, The, 132
Sturges, John, 77
Suchet, David, 4
Swing Time, 153

Taming of the Shrew (film, Zeffirelli), 74
Taylor, Elizabeth, 74
Taymor, Julie, 79

"There's No Business like Show
    Business," 153, 160
"They Can't Take That Away From Me,"
    156, 157
Thomas, Tamar, 187
Thompson, Alex, 15, 139
Thompson, Emma, 7, 11, 13, 21, 33, 41,
    44, 45, 47, 55, 62, 67, 74, 77, 82,
    83, 86, 100, 101
Throne of Blood, 78
Toland, Gregg, 114
Top Gun, 65, 69
Top Hat, 153, 156
Touch of Evil, 138
Tracy, Spencer, 10
Trilling, Lionel, 194

"Underground Song, The," 57, 59, 68
Unforgiven, The, 10
Updike, John, 164, 197

Vietnam War, 32
Villa Vignamaggio, 6, 13, 73

Walton, William, 15, 32
Washington, Denzel, 13, 44, 74, 81, 83, 93
Wasserstein, Wendy, 162, 197

"Way You Look Tonight, The" 63,
    153
Wayne, John, 10
Weber, Bruce, 38, 189
Weinstein, Bob, 149, 158
Weinstein, Harvey, 149, 158
Weir, Peter, 66
Welles, Orson, 8, 9, 10, 11, 19, 35, 40, 42,
    46, 70, 165
Whale, James, 96
Whiting, Leonard, 15
"Why Must the Show Go On?," 120,
    126
William Shakespeare's Romeo + Juliet
    (film, Luhrmann), 93, 97
Williams, Michael, 29
Williams, Robin, 11, 13, 43, 44
Winslet, Kate, 135, 136
Witness, 66
Wizard of Oz, The, 117
Wray, Ramona, 163, 197

Young Mr. Frankenstein, 97
Yuill, Jimmy, 92, 115, 152, 167, 179, 180,
    181, 182, 195

Zeffirelli, Franco, 10, 15, 19, 129

About the Author

SAMUEL CROWL is Trustee Professor of English at Ohio University where he has taught since 1970. He is the author of two books on Shakespeare, as well as numerous essays, articles, reviews, and interviews on all aspects of Shakespeare in performance. He has been honored many times for outstanding teaching and has lectured widely on Shakespeare at universities and conferences here and abroad, including the Shakespeare Institute and the International Globe Center.